# FRAMING
# IDENTITIES

Frontispiece. From the *Untitled Mirrors* series (1990), by Lillian Mulero.
Used by permission of the artist.

# FRAMING IDENTITIES

*Autobiography and the
Politics of Pedagogy*

Wendy S. Hesford

 University of Minnesota Press
Minneapolis
London

The University of Minnesota Press gratefully acknowledges permission to reprint the follow-ing essays. Chapter 2 originally appeared in a different form as "Autobiography and Feminist Writing Pedagogy," in *Genre and Writing: Issues, Arguments, Alternatives,* Wendy Bishop and Hans Ostrom, editors, copyright 1997, Boynton/Cook. Chapter 3, a revised version of "Writing Identities: The Essence of Difference in Multicultural Classrooms," is reprinted by permission of the Modern Language Association of America from *Writing in Multicultural Settings,* Johnella Butler, Juan Guerra, and Carol Severino, editors, copyright 1997, Modern Language Association of America. Chapter 4, a revised version of "'Ye Are Witnesses': Peda-gogy and the Politics of Identity," is reprinted by permission of the Modern Language Associa-tion of America from *Feminism and Composition Studies: In Other Words,* Susan Jarratt and Lynn Worsham, editors, copyright 1998, Modern Language Association of America.

Published by the University of Minnesota Press
111 Third Avenue South, Suite 290
Minneapolis, MN 55401-2520
http://www.upress.umn.edu

Printed in the United States of America on acid-free paper

Library of Congress Cataloging-in-Publication Data

Hesford, Wendy S.
    Framing identities : autobiography and the politics of pedagogy / Wendy S. Hesford.
        p.   cm.
    Includes bibliographical references (p.  ) and index.
    ISBN 0-8166-3153-0 (hc). — ISBN 0-8166-3154-9 (pbk.)
    1. Critical pedagogy—United States. 2. Education—United States—Biographical methods. 3. Multiculturalism—United States. 4. Education, Higher—Political aspects—United States. 5. Minorities—Education (Higher)—United States. 6. Ethnicity—United States. 7. Oberlin College—Students. I. Title.
LC196.5.U6H47   1999
370.11'5—dc21                                                                              98-45127

The University of Minnesota is an equal-opportunity educator and employer.

10  09  08  07  06  05  04  03  02  01  00  99        10  9  8  7  6  5  4  3  2  1

*For Matthew*

*In memory of Paulo Freire*

# CONTENTS

# Preface

## FRAMES WITHIN FRAMES

*Experience is contingent; it is unstable; it is invoked within a framework of memory, consciousness, context, its fictionality slipping through its fissures. (Puar, 81)*

When spring returns to northern Ohio, the grey pall that for months has held sway over the countryside begins to break, and the first signs of Oberlin College's carefully landscaped gardens appear—a few crocuses outside the Oberlin Inn, the first green shoots of daffodils arranged in wide swaths across Tappan Square, the banks of phlox that overhang the walls before Carnegie. The gardens have been carefully scripted to keep the campus in bloom from April to October. This pastoral panorama is a painstakingly maintained work of living art, a constant reminder of the urge among early settlers to create detached colonies from which they might realize their vision of a pure society and a "sense of separation from the world of orthodoxy" (Blodgett 1972, 7). Oberlin's militant Christian founders established the institution to train teachers and Christian leaders to advance the faith to the West (Oberlin Course Catalog 1996).

From the steps of Allen Memorial Art Museum, where I'm standing with a group of my students, beneath the tiled and multicolored mosaic ceiling, more of Oberlin's construction of its own history becomes visible. Before us is a small stone marker commemorating Oberlin College as the first coeducational college in the United States. Founded in 1833, Oberlin was among the first colleges to grant undergraduate degrees to women and the first primarily white college to educate African-Americans. The Memorial Arch across the square honors the Christian missionaries from Oberlin who died in China's Boxer Rebellion in 1899. Beyond that, down Professor Street just out of sight, a fifteen-foot-long set of railroad tracks emerges at a forty-five degree angle from the ground outside a student co-op, signifying Oberlin's role in helping fugitive slaves to freedom. These gardens, monuments, and narratives of Christian expansion and social reform frame Oberlin's image of itself.

A frame surrounds an object, shapes its contours, re-presents it. Frames offer perspective; they style how an object or subject is seen. Frames imply boundaries; they limit what and how we view something. Window frames. Eyeglass frames. Analytical frames. Methodological frames. Institutional frames. Cultural frames. Historical frames. Frames of reference. To frame: to fake the evidence against. The frame-up. Frames are structures that enclose, encircle, expose. Picture frames. Frames structure from the inside. A skeleton. A chassis. The frame of a car or house. Frames support. A scaffold. A cadre. Frames mark a place in a series. Motion-picture frames. The frames of a storyboard. An inning in baseball. A round in bowling. Frames are states of mind. Formulations. Constructs.

The permanent collection in the Allen Memorial Art Museum, a structure established on the Oberlin College campus in 1917, houses pastoral landscapes of the European masters of the past: Cézanne's *Pine Tree at Bellevue,* Turner's *View of Venice,* Monet's *Garden of Princesses.* Paths are clear: the students and I must walk past these landscapes in order to get to the temporary exhibit "Interrogating Identity," which is comprised of work solely by contemporary artists of color. The students disperse, and I find myself standing alone before a series of rectangular canvases coated in metallic green and silver paint. They look like mirrors but elicit no self-recognition. Identification continually slips away. They are mirrors that are not mirrors. The nameplate below the first canvas reads, "Lillian Mulero, *Untitled Mirrors*" (see figure 1).

Each canvas looks like a mirror that has been painted in. Frames are painted directly onto the canvas; they are part of the illusion. Mulero's mirrors prompt me to think of myself as a subject in their making. Paradoxically, the *Untitled Mirrors* prevent me from seeing my brown eyes, my shoulder-length auburn hair graying at the temples, my white skin, its discolorations and scars; yet in their literal denial of my bodily image, the paintings expose the partiality of my vision. Who am I when I'm looking? Who am I *not* when

Figure 1. From the *Untitled Mirrors* series (1990), by Lillian Mulero. Used by permission of the artist.

I'm looking? Am I not a teacher of writing? Am I not a woman? Am I not white? Am I not able-bodied? Is this who I am when I'm looking?

While these categories reveal aspects of my identity and institutional affiliation, they too are deceptive, partial. It is precisely the partiality and instability of social-identity categories that Mulero's mirrors throw into relief by rendering them invisible. These mirrors that are not mirrors set an unavoidable trap. A snare snaps back in this self-referential field where the visible is made invisible in order to reflect what is not seen: the ideology of looking. The mirrors summon viewers to observe how art is framed by historical contexts, paradigms, and conventions. They elicit an awareness of the lenses that frame the stories we tell about ourselves and our institutions. They expose the frames within the frames.

The *Untitled Mirrors* frame perception as a process of self-(re)presentation. The fluctuating and contestatory nature of identification is perhaps best illustrated through the ironic relation between the paintings and their title. The title *Untitled Mirrors* recovers the mirror's function in order to disturb it. Like René Magritte's painting *Ceci n'est pas une pipe,* these mirrors interrogate the language of representation itself. Bound together by spatial positioning, the paintings and their title enter into a reciprocal complicity, each denying the other. Together, they unsettle the traditional view of language as a mirror of reality. Moreover, Mulero's mirrors undermine the power of the viewer to control what is seen. They call into question principles of authenticity and privileged vision and renounce vision as the predominant indicator of difference. In other words, they challenge the conflation of identity with visibility and interrogate the "discursive and disciplinary place from which questions of identity are strategically and institutionally posed" (Bhabha 1987, 5). To enter this self-referential game is to play among the stylized language of mirrors—instruments of adornment and exhibitionism—and theories of spectatorship and subjectivity.

As I walk through the Allen Memorial Art Museum with students from my writing course, I realize that these mirrors tell a story about the dynamics of autobiography, pedagogy, and the culture of the academy. Mulero's mirrors are an image metaphor for this book, which focuses on how social identities and differences are framed by particular theoretical, historical, and institutional contexts. The very placement of the exhibit "Interrogating Identity"—in an institutional space where the works of European white male artists have been favored—exposes the institutionalization of the white male body and how historically white men have been licensed to look. The placement of the paintings, and the exhibit as a whole, could be interpreted as a gesture of institutional tokenism, in that artists of color are strategically positioned in a predominantly white institution as interrogators and thus educators of differ-ence. Mulero's *Untitled Mirrors* play against institutional tokenism by chal-lenging the viewer to recognize how differences are produced through cultur-al practices and social categories of representation.

Mulero's mirrors reveal how power relations in the academy are enacted through a "regime of visibility" (Bhabha 1983, 33). Mulero's mirrors deny the historically privileged viewer the luxury of seeing himself in the paintings. By not reflecting the viewer's bodily image, physique, and frame, Mulero play-fully suspends unreflective and ritualized practices of self-representation and disables the habitual tendency to render the other exotic. But visibility is more complex than not showing the white male viewer. Other viewers may identify with the image of absence, seeing it as a visual prototype for their own marginalization. Historically privileged groups may feel that the process of imaging their own absence enables them to understand better the alien-ation and marginalization of historically oppressed groups. Notwithstanding the shifting and multiple frames that viewers bring with them, Mulero's *Un-titled Mirrors* provide a visual space, an openness, a frame through which viewers may join with one another in identifying how ideology works so well when it is invisible.

> There is no clear or obvious "message," no language that is not punctu-ated by its contexts, by our bodies, by our selves, just as there is no neu-tral means of representation. (Chambers, 22)

By invoking the multiple metaphors of frames, I am *not* suggesting that as teachers-researchers we can situate ourselves beyond all frames. But I am urging that we recognize how particular frames—theoretical, pedagogical, or otherwise—shape and limit the knowledge we produce, and how power is lo-cated in the cultural practice of enframing. Mulero's mirrors expose the power of selection and the social and aesthetic logic that shape the museum's perma-nent collection. They elicit recognition of the bodies that look and the bodies that are seen, of the material and historical embodiment of vision, and thus foreground self-representation as a field of struggle. Paradoxically, the struc-tures that frame Mulero's critical vision are the very structures with which such critiques and visions must compete (Lakritz, 6). In this sense, Mulero's *Untitled Mirrors* point to the themes at the heart of my project: my interest in cultural struggles over self-representation, the distribution of power and knowledge in the academy, and the contradictions critical educators, artists, and activists face working within institutions resistant to change.

The postmodern concept of embodied vision contrasts with traditional views of knowledge and vision as something that leaps out of the body—

what Donna Haraway calls the "conquering gaze from nowhere . . . that mythically inscribes all the marked bodies, that makes the unmarked category claim the power to see and not be seen, to represent while escaping representation" (1991, 188). In contrast to those who argue for an unconditional objectivity, which isolates the historical and material body from the realm of discourse (a form of identity politics wherein authorial authority is masked ), I am interested in the political and pedagogical dimensions of reflexivity and the relationship between the voices of those represented and those doing the representing.

Like Mulero's mirrors, I maintain that the material and discursive realms are fundamentally inseparable. Hence, I urge readers to "read" autobiographical acts, whether spoken, visual, or written, as material-discursive meeting grounds and writing and reading subjects as located across, and continually moving through, institutional spaces and their truth-telling discourses of identity and difference (e.g., medical, pedagogical, legal, religious, and so on). I use the term *discourse* in the Foucauldian sense to indicate a configuration of possibilities that structure what can have a truth value through rules of exclusion, prohibition, and classificatory divisions. I find what Mulero's mirrors say about the hierarchization of discourses on identity and difference and their implicit self-reflexivity useful for thinking about how the material writing body and textual bodies are represented and negotiated in the culture of the academy. The textual body is not a mirror of the material self that writes. In much the same way as the written body can be said to be intertextual— comprised of various and contesting social languages and codes—the material writing body is intercorporeal; it cannot be conceived outside of the interrelations and contexts of which it is a living part (Holquist, 90).

> The body becomes a flexible zone, interleaved, crossed and composed by multiple discourses, constructed in different languages, tempos and places, received and lived with disparate meanings that are diversely embodied. (Chambers, 23)

My goal in *Framing Identities* is to "read writing so that bodies speak" (Kraemer, 65), and to investigate the process of self-(re)presentation and the social, spatial, and discursive frames within and through which academic bodies and identities are constituted. Throughout the book, I attempt to hold the material and discursive in productive tension, as Mulero's *Untitled Mirrors* do, to frame the complicated workings of self-representation as they are inflected, given expression, and grounded in institutional spaces, themselves defined by radical inequalities and contesting ideologies and narratives of identity.

Everyday autobiographical practices are enmeshed in the technologies of selfhood dispersed across a heterogeneous field of institutional locations . . . individuals move into, through, and out of these disparate social spaces, and participate in specific, yet different, narrative practices through which we become subjects in and of our stories. (Smith and Watson 1996, 10)

Outside, it has been raining a little. In the reflection along the slate sidewalk, another Oberlin appears, an image that reframes the college's representation of itself. It is precisely this process of turning the image upside down, of making the familiar strange, that allows us to see how we have become part of the reflection and how the process of enframing shapes and moves through our investigations.

# ACKNOWLEDGMENTS

I am grateful to many friends, colleagues, and editors involved with earlier versions of this work who enriched my written accounts: Ann Cooper Albright, Cristelle Baskins, Wendy Bishop, Purnima Bose, Jan Cooper, Pat Day, Paul John Eakin, Christine Farris, Leela Fernandes, Sibelan Forrestor, Juan Guerra, Susan Jarratt, Eileen Julien, Joan Pong Linton, Camille Guerin-Gonzales, Maggie Kamitsuka, Nancy Matthews, Audrey McCluskey, Hans Ostrom, Len and Joanne Podis, Angela Pao, Yopie Prins, Paula Richman, Judith Roof, Carol Severino, Sidonie Smith, Lynn Worsham, and Sandy Zagarell. I can only hope I have approximated their suggestions. I am deeply appreciative of Wendy Kozol, an extraordinary friend and colleague, whose generous and challenging readings (and rereadings) of these chapters over the years substantially enriched the book as a whole.

I am indebted to my former students at Oberlin College, whose commitment to social change and spirit of inquiry was a never-ending inspiration and joy for me as a teacher. I especially want to thank those students who gave me permission to include their work as part of this study. Likewise, I would like to thank former Oberlin colleagues who contributed to chapter 5 by sharing their thoughts with me in private interviews. For reasons of confidentiality, I cannot list their names here, but thank you all; your generosity and insights have been invaluable. Thanks also to Roland Baumann, Oberlin College archivist. I'd also like to thank my graduate students at Indiana University from my spring 1998 seminar "Autobiography, Pedagogy, and the

Culture of the Academy," whose insights helped me clarify aspects of the manuscript in its final stages.

I want to express my sincere gratitude to Chandra Talpade Mohanty and Henry Giroux for their enthusiasm for the project in its early stages. I am likewise thankful to Lisa Freeman, former director of the University of Minnesota Press, Roger Simon, and an anonymous reader; their critical reading of the entire manuscript helped bring the project to fruition. The production process was beautifully handled by Laura Westlund, managing editor, and Robin A. Moir, editorial assistant, and the manuscript much improved by the copyediting of Susan C. Jones. Thanks also to Kathleen Fallon, my research assistant, who did exceptional work on the bibliography in its final stages, and to Kelly Wissman for assistance on the index.

Financial aid from various sources provided valuable time for writing, research, and course development. I want to thank Indiana University for a summer research fellowship that enabled me to revise the manuscript for publication. Thanks also to Oberlin College for curricular-development grants that helped me refine my pedagogy and to the Rockefeller Brothers Foundation for selecting me as a mentor for minority students in education, an exciting fellowship program that put me in contact with students and teachers with similar interests at a variety of U.S. institutions.

One person deserves special mention. Matthew Cariello has been an unswerving source of support. I thank him for his unyielding love and patience over the years. I would like to acknowledge my parents, Phyllis and David Hesford; my brother and sister-in-law, Darrell and Deanna Hesford; and my in-laws, Michael and Norma Jean Cariello, for their generosity and support. Finally, I send a spiritual embrace to Amy Cariello, however insufficient a tribute words may be to acknowledge the loss of your presence in our lives.

# Introduction

## AUTOBIOGRAPHY AND THE POLITICS OF IDENTITY ON CAMPUS

> The "Oberlin" we must fight for is a community that we ourselves con-
> stitute, uphold and define; furthermore, our efforts here must be in the
> context of a larger social system in which Oberlin is merely a tiny, privi-
> leged part. . . . We must not only reclaim these spaces but transform
> them; for we must realize that our very presence as tokenized individu-
> als within these spaces of privilege more often serves not to expose but to
> obscure the oppression faced by those very populations we are supposed to
> represent. (Schleitwiler, 24)

> I am a second generation Asian American. Specifically, I am a Filipino
> American. More specifically, I am a neo-colonial diasporic Filipino
> struggling to exist in this predominantly white liberal institution we call
> Oberlin. It is absolutely necessary for me to state that for us as Asian
> Americans to be denied the opportunity to learn about our history and
> experience in this neo-colonial construct we call America is an absolute
> violation of our rights as tuition-paying students. . . . As we fight for
> Asian American Studies, it is imperative to constantly remember our
> long struggle. Remembering is part of a decolonizing process . . .
> (Cabusao 1996, 19–20)

Asian-American students at Oberlin College organized a speak-out during
the fall of 1995 to increase support for Asian-American Studies and to educate
the community about the twenty-five-year struggle for its development at the

college. Speakers at the rally summoned administrators, faculty, and their fellow students to interrogate the promises of Oberlin's progressive legacy upon which the college has built its image. Oberlin College is a selective residential liberal arts college with a long history of social consciousness and commitment to equal rights shaped by the values of Western liberalism and by missionary imperatives.[1]

Despite Oberlin College's legacy of progressivism and its self-image, expressed in a 1996 college catalog, of being "dedicated to recruiting a culturally, economically, geographically, racially diverse group of students," historically oppressed groups at the school continue to fight for representation and rights. For instance, a 1995 survey revealed that approximately three-quarters of the Oberlin student body is white and middle-class.[2] Students at the rally called attention to the gaps among Oberlin's goals of diversity and equality, the institutional narratives that become fixed in the social imagination of Oberlinians, and the material reality of life at the college. I cite these gaps not to embark upon a critical history of Oberlin College's admission policies but to underscore some of the questions that frame my exploration of the pedagogy and politics of representation. These larger framing questions include: How are the stories we tell about our educational institutions used to justify local resistance or institutional complacency? How do historically marginal groups expose the partiality and presumptions of institutional histories and truths through autobiographical acts?

In order to address these questions, I return to the two epigraphs of this Introduction. These two excerpts were taken from a student-run publication *As I Am,* whose purpose is to give voice to the concerns of the Asian-American community on campus, shortly after the rally for Asian-American Studies; the second excerpt is a transcript from a speech given at the rally. *As I Am* claims a kind of insider-outsider status; it is both in the academy and an alternative to dominant discourses of the academy that seeks to give voice to groups traditionally silenced. While alternative publications may reinscribe the very categories of difference they seek to transform, their presence and need indicate that students from historically oppressed groups must negotiate their way through the contradictions produced by the very structures they challenge. I selected these extracts because they exemplify the complex and contradictory ways that autobiography is mobilized on our nation's campuses in debates over the curriculum, the configuration of disciplines, the composition of the student body and faculty—issues at the heart of this study.

These excerpts foreground the institutionalization of particular subjectivities, and thus provide the opportunity to discuss how institutional needs frame the details of a life, selectively legitimating and mapping out certain subject-positions and projecting autobiographical scripts onto particular in-dividuals and groups. I use the term *autobiographical scripts* to refer to the cul-turally available models of identity and narrative templates that structure ex-periential history (Smith and Watson 1996, 9). Consider, for example, how these two students claim authority and negotiate their positions through sig-nification and how such insider-outsider identity narratives get used by insti-tutions in essentializing ways. For example, individual minorities are far too often positioned as institutional tokens upon whom authority is granted be-cause of visible appearances and assumptions about their affinities with a par-ticular subject matter.

The two students of color quoted here invoke and critique social-identity categories that have been used to define their marginalization. Vincent Schleitwiler suggests that his identity as an Asian-American in the academy simultaneously authorizes his claims and positions him as a token other—that is, people in powerful positions essentialize him as a representative of the Asian-American community. Like Schleitwiler, Jeff Cabusao is critical of es-sentialist uses of identity categories (the idea that a core identity and fixed characteristics unite communities); he contends that identity is shifting and multiple. But in his refusal to be reduced to fixed, categorical distinctions, he endorses a racially and ethnically based group identity. These two epigraphs thus exhibit the kind of "double-consciousness" that Du Bois defined as "the sense of looking at one's self through the eyes of others" (quoted in Bow, 40). Schleitwiler reveals the contradictory nature of his position of speaking both *for* and *as* a minority within the privileged confines of the academy and of contemplating the institutional structures of authority through which such representations are channeled.

Jeff Cabusao exposes the racist ideologies behind conceptions of diversi-ty that homogenize the other and, at the same time, appropriates the lan-guage on which such ideologies are built. For instance, he invokes the dis-course of rights and consumer rhetoric within his critique: "this neo-colonial construct we call America is an absolute violation of our rights as tuition-paying students." In his attempt to define himself and to engage with repre-sentations others have made of him, we see the clash of dominant and resis-tance discourses. That Cabusao and Schleitwiler work both *with* and *against* dominant structures and discourses suggests that strategies of resistance with-in the academy often are borne out of the "very gaps, fissures, and silences of hegemonic narratives" (Mohanty 1991, 38).

These students use autobiography and the language of identity to ex-pose the partiality and presumptions of institutional histories and truths and, like many scholars of color, to fracture fixed autobiographical scripts and to represent the shifting identities and multiple identifications among communities. Leslie Bow points out that identity categories such as Asian-American are not culturally coherent or natural. Rather they are used for political expediency and thus "specify a coalition based on a similarity of treatment within the U.S." (32). Bow argues that Asian-Americans share a history of issues including immigration policies, labor patterns, bilingualism, and racist structures that reduce identity to a commodity. Despite these similarities, as Cabusao proposes, this is a time when issues of representation and authenticity are points of contention within nondominant communities. For example, the category of Asian-American often excludes the histories and experiences of Filipinos in this country; their immigration experiences, differentiated by U.S. colonialism, are not necessarily those of other Asian-Americans (Cabusao 1995). There are, therefore, strategic reasons why student organizations premised on identity and publications such as *As I Am* continue to exist. Oberlin student Narges Kakalia, editor of *DESI* (a slang term for Indian, which functions here as an acronym for Discourse Expressing South Asian Issues), puts it this way:

> Until I came to Oberlin I had always defined myself as Pakistani. In 1992, encountering the fact of suddenly being the visible minority in a new country, I called myself South Asian. As a Pakistani I am one of approximately ten students at Oberlin. As a South Asian I am one of around a hundred. There is safety in numbers. (5)[3]

Like Schleitwiler's and Cabusao's, Kakalia's statement illustrates the double discourse of autobiography: how, when expressed at the level of historical consciousness, autobiography can be used to resist hegemonies and to negate imposed identities, and how it can be used to disguise differences and reinforce essentialist notions of community (Higginbotham, 267–68). What Kakalia importantly points out then is the relational nature of autobiographical positioning, how the position of the speaker and the context of the utterance shape both its production and reception.

The conflicts and concerns raised by these students may have a particular history at Oberlin College, but they are not peculiar to Oberlinians. These students' struggles resonate with the experiences of historically marginalized groups at colleges and universities throughout this country.[4] Although these issues reverberate at the national level, there is a great need for studies of the pedagogy and culture of the academy that are situational—located specifically and elaborated contextually. There is also a need for a sustained analysis of the political stakes of invoking the autobiographical in academic sites and the contradictory effects of such acts. We must not, however, romanticize the primacy of the local or mythologize local sites as independent from larger power structures, social relations, and discourses. As the student excerpts suggest, the local and the national (themselves shifting sites) have a dialogic relationship; national narratives are embedded in the local and local narratives in the national. While it is important to account for the local contours of each site, it is equally important to realize that the local and national are interlocking and that they have a mutually defining relationship. It is my hope that *Framing Identities* will exemplify the type of pedagogy scholarship necessary to deepen our understanding of how autobiography shapes the culture of the academy.

*Framing Identities: Autobiography and the Politics of Pedagogy* contributes to the debates over the culture of the academy by investigating how various constituents use autobiographical practices to constitute themselves as social, political, and intellectual subjects. Autobiographical acts (whether speech acts, written texts, visual forms, or symbolic gestures that reference the autobiographical subject or body) do not reflect unmediated subjectivities; rather, they are acts of self-representation that are ideologically encoded with historical memories and principles of identity and truth. My interest in acts of self-representation contrasts with expressionist viewpoints, wherein autobiography is framed as a doorway to the apprehension of an original experience or unchanging essence. I am less interested in autobiography as a chronological record of a life already lived or as the retrieval of an essential essence or truth (the traditional view) than I am with examining autobiographical acts as social signifying practices shaped by and enacted within particular institutional contexts and their histories. Inquiry into the pedagogical dynamics of autobiography can reframe and renew contemporary discussions about the academy as a site of struggle, collaboration, and transformation.

## Multiculturalism and the Politics of Identity

Beyond introducing the struggles over self-representation and power at the local level, the issues and questions raised by the two epigraphs are points of contention in many academic communities. Who can speak for whom and in what contexts? Can I as a white feminist speak *for* or *on behalf of* Asian-American students? What is the relationship between authenticity and oppositional politics? How do/can we reconcile the articulation of multiple identities and shifting subjectivities with collective struggle? These questions point to a crisis of representation and concern about the institutionalization of difference, which reflects the current scrutiny of identity politics and autobiography in the academy. The term *identity-based politics* has put autobiography and self-representation at the center of campus politics and has come to signify a range of political, scholarly, and pedagogical projects. For instance, identity politics has shaped the debates over affirmative action policies, sexual harassment, the curriculum, and the focus of writing instruction. Indeed, critiques of autobiography and identity politics are intrinsically linked: when you begin to question the premises of autobiography, you unveil the relationship between identity and power.

*Framing Identities* is distinctive in its focus on autobiography as an especially weighty discourse of identity. Autobiography, like identity politics, can be used to refuse the boundaries and identities imposed by dominant groups. For instance, the students quoted at the beginning of this Introduction reclaim imposed labels while they challenge Eurocentric ideas of the homogenous other and frame naming as a political activity. But as the students imply, identity politics also can disguise differences and reinforce dominant structures and relations of power. Two examples of this use of identity politics are institutionalized practices of tokenism and essentialism. Likewise, autobiography is not an unequivocally empowering medium but a contradictory form of cultural politics that has both progressive and reactionary forms. I contend that greater awareness of how power is claimed and negotiated through autobiographical acts can enable historically oppressed groups to better gauge the risks of autobiography and develop more effective strategies and pockets of resistance. Autobiography is indispensable to the study of intellectual and political resistance, because the capacity to transform oppressive relations, practices, and structures is tied closely to the sociopolitical struggles of the groups making the challenges.

The New Right has blamed minority communities for the rise in racial tensions on campus and targeted them for practicing separatist politics and tribalism (which they refer to as the balkanization of American campuses). As Norma Alarcón perceptively points out, "Because 'multiculturalism' is often perceived through the ongoing ethnic genocide and fighting in Eastern Europe, it gives rise in the United States to paranoia" (142). To curtail so-called tribal identity politics, the New Right has called for a return to traditional standards of excellence (the "Great Books") and the formation of a "common culture," which they argue are endemic to national identity and security (Bennett, A. Bloom, Cheney, D'Souza, Kimball, and Ravitch, among others). E. D. Hirsch's best-selling version of this is the push for a common cultural literacy. The common-culture-literacy argument is in part a national apocalyptic narrative in which neoconservatives position themselves as defenders of Western civilization, a narrative reflecting the anxieties of dominant groups threatened by an increasingly multiracial America and the fracturing of a relatively homogenous educational citadel (Graff). Elizabeth

*Shakespeare is an acquired taste for white people too*

Kamarck Minnich describes this false universalization as the "root" problem in academe, which regards the views of a few white privileged men from a particular tradition as the norm and ideal for all (2). It should come as no surprise, then, that conservatives accuse minority communities of identity politics. They have seldom if ever seen themselves as engaged in identity politics; they have framed identity politics as something that "others" do.

Historically, identity politics is associated with social movements such as the Black Power movement, the women's movement, and the gay and lesbian movement, all of which sought to reclaim identity and to revalue the devalued pole of dichotomized hierarchies such as white/black, male/female, and straight/gay. What started as a broad-based identity politics in the civil rights, anti-war, gay rights, and women's movements has turned, according to some critics, into a narrow politics of identity. Recently, some feminists have argued that reclaiming positive identities is important, but engaging in politics that emphasize national and social identities hinders a group's ability to create common ground and to work for an egalitarian society. Liberal cultural critics also have argued that identity politics has fractured political action on our campuses and produced "a grim and hermetic bravado celebrating victimization and stylized marginality" (Gitlin, 311). Undeniably, some individuals do celebrate their own victimization; this occurs as often in the academy as it does on television talk shows and in tabloid publications. However, critics who claim that a focus on identity can only lead to divisive politics or "stylized marginality" ignore the particularization of knowledge and the fact that identity-related conflicts remain integral to many political and pedagogical projects. Identity politics is about material bodies, social relations, labor, and power. Cornel West puts it this way:

> We cannot talk about identity without talking about death . . . Persons who construct their identities and desires often do it in such a way that they are willing to die for it—soldiers in the Middle East, for example—or, under a national identity, that they're willing to kill others. And the rampant sexual violence in the lives of thousands of women who are attacked by men caught up in vicious patriarchal identities—this speaks to what we are talking about. (16)

Although contemporary identity politics on U.S. college campuses may appear to privilege cultural representations as the site of identity, we must not forget that material bodies and institutional structures are surfaces and sites of identity production. Moreover, we must recognize the volatile and changing nature of identity in the late twentieth century due to the globalization of capitalism, decolonization, emigration flow, ethnic cleansing, and so on. The times demand, as Coco Fusco contends, a critical position that recognizes identity as historical and changing yet still a political reality (27).

Debates over the politics of identity prompt questions about autobiography, authenticity, and agency that are central to this study. How, in reclaiming certain identities, do nondominant groups in the academy reaffirm the very categories they challenge? How do these contradictions give rise to resistance? How do subjects from historically marginalized groups negotiate authority? How can we create sites of resistance if the spaces framing our resistance are fractured and conflictual? How can an interrogation of the dynamics of autobiography inform resistant acts? What political and pedagogical strategies can acts of self-social reflexivity produce? How do the dominant paradigms appropriate or reclaim strategies that marginalized groups have used in their own struggles for power? To sidestep these difficult questions is to ignore the interpretive and historical frameworks that shape and, in many cases, force assertions of identity and difference.

Critical educators are caught in a conundrum, juggling tensions provoked by attacks on the relevance of cultural identity to the production of knowledge and to the governance of institutional affairs, claims that we live in a postracist era, and a suspicion that race and ethnicity are synonymous with the weak's self-destructive threats to the strong (Newfield and Gordon, 77). The backlash against affirmative action, race and gender consciousness, and welfare reforms has reintroduced the image of common culture into the national narrative. The contradictions produced by the institutionalization of difference and multiculturalism exacerbate these tensions.

Multiculturalism holds the promise of giving historically oppressed groups a sense of place and history in the academy. For example, the formation of programs based on identity—African-American Studies, Asian-American Studies, Ethnic Studies, Gay and Lesbian Studies, and Women's Studies—has encouraged the exploration of links among history, identity, and knowledge, demanded integration of the histories of people of color in the United States, called for structural changes in more traditional disciplines, made visible veiled universalism and assimilationist pluralism, and uncovered interpretive errors in research about women and communities of color (Newfield and Gordon, 102). At the same time, these programs, more often than not underfunded, are marginalized and kept in a manageable space that does not substantially affect the process of restructuring authority and power. Multiculturalism can be seen as an attack on the common-culture argument. For many, however, its institutionalization has amounted to the common-culture argument in drag (Gordon and Newfield, 4–8).

Cultural-diversity requirements in colleges and universities nationwide

reveal the limits of multiculturalism and the institutionalization of difference. Far too often, such curricular reforms abstract identity from issues of
power and reflect a consumer approach to difference. Cultural-diversity requirements that entail little more than relabeling existing courses, for example, do not fundamentally transform the curriculum or open up institutional
structures to those who have traditionally been denied access. Such reforms
are an academic version of ethnic fast-food franchises; ethnicity and difference have entered the kitchens and malls of mainstream America, but they
have not altered the fundamental inequalities of our economic or social structures. Cultural-diversity requirements that are not supported by larger structural reforms put dominant groups in the privileged position of consuming
the other. Additionally, a multiculturalism that simply adds or celebrates the
voices and histories of oppressed groups does not necessarily alter the way the
center is read or affect the political core of power; instead, it often perpetuates
a kind of "pluralism structured in dominance" (Erickson quoted in Newfield,
102). Moreover, multiculturalism that avoids talk of racism, reframes race
solely as an issue of personal identity, and idealizes equality among multiple
cultures does not challenge the workings of capitalist democracy. Repeatedly,
multiculturalism in predominantly white institutions remains little more
than an attitudinal engagement with diversity and the academy, a museum
displaying difference at the level of culture.

What we need in American education is a multiculturalism that analyzes
power differentials at the structural level and recognizes intersections of difference based on gender, race, class, language, and sexuality. We need a strong
multiculturalism that emphasizes political equity and takes responsibility for,
and action toward, the divestment of institutional and historical privileges
(Newfield and Gordon, 106).

## Contact Zones and Contradictions

In order to understand the politics of autobiography as it shapes the pedagogy of the institution, we must first acknowledge that colleges and universities are historical sites where radical inequalities exist and heterogeneous
identities and ideologies collide. As Gerald Graff points out, the modern university always has "rested on a deeply contradictory mission." It is expected
to preserve and transmit traditions and, at the same time, produce new
knowledge (7). Graff proposes that teachers recognize the legitimacy of
today's social conflicts, including conflicts over the production of knowledge
and construction of disciplines, and teach the conflicts rather than shield
students from them—the common culture platform (5). I maintain that we
not only "teach the conflicts" but that we also view our campus communities

and classrooms as "contact zones" and use this concept to help us better understand the pedagogy of the institution—its affiliations, structures, policies, curricula, programs, student protests, and coalitions.

In *Imperial Eyes*, a book about European travel writing and its role in the possession of new territories by industrial nations, Mary Louise Pratt defines "contact zones" as "space[s] in which peoples geographically and historically separated come into contact with each other and establish ongoing relations, usually involving conditions of coercion, radical inequality, and intractable conflict" (6). Pratt's primary interest is in the "dynamic of self-representation in the context of colonial subordination and resistance" (5). She focuses, therefore, on the social and discursive spaces where disparate cultures collide, a phenomenon she calls transculturation and defines as the process by which "subordinate or marginal groups select and invent from materials transmitted to them by a dominant or metropolitan culture" (6). Autoethnographic expressions—those instances wherein colonized peoples engage with representations others have made of them—exist in dialogue with ethnographic representations, when privileged groups represent "the other" to themselves, in both their production and reception (7). Pratt's notion of the contact zone, transculturation, and autoethnographic expressions are important to my critical investigation of the pedagogical dynamics of autobiography in the academy. Like Pratt, I am interested in how marginal groups appropriate dominant modes of representation and, conversely, in how privileged groups appropriate the strategies of marginalized groups and, subsequently, how the oppressed/oppressor binarism is traversed.

Contact zones are not only spaces on the colonial frontier; they also are material, conceptual, and linguistic spaces that we encounter in our cities, at the workplace, and in the academy. My intention is not to perpetuate the conditions of academic contact zones but, rather, to recognize and engage their political and pedagogical dynamics. The term *pedagogy* in the title and as used throughout this book refers not solely to teaching methods and curricular content and design but also to the processes by which teachers, students, administrators, staff, and others negotiate and produce knowledge, identities, and social relations (McLaren 1995, 34). To say that pedagogy is a form of cultural politics is to see practice as living theory—living in the sense that it is situated historically and thus open to change, debate, and contradiction.

This conception of pedagogy expands our understanding and enables us to see that pedagogy is not limited solely to classroom practice. The pedagogical occasions I consider in this study include writing and women's studies classrooms; meetings at which faculty, students, and administrators discussed revisions of the college's sexual-offense policy; and student activism and protests against violence toward women, institutional racism, and hate crimes. I argue that faculty meetings and student protests, like classrooms, are sites with pedagogical investments and imperatives. The pedagogical occasions represented in this study are not intended to reflect the views of all faculty, students, or administrators at Oberlin College, past or present. Nor are my interpretations presented as incontestable evidence. The pedagogical occasions selected are those I believe best represent the dynamics of autobiography and politics of identity as they shaped the pedagogy of the institution during the period under study.

The speak-out in support of Asian-American studies exemplifies how autobiographical and pedagogical acts come together as a form of cultural politics. Students linked their call for transforming the curriculum and disciplinary structures to the historical struggles and identities of particular groups. They attested to the conflicts in the contact zone of the academy and depicted how, as historically marginalized subjects, they must negotiate their authority among contradictory positions. These negotiations of dominant and oppositional discourses (themselves heterogeneous) could be considered critical pedagogical acts—or, in Pratt's terms, autoethnographic expressions—because they arise out of contradictions and in spite of them. Critical pedagogical interventions involve recognition of the contradictions that define and constitute one's authority. Like students, teachers-researchers work among a multitude of forces (institutional, social, and personal), none of which exclusively dominates or liberates but all of which are caught in contradictory relations. These contradictions suggest that a subject's agency is fluid, not static, and that both personal and political agencies exist in relation to particular historical struggles and contexts. My goal is not to resolve these contradictions but to focus on their pedagogical implications and how personal and political agency emerges from, or is borne out of, such tensions.

I do not intend to conflate the positions of students and teachers or to deny that student-teacher relations are hierarchically structured. My goal is to explore multiple articulations of authority and identity and to discover how authority and agency shift from one pedagogical context to another. A relational understanding of power thus prompts a new set of questions about how teachers and students claim authority within the academy. Is Vincent Schleitwiler's authority established through his own assertion of difference in an elite and largely white liberal arts college? Does Schleitwiler gain authority and agency by being on the edge or in the margins? Or is the authority from which he speaks presumed to be given to him by dominant groups that position him as the representative or tokenized other? This last question illustrates the problem of positioning minority students and scholars of color as the sole educators of difference; that is, white students and faculty often displace the burden of understanding and working through differences onto students and faculty of color. Consider the displacement of authority in the present example, in which I speak about Vincent speaking about his problem of speaking for his community. I draw attention to the relational nature of authority because it raises important pedagogical questions about the power of representation. How might my engagement with the experiences and protests of students of color re-ignite the problems they address? How can educators and scholars research and teach students about the struggles of historically marginalized groups without appropriating their experiences and neutralizing counternarratives? These questions expose the risks inherent in this kind of pedagogical work, specifically, the risk that I might speak *for* students rather than *with* them. There is, however, more at stake in *not* pursuing transformative pedagogical projects, and that is the risk of re-creating the silences. Critical educators must bear witness to the struggles of others. Bearing witness, as I argue in chapter 6, is not a passive pedagogical act but one with interventionist implications. Bearing witness, like giving testimony, is a form of action.

Although I began with statements from students of color, I do not intend to position myself or my readers as mere spectators of cultural difference or to reproduce a kind of illustrative tokenism—versions of identity politics practiced from locations of privilege. Instead, I propose that teachers-researchers, particularly white critical educators, turn the othering gaze on ourselves and envision new ways of speaking and listening that acknowledge cultural differences and work against the historical tendency to situate ourselves at the center (Ellsworth 1992, 9).

Antiracist and antisexist pedagogical work often puts one in an uncomfortable and tenuous position in the institution, but such risks must not paralyze us. Nor must we be complacent. Instead, we must examine how we participate in the construction of the "other" at the level of practice. I urge all educators to be accountable for the narratives of gender, race, and class that they inhabit. Coalitions and dialogues across differences are not possible without this knowledge. As Peter McLaren puts it, we "need to be able to read critically the narratives *that are already reading us*" (1995, 89, emphasis in original). "The degree to which we resist certain narratives depends upon how we are able to read and rewrite them" (98). Critical educators must ask themselves: What narratives of identity and difference shape our authority, and how can we use the authority conferred on us to challenge and expose these narratives? I'm not suggesting that teachers-researchers frame each pedagogical and critical act with an identity mantra—for example, "I am a white heterosexual middle-class woman, a granddaughter of English immigrants"—

Figure 2. From the *Untitled Mirrors* series (1990), by Lillian Mulero. Used by permission of the artist.

but that we ask how identities and differences are framed by the institution and that we use this knowledge self-critically.

## Convergences: Composition, Feminist Studies, and Critical Pedagogy

*Framing Identities* participates in the autobiographical wave sweeping feminist scholarship and pedagogy across the disciplines.[5] Dale Bauer suggests that the feminist turn toward the autobiographical represents the need to establish a sense of community dissipated through the institutionalization of feminism (66). The urgency of autobiographical criticism and feminist interventions represents an effort to establish community but also to reclaim writing and teaching as forms of resistance. This push for the personal voice in scholarship and pedagogy has not gone unchallenged; indeed, it has provoked fury and indignation.[6] Nevertheless, more and more scholars, particularly in composition and literacy studies, are integrating autobiography as a form of cultural criticism into their pedagogy scholarship.

The convergence of autobiography, cultural criticism, and pedagogy can be seen in recent calls for site-specific pedagogy studies and the cultural materialist reframing of experience and the ethnographic project in composition (Brodkey, Chiseri-Strater, Farris, Lu and Horner, Kirsch and Ritchie), and in the proliferation of literacy testimonies by teachers themselves (Brandt, Brodkey, Gilyard, Royster, Lu, M. Rose, Soliday, N. Sommers, Villanueva). Min-Zhan Lu and Bruce Horner, for example, call for site-specific pedagogy studies that expose the problematics of experience and its interventionist potential and that reframe the ethnographic project "not strictly in terms of its efficiency in producing or transmitting knowledge to inform *subsequent* (social) practices but in terms of its effects *as* social practice" (1998, 257). Gesa E. Kirsch and Joy S. Ritchie call for a "politics of location" in which teachers-researchers in composition "theorize their locations by examining their experiences as reflections of ideology and culture"(8). Kirsch and Ritchie urge teachers to examine how their "conflicting positions, histories, and desires for power [are] implicated in [their] research questions, methodologies, and conclusions" (9). Many composition scholars call for a reflexive and rigorous revisioning of ourselves as teachers-researchers and for a use of autobiography that reinterprets experience and situates the personal in historical, political, and social contexts (10). John Schilb makes a similar point in *Between the Lines*, when he argues that autobiographical writing can be valuable when pedagogically "it recognizes (1) the self's often dynamic and mutable thoughts and feelings; (2) the role of interpretation and social context in the self's construction of experience; (3) the provisional quality of self-description; (4) the relation of the self to others in the world, including people who are more oppressed; and

(5) the ways that personal experience can problematize as well as produce theoretical generalizations" (174–75). Likewise, my goal in *Framing Identities* is to practice "autobiography as cultural criticism," to weave critically self-reflexive narratives into theoretical, pedagogical, and political arguments, and to formulate a cultural materialist pedagogy of autobiography (N. Miller 1).

The pedagogical implications of the cultural materialist approach to autobiography are significant for the teaching of writing and, as Horner and Lu suggest, for critical ethnography (259). First, it urges writing teachers to reconsider the role of the personal in the classroom and to challenge the idea that personal voice can be achieved apart from constraints of social material realities. Second, it encourages teachers-researchers to recognize how writers struggle with inherited social narratives of the self and how students negotiate their identities in response to perceived power relations, including teacher expectations. Third, it asks teachers-researchers to acknowledge the tensions between experience and discursive understanding, and the risks of autobiography in the classroom—that is, how power may be resecured through autobiographical acts.

Methodically, my study falls under the categories of autoethnography and critical ethnography. David M. Hayano in "Auto-Ethnography: Paradigms, Problems, and Prospects" defines autoethnographies as studies in which anthropologists and sociologists write ethnographies of their own people. There is a trend toward autoethnography in specializations such as urban anthropology, action anthropology, and research emerging from interdisciplinary and education studies (99). Autoethnographies do not follow one distinctive theoretical framework or paradigm, and there are several types of studies included in the autoethnography category. Among these are works by ethnographers who study their own cultural, social, ethnic, racial, or religious group and those who have acquired an intimate familiarity with, and write about, certain subcultures or recreational or occupational groups (100).

*Framing Identities* is autoethnographic in the sense that I have conducted research at a location where I was a member and with which I self-identify; I'm familiar with the language of academia, with the occupational group of teachers, and with the subculture of college students. My study is also self-ethnographic in the sense that I attempt to become a student of my own practice—to develop an antagonism in myself, to step back and examine my interpretative frames and presentations. This means being open to the possibility of *unlearning* certain historical narratives, institutional and personal. There are three main lines of inquiry that constitute my study as critical autoethnography: (a) the "emphasis on the narrative character of cultural representation" and view of experience and autobiography as an "ongoing process rather than a self-evident thing"; (b) attention to how I, as researcher-writer, mediate and translate experience and subjectivities; and (c) the emphasis on pedagogical implications of autobiographical acts and the politicization of experience is such that "the ethnographic project ceases to be purely hermeneutic, instead being understood as interventionist praxis" (Horner and Lu, 262). Thus, I attempt to resist and subvert the traditional ethnographic gaze by practicing a form of critical autoethnography that articulates my place within the contact zones of the academy and the theoretical and pedagogical frameworks that shape my analysis of these shifting and contested localities (Spurr, 9). The larger pretext narrative of *Framing Identities* is predicated on my ability to claim an insider-outsider status and to negotiate the scripts that one projects onto the other. I may resist the dominating gaze, but I nevertheless retain the power of representation. Unlike traditional ethnographic studies, in which researchers explain their presence through an introductory personal disclosure, I attempt to sustain this reflexive autoethnographic quality throughout the study, examining the relational nature of power and how my authority and agency shift from one pedagogical and institutional contact zone to another. In contrast to the authoritative positions commonly held by ethnographers, I don't seek to contain or fix the voices of those I'm studying, nor do I assume that by turning inward I can comprehend the totality of my experience or the experiences of others. Instead, I seek partial truths, what Donna Haraway calls a "critical positioning" [what I would call a pedagogy of location] "where partiality and not universality is the condition of being heard" (1991, 195). The autobiographical process necessitates constant reflexivity and the realization that interpretations fixed through print are provisional—part of the historical moment.

The most challenging aspect of conducting research while teaching at Oberlin College has been examining the contradictions between the college's ideals and the contested material realities and discovering how these contradictions shaped my position and authority in that context. As I suggested earlier, colleges and universities consist of multiple forces and discourses, institutional, social, and personal, none of which is exclusively dominating or liberating but all of which are often caught in contradictory relations. I soon realized that implementing critical feminist pedagogy in an elite institution involved the continual recognition of the contradictions I lived and the negotiation of projected and assumed autobiographical scripts and identities. I am not only concerned with how dominant institutional narratives and relations shape pedagogy but I also am interested in articulating the contradictions in the system that make those barriers vulnerable to change.

*Framing Identities* represents critical intersections among composition, critical pedagogy, and feminist studies, particularly materialist feminism, as each wrestles with the problematics of experience and the contradictory uses of autobiography in the academy. I see this project as an interdisciplinary and bridge-building pursuit that traverses the boundaries of traditional disciplines. This overlay of frames enables me to formulate a mode of analysis to study the politics and pedagogy of autobiography at the intersections of the material and discursive realms. It is precisely the convergences of these analytical and disciplinary frames, which are newly animated as they move from one pedagogical context to another, that makes this study unique. I hope that *Framing Identities* will provide a conceptual model for teachers-researchers across the curriculum to study the contradictory uses and social consequences of autobiography in the pedagogical contact zones at their own institutions and to enable them to imagine new pedagogical spaces for the practice of autobiography as cultural critique.

Concerns about power and agency motivate the questions at the heart of this pedagogical project. While I investigate how individuals and collectives are constrained and determined by social forces, cultural practices, and institutional structures, I'm equally interested in how subjects engage or transgress the co-option and commodification of their experiences by institutions of higher education. In other words, I give explicit attention to how a subject's recognition of social, rhetorical, and ideological frames and constraints can enable the production of transformative cultural projects and subject-positions.

The distinctions I draw here between negative ideological criticism and one that takes seriously the possibility of human agency have a long history in critical education theory. One of the major theoretical distinctions made by critical education theorists (Giroux, Freire, Simon, Weiler) is the difference between reproductive theories of education (sometimes called correspondence theory) and cultural-production theories of education. Reproduction theory, influenced by Marxist materialist analysis and Althusserian theories of ideology, focuses on the macrostructural relationships between individuals and schools and the reproduction of class structures, class cultures, knowledge, and power relations. Educators and critics whose work is informed by social reproduction and cultural-production theories both are critical of technocratic approaches to education. However, unlike reproduction theorists (Althusser, Bowles and Gintis), cultural-production theorists (Bourdieu, Bernstein, Freire, Giroux, Weiler) are more concerned with the *flesh and blood* of human beings; they tend to emphasize the dialectical and dialogic relation between the structural and the personal. Likewise, I don't see the relationship between institutions and individuals as a top-down, unilinear one or hegemony as an imposition from above. Rather, I take a Foucauldian view, which looks at power as a network of relations, constantly in tension. In each chapter, I have worked these tensions out in different ways.

Critical pedagogy, which is inspired and articulated by the theory and practice of the Brazilian educator Paulo Freire, calls for participatory learning (interactive, cooperative, and situated in students' experiences) and critical self-reflexivity and dialogic formats (frontloading questions, backloading lectures). Those who espouse the principles of critical pedagogy expect both students and teachers to be researchers and activists (Shor, 33–34). The primary goal of critical pedagogy is to empower students to understand the links between knowledge, history, and power and to use this knowledge to resist hegemonic structures and dominant ideologies. Critical pedagogy, informed by cultural production theory, is concerned with both the structural aspects of oppression and individual and collective resistance.[7] However, because critical pedagogy is a form of praxis (action informed by social theorems and critical analysis), it is something one struggles constantly to attain but can never fully achieve.

Teachers-researchers whose work is informed by feminist theory, particularly materialist feminist theory, have been most outspoken about the difficulties of implementing critical pedagogy in American classrooms. Elizabeth Ellsworth, for instance, argues that dialogue, a central principle of critical pedagogy, assumes a sharing of power, a free exchange of ideas between equal individuals. In order to reflect more accurately the contradictory ways individuals and groups undergo and exercise power, Ellsworth suggests that we should think of our pedagogical relationships not as dialogic but as multivocal alliances. The concept of multivocal alliances reframes agency as relational and contextual, an enframing that is particularly useful when studying educational sites where there may not be direct coercive or authoritarian forces but which are nevertheless characterized by hierarchical relationships and structural inequalities. The relational understanding of power and agency has been animated most vividly in the theoretical work of materialist feminists and resistance postmodernists.

I explore the relationship between materialist feminism and postmodern feminism in depth in chapter 4. Here, I will briefly review the distinctions necessary to understand my framing of autobiography and pedagogy as a form of praxis. Teresa Ebert categorizes differences within postmodernism as ludic and resistance postmodernism. Ebert defines ludic postmodernism as a textual practice and politics that "seeks open access to the free play of signification in order to . . . deconstruct and dehierarchize dominant discourses through textualizing strategies" such as mimicry, parody, pastiche, and free association (1991, 887, 894). Although ludic postmodernism is subversive, it is not, Ebert maintains, materially transformative; it is formalist in nature and concerned primarily with a microlevel analysis of difference; it is, therefore, perhaps better described as conceptually transformative.[8] In contrast, resistant postmodernists investigate social structures and identity formation at both macro and micro levels.[9] Resistance postmodernists challenge the modernist notion of the subject as the originator of meaning, and view the subject as dynamic and shifting and as historically and discursively positioned. Resistance postmodern feminists, however, do not abandon issues of agency. Moreover, power and resistance are not considered stable or fixed but are perpetually in construction and contradictory. Joan Scott puts it this way:

> To claim that the subject is discursively positioned is not "to introduce a new form of linguistic determinism, nor to deprive subjects of their agency. . . . Subjects are constituted discursively, but there are conflicts among discursive systems, contradictions within any one of them. . . . And subjects do have agency. They are not unified, autonomous individuals exercising free will but rather subjects whose agency is created through situations and statuses conferred on them. (793)

The advantage of resistance postmodernism for understanding the pedagogical dynamics of autobiography in the academy is that its relational understanding of power makes problematic the image of the critical pedagogue as savior or empowerer. Instead, it encourages teachers-researchers to acknowledge their distinctive standpoints and authority and to consider how their authority and power may shift as they move from one pedagogical contact zone to another. Power, then, cannot be given to students outright; it emerges from struggles within the hierarchical system of institutional relationships. Being a reflective practitioner involves engaging yourself in a sustained activity of inquiry into the situatedness of your practice—that is, how it is shaped by institutional, disciplinary, and social constraints. Critical reflexivity is the necessary first step on the road to critical action. As teachers-researchers, we must acknowledge that we do not work from positions of neutrality; we frame the realities we study, and we define the borders for investigation theoretically and pedagogically. Not passive onlookers, we intervene in learning contexts and respond (sometimes in institutionally complicit ways) to emergent pedagogical occasions at the intellectual level and at the level of action (Grundy, 105). One of my goals in *Framing Identities* is to account for the relational nature of power and resistance as it is articulated through particular autobiographical acts, and to urge teachers-researchers to express the contradictions and struggles they face as they work for institutional change. The convergence of composition, feminist studies, and critical pedagogy lies in the *act* of doing—in praxis.

I argue for a pedagogy scholarship (an oxymoron for some) that recognizes the theories and constraints that guide its perceptions and that acknowledges pedagogical activity as the practice of theory. As Giroux puts it, practice is living theory (1994a, 116–17). I recognize that theorizing and writing about practice require time and resources (which many teachers lack), that theory is not always accessible and can be exclusionary, and that few working-class people and people of color are in a position to produce what is recognized as theory (Griffiths, 35). To assume, however, that only privileged groups create theory is to ignore the theoretical work of historically disempowered groups that emerges from classroom practice and communities outside the academy, even though these groups may not have used the term *theory* to describe their efforts. Moreover, critics who argue that theory is an inherently elitist concept ignore the important liberating or interventionist role that theory can play. For example, theory helped me situate the lessons I learned at school within particular historical and pedagogical traditions. The disassociation of students from the production of knowledge permeated my education. I was positioned as a passive recipient of knowledge, not as a maker of meaning. Theory, particularly Freire's theories of teaching, helped me ask certain questions about how I came to know and what I knew. Theory initiated this reflexive turn. Theory is not simply a by-product of inquiry; rather, it is a process of knowledge making, a way of seeing (Ray, 65). Robert Scholes puts it this way: "Practice is never natural or neutral; there is always a theory in place, so that the first job of any teacher . . . is to bring the assumptions that are in place out in the open for scrutiny" (quoted in Ray, 70).

Too often, studies of the culture of the academy depend heavily on theoretical and pedagogical abstractions. I bring to this project an analysis of the uses of autobiography by "real" students, faculty, and administrators. This is not to say, however, that I don't interrogate notions of the "real" or consider the problematics of experience and self-representation; in fact, such investigations are central to my project. Rather than accept the traditional dichotomy between theory and practice, I put practice at the center of theorizing. To assume that theory is only jargon-filled discourse of a particular field is to ignore that theories are generated by activists and teachers. Historically, activities at the grassroots level have not been seen as resources for theory or as actively negotiating theory (Ackelsberg, 97). But activism, like teaching, is a form of knowledge making. Theory is not inherently exclusive; it is simply defined in ways that reinforce an "intellectual class hierarchy" that characterizes only the work of certain groups as theoretical (hooks 1994, 64). In summary, critical educators must not only seek out the expression and generation of theory in our daily lives and classrooms but we must also examine the politics that shape the institutionalization of what counts as intellectual work.[10]

1

MEMORY WORK

*To remember* in a critical mode . . . *means, in Freirean terms, to con-*
*front the social amnesia of generations in flight from their own collective*
*histories. (McLaren and Tadeu da Silva, 73–74)*

In the basement of my parents' home is a photograph that was once prominently displayed on the fireplace mantel in the family room with other representations of such rites of passage as weddings and school graduations. The
photograph stood beside the sacred family heirloom, a large, black, leather-
bound Holy Bible, with pressed birth announcements, engagements, and
obituaries crumbling between the pages. It is a "portrait" of my maternal
great-grandfather, Edward William Trevenan, who left his wife, Amelia, and
their five children in Cornwall, England, in 1910 to work as a supervisor of
operations at one of the gold mines in Johannesburg, South Africa (see figure
3). Edward, in his midthirties, is seated in a small room on a simple wooden
chair. The other furnishings are well-worn and merely functional: two low
cots, a small wooden table, two battered steamer trunks. The floorboards are
rough and paint is peeling off the walls. Edward wears black leather shoes,
dark cuffed pants, a button-down shirt (without a collar), and what he would
have called "braces" to hold his pants up. He has rolled his shirtsleeves up to
his elbows, which are placed casually on the chair back and tabletop. His legs
are comfortably crossed, and his shoes shine in the camera's light. His appear-
ance suggests a sense of control over his modest domain.

1

Figure 3. Edward William Trevenan with young man, Johannesburg, South Africa.

On the table are what appear to be the deliberately chosen necessities of an English workingman's life at the turn of the century: two tobacco pipes, two brushes (one for shoes, one for hair), a pot of ink containing a pen, a tin canister and several bottles, some papers (letters home?). The walls, too, are covered with "civilizing" touches: a pocket watch and chain hanging where a clock might be kept at home, a felt pincushion (identifiable as such only because my grandmother, Edward's daughter, still has the memento). Most prominent, however, are what appear to be pages torn from newspapers or magazines of British popular culture, which are tacked up in rather random fashion on the wall behind the beds. For example, one of the images seems to be a cover from *The Graphic*, a popular magazine of the British middle-class in the early twentieth century, the contemporary equivalent of our *Life* and *People* magazines. In addition, there is a page of nine portraits of formally dressed white men and women, each accompanied by a printed caption, illegible at this distance; a full-page photograph of a woman, perhaps a popular actress or singer in costume for some role; and two indistinct images, one of which appears to be men on horseback, some with arms in slings and others with guns. Finally, behind Edward's right arm is an image of two smiling women leaning coyly toward each other.

Before Edward, perched on the edge of a steamer trunk beside the cot on the left, sits a young black man in his mid-teens. My great-grandfather looks neither at the camera nor at anything within the frame of the picture, but gazes out, over, and beyond the visual field; the black youth, on the other hand, looks directly into the camera. He is dressed in baggy plaid pants that end above the knee and a plain long-sleeved shirt. His clothes do not fit well: the pants are clearly too large, gathered at the waist by a thick black belt, and his shirt is too small and rises up his back. Upon his head sits a misshapen felt slouch hat turned up in the front, and on his feet are scuffed and poorly soled white boots.

This description of the photograph may appear fairly straightforward and objective. But, in truth, it is far from neutral, because I have highlighted certain details and rejected or ignored others. In fact, one could argue that my description, like the photograph, reinvents the all-powerful gaze of the white European patriarch, because it does not question or reveal the logic of representation or the moral economy of the photograph and its relation to material realities. For instance, the description does not mention that there are no pictures of my great-grandmother or their children, nor does it shed any light on other social systems or relations that are not in the immediate field of vision. What exists on the other side of the interior walls is not known. Neither the photograph nor the description depicts the struggles that my great-grandmother Amelia must have faced in raising five children on her own or what must have been conflicting emotions over her husband's absence, which lasted more than eighteen months. Through omission, the description, like the photograph itself, also ignores the dangerous working conditions in the mines and the black workers' resistance to these conditions, as expressed in riots, strikes, and work stoppages, as well as the brutal suppression of such acts by those in power. The opening description and its focus on what can be seen could be interpreted as a controlling act that reinforces the domestic order of the room—a kind of cartography of the privileged—to see only what we want to see. Yet what is *not* seen is as much a part of the context of the photograph as what *is* seen. And in that respect, the opening description mirrors the patterns of detachment common to the Western ethnographic and autobiographic gaze, of which the photograph is emblematic.

Unlike this image of my great-grandfather, which could be seen as a study in detachment, one of my primary goals is to show how autobiographical acts can only be understood by means other than detachment. An engaged, critically reflexive reading of the photograph illustrates how detachment has become part of the social memory. This photograph and the process of reading it provide an opportunity for me to present the governing theme of this chapter: the relationship between self-representation and historical realities and the implication of this relationship for understanding "the complexity of the momentarily situated subject" (Faigley, 239). It also serves to further highlight the critical gestures I bring to my study of autobiographical acts in the contact zones of the academy. Thus, this chapter is both critique and construct—a lesson in point of view. My interest is heuristic rather than documentary. I propose that we take a rhetorical approach to the study of autobiography, investigating its pedagogical and cultural dynamics at particular historical moments and within specific material circumstances (Mailloux, 83). As Steven Mailloux suggests in "Rhetorically Covering Conflict," a study of cultural rhetoric "attempts to read the tropes, arguments, and narratives of its object texts (whether literary or nonliterary) within their socio-political contexts of cultural production and reception" (83). What I propose is a cultural materialist approach that investigates how one attempts to position oneself, or is positioned, among competing discourses and that relocates autobiography in the rhetorical and historical moments of its production and reception. Moreover, as a mode of analysis, cultural-materialist reading practices that foreground rhetoric open up the space to consider how autobiographical subjects negotiate and claim a sense of agency among contrary discourses and how the autobiographical subject and material body are cultural and linguistic sites of contestation.

The photograph and the process of interpreting it can serve as a heuristic for thinking about my shifting roles as author—great-granddaughter and keeper of the tales (a generational space that involves feelings of betrayal as much as pride), teacher, and social critic—and the cultural and social narratives that shape my authorial location. I began with a reading of this photograph and its accompanying narratives of interpretation to demonstrate that autobiography is a situated, fragmented, and negotiated performance, which has an "ambiguous relation to reference" (M. Hirsch, 83). I thus use the mobile and intersecting visual and verbal narratives to interrupt any naturalized temptation to construe autobiographical acts as static or mimetic. In the second part of the chapter, I focus on theories of autobiography informed by deconstruction and poststructuralism, and I argue that positions adopted by critics such as Roland Barthes and Paul de Man theoretically parallel the social posture that my great-grandfather exhibits in the photograph. I call for a theory of autobiography that accounts for the socially constructed positions of the critic, autobiographer, and reader and an understanding of the historical context in which these constructions are produced. In the last section of the chapter, I reveal how tropes of detachment and privilege, which characterize both the production and reception of the family photograph and the theoretical stances of critics of autobiography, are common pedagogical stances, and I argue for a pedagogy that enables teachers and students to become sensitive to the autobiographical scripts and cultural narratives that shape their relations to each other. The intent of this chapter, then, is to perform autobiography as a form of cultural criticism (N. Miller's coinage) and to cross disciplinary boundaries and blend personal observations with social critique, cultural theory, and political analysis common to such projects.

Let us turn, then, to the logic of representation and its relationship to material and economic realities, which are no less constructed than the stories we tell about them. Consider, for example, how my description of the photograph simultaneously reinforces and lessens my great-grandfather's position of privilege. First, I call the image a "portrait" of my great-grandfather, which highlights his presence and awards him ownership of the image. Second, I suggest that his self-assured posture conveys a "sense of control over his modest domain" (referring to the actual space, although surely both the space and the black youth were considered part of his "domain"). Third, my use of the term "modest"—a minimizing phrase—places limits on my great-grandfather's power and suggests he was not the "grand colonizer" (a descriptor that is informed by the knowledge that my great-grandfather was in a lower-management position in the mining company).

Hygiene is another cultural concept that seeps into the description by separating order from disorder and distinguishing the powerful from the powerless. My great-grandfather's well-fitted clothing and shoes—shined, I suspect, by the black youth—contrast with the black youth's ill-fitted clothing and worn-out boots. The white male body is presented as neat and controlled, whereas the black male body appears ill-kempt. In other words, the clothing and descriptions of the subjects indicate social boundaries of race and class. Whether the photograph was commissioned by the mining company as a promotional piece or taken at the request of my great-grandfather, the construction of the room—namely, the parallel alignment of beds and trunks—conveys an ideal of domestic order. Interestingly, this image of domesticity lacks women, although the black youth is effeminized in the colonial, homosocial domestic relationship. In this instance *domesticate* is akin to *dominate*. The pocket watch, caught by the camera at 10:35, is an emblem of mechanical time and, along with the light bulb, reflects industrial progress, scientific advance, and the functionalism of male colonialists. By visually reproducing an image of imperial aggression and capitalist civilization, the photograph is a vivid reminder of the privileged group's anxiety and discomfort over changing social boundaries and its need to create a "home" far from home.

This photograph of my great-grandfather recalls nineteenth-century portraiture and foregrounds the paradoxical status of photography in bourgeois culture. In the early 1800s, within the developing context of global economy and a professionalized penal climate in Britain, photography was used as a technology of surveillance that "fixed" an image of the "other" through the photographic regulation of the subproletariat in police procedures and anthropological records. Paradoxically, photography both promised the "mastery of nature" and threatened to level the existing cultural order—that is, it represented the "triumph of a mass culture" (Sekula, 4). Photography, as a technology of representation and power, thus was used both to repress and signify the "other" through the imperatives of medical and anatomical illustration and of criminal documentation (which was informed by constructs of deviance and social pathology) and to celebrate the bourgeois tradition through the honorific portrait tradition (Sekula, 7). As Allan Sekula points out, in the nineteenth century, photography "introduce[d] the panoptic principle into daily life" (10). For example, criminal-identification photographs were used to "facilitate the *arrest* of their referent" (7) and, presumably, to "unmask the disguises, the alibis, the excuses, and multiple biographies of those who find or place themselves on the wrong side of the law" (Sekula, 6). However, the moral economy of the photographic image served socially cohesive functions, particularly in the United States, where "family photographs sustained sentimental ties in a nation of migrants" and articulated a "nineteenth-century familialism that would survive and become an essential ideological feature of American mass culture" (8–9).

As the photograph of my great-grandfather and his black servant vividly illustrates, "photography welded the honorific and repressive functions together" (Sekula, 10). The family photograph of my great-grandfather and the black youth placed on the mantelpiece—the family shrine—"took its place within a social and moral hierarchy" (10); it monumentalized, commemorated, and reproduced an idealized image of the family and its value—that is, its accomplishment of social conventionality and status. The seemingly private moment of sentimentality and individualization was shadowed by the two other, more public looks: the averted gaze of my great-grandfather and the black youth's arrested gaze at the camera (Sekula, 10). As the family narratives that accompany this photograph suggest, photography asserts its instrumental power by "naturalizing cultural practices" (M. Hirsch, 7). Presumably, the photograph unveils, captures, and *arrests* the truth. But, we must ask, whose truth does the photograph of my great-grandfather and his black servant capture? Who is looking? Who is being seen? To whom does the terrain of representation belong? Is the black youth's look back at the camera an oppositional gaze?

Historically, in the visual structure of representation, black slaves were punished by white slave owners for looking back; as hooks puts it, "The politics of slavery, of racialized power relations were such that the slaves were denied their right to gaze" (1992, 115). Ironically, the black youth's gaze at the camera is not an unequivocally insurgent act of looking back, but rather his visibility produces a kind of public invisibility. Within the framework of late-nineteenth and early-twentieth-century photographic conventions, he is positioned as an object to be surveyed and regulated. He is caught in the exploiters' (both my great-grandfather and the photographer) production of him as "other." As a colonized subject, he is also positioned as a feminized object, capable only of offering himself up to the gaze of the paternal state (Tagg, 11–12). His gaze at the camera is not, then, an act of resistance. As David Spurr points out in *The Rhetoric of Empire*, "For the observer, sight confers power; for the observed, visibility is a trap" (16). The black youth's gaze at the camera contrasts with my great-grandfather's posture, which intentionally refuses the camera's probe and expresses the omniscience of Western European male culture. His commanding view suggests the colonialist surveying his dominion; it is a statement of control. From this perspective, one could look at the "portrait" of my great-grandfather as a use of visualizing technology for the self-authorization of the proto-typical Western white male, what Mary Louise Pratt calls "the monarch of all I survey" (quoted in Shohat and Stam, 156).

One challenge of reading this photograph is recognizing how it situates me, heir to my great-grandfather, as if I too were looking through the eyes of the colonizer. Here, we see how the context of imperial power shaped the uses of visual technology and how the I/Eye of empire traveled around the globe (156). Reading this photograph is like entering an autobiographical contact zone, a space where the narratives of my great-grandfather's generation and my own connect. More particularly, it is a space where the narratives that shape our lives collide. This is not to suggest that I'm caught in the grip of my great-grandfather's historical consciousness or that my gaze simply replicates his, but rather that I face the challenge of unsettling the historic and familial impulse to position myself at the center and of turning the "othering" gaze back on itself (Ellsworth, 9). In order to expose and transform the family narrative, I must resist the historical impulse to construct myself as a neutral cartographer recharting the circumspective force of the colonial gaze and must, instead, move beyond self-centering ethnocentrism. Moreover, I must avoid inscribing the same privileged mobility that my great-grandfather brought to his supervision of South African gold mines. Mary Louise Pratt claims that the representational phenomena of contact zones produce texts that are heterogeneous in their production as well as their reception. Reading a visual text, which to a certain degree circumvents narrative, nevertheless reinforces a kind of discursive mobility and academic literacy that casts an illusionary meta-narrative of control and coherence. My challenge is to inflect heterogeneity in my re-creation and to simulate it in narrative form by constantly unsettling the narratives themselves by showing how they are transformed as they move from one historical, cultural, and familial space to another. In this chapter, I appropriate Pratt's spatial metaphor in order to examine the production and reception of the family photograph and the clashing and collision of family identities, narratives, and networks of looking.

Despite the temporal, spatial, and cultural distance that separates me from the historical location of this photograph, the passage of the unframed "portrait" from one generation in my family to the next (it has traveled from my great-grandmother to my grandmother in Cornwall, England, to my mother in Essex County, New Jersey, to me in Oberlin, Ohio) indicates a lingering commitment to a sense of public history and the power of self-representation. This photograph can be described in Pratt's terms as an "ethnographic text" that captures my family's privilege and historical role in the objectification of the "other." My goal in this chapter is not to re-create yet another dominant ethnographic reading but to reach beyond a historical dominating sensibility to a reading that does not reproduce a colonial encounter. But in writing my first description of the photograph, I learned I cannot interpret it within the culture I live "without also apprehending the imperial contest itself" (Said, 217). "And," as Edward Said rightfully points out, "This . . . is a cultural fact of extraordinary political as well as interpretive importance" (217). In other words, "representations bear as much on the representer's world as on who or what is represented" (224). Spurr elaborates on the "metaphorical relation between the writer and the colonizer":

> The problem of the colonizer is in some sense the problem of the writer: in the face of what may appear as a vast cultural and geographical blankness, colonization is a form of self-inscription onto the lives of people who are conceived of as an extension of the landscape. For the colonizer as for the writer, it becomes a question of establishing authority through the demarcation of identity and difference. (7)

While my opening description of the photograph illustrates the power of self-representation and my own role in the reconstruction of my family's history, it also suggests, as revealed through my analysis, that points of contact and collision lie within the "social moment of making memory" (Kuhn, 13). The challenge of reading this photograph is recognizing that the contact zone is *within* my gaze. Indeed, my goal in this chapter is to articulate the dominant narratives that define the historical moments of the photograph's production and reception and to consider how these narratives are now shaped by and mediated through my gaze.

Having presented some of the basic tenets of Pratt's concept of the contact zone in the Introduction and how it shapes my approach to autobiography— namely, my focus on the production and reception of autobiographical acts— I will now consider the particular narratives that shaped my reading of this family photograph as a young girl. This photograph has always fascinated and, at times, embarrassed me. My fascination sprang originally from wanting to know about the lives of my ancestors: where they lived, what they did, whom they knew. My sense of embarrassment is less readily identifiable, although I suspect it stems in part from guilt. When I asked members of my family about the relationship of the young black man to my great-grandfather, I was told that he was one of my great-grandfather's friends. Although I wanted to believe this interpretation, something about the image told me otherwise. Even at age ten, I knew the world was not that simple: a fairly well-dressed white man in South Africa was not likely to be "friends" with a black youth dressed in rags. My lingering sense of guilt arose from the nagging fear that the young black man seated across from my great-grandfather was actually some kind of indentured servant, or worse.

Perhaps it *is* possible that my great-grandfather Edward and the black youth were friends, although the fact that the latter was never named in this narrative of friendship is telling and perhaps another sign of colonial rule. As Spurr points out, "The very process by which one culture subordinates another begins in the act of naming and leaving unnamed, of marking on an unknown territory the lines of division and uniformity, of boundary and continuity" (4). Indeed, as Edward's only living son told me, the youth was referred to as my great-grandfather's "valet," a title that simultaneously suggests the imposition of British social norms onto the South African life and efforts to legitimize the relationship between the two: a personal valet is, after all, no mere servant. Not only is the young man's name unknown, but there is no definitive way to identify his language or place of origin. The colonial government recruited white miners from overseas, but most of its labor came from the indigenous black populations in southern and northern parts of Africa. Perhaps my great-grandfather's servant was initially recruited to work in the mines, but after a cursory medical examination revealed he was unfit or underage, he was relegated to employment outside the mines.[1]

This narrative of friendship may provide a paradigm for the rhetoric of colonial rule, because it allowed certain members of my family to deny their historical position of privilege and, at the same time, reinforced it. But because this narrative emerged in the contact zone of colonial relations, it rewrites the colonial situation in curious and complex ways. For example, reading their relationship as one of friendship or camaraderie rewrites the national colonial narrative at a time when colonial discourse constructed native black South Africans as savages. In other words, the South African youth gets reclassified from the "primitive savage" class into a Europeanized South African—a valet, part of an "advanced" community within the national and local hierarchy. Even if they did share the same living space, which is unlikely (the black youth probably lived with other black workers in overcrowded and unsanitary barracks), this imagined fraternity nonetheless speaks to the economic dependency of British imperialism on black African men's labor.

This narrative of friendship is also complicated by and intertwined with national narratives of immigration. In fact, the very multiplicity of the friendship narrative lies in its capacity to absorb distinct cultural and national narratives together (Jameson, 142). For instance, the constructed parallelism and imagined fraternity between my maternal great-grandfather and the South African youth, a reading that was formed well after my great-grandfather and his family had immigrated to America, rewrites my great-grandfather's privileged status as colonizer, replacing it with a narrative about his subordinate status as an immigrant "other" in the United States. By immigrating to this country, Edward became the "other" when his position relative to the culture in which he worked changed: in South Africa, he was situated as the foreigner as colonizer, yet in the United States, he was reconstituted as the foreigner as immigrant (a position of considerably less power). These positions of "otherness" are not historical equivalents. In fact, the allegory of alliance and projected fraternity actually disguises neocolonial relationships between First and Third World powers. I suspect, however, that my great-grandfather regarded immigration as an abandonment of the colonial system. Thus, in this friendship narrative, we see both anxiety and hope—a kind of double-sided consciousness.

Like most European immigrants in the late nineteenth and early twentieth century, my great-grandfather sought a better life for his family. For example, he was adamant about living where his sons would not have to work in the mines. As it was, they lived in New Jersey and worked for Du Pont, a plastics company. Although the friendship narrative may reflect the family's anxiety over its own differences in America, as white Anglo-Saxons they were less subordinate than other immigrants. They did not have to learn another language or a new economic system. Nevertheless, we may read into the family's interpretation of this photograph the double-sidedness of my great-grandfather's movements between England and South Africa and, later, the family's immigration to America. More particularly, the narrative of friendship between my great-grandfather and the South African distances my great-grandfather from the British social system of which he was originally a part, and contributes to the process by which he and his family were to invent and assimilate themselves as Americans. Reading this photograph at the moments of its production and reception involves reading into it the colonial relationship and expansion of Western interests, as well as the family's reconception of itself as Americans. When taken together, the friendship and immigration narratives challenge understandings of power relations that are constructed as fixed binaries (white/other, colonized/colonizer), and call for an understanding of the contradictory nature of subject positions, different national and cultural systems of stratification, and the historically situated nature of power (Friedman, 7).

The anxiety over the unsettling of cultural and geographical boundaries between the "First" and "Third" Worlds created narratives that constructed South Africa as a place where England (and Europe more generally) "projected its forbidden sexual desires and fears" (McClintock, 22). Similar narratives of sexual desire shaped my family's reading of this photograph and its understanding of my great-grandfather's movement abroad. For instance, when I visited Cornwall, England, in the mid-1980s on a foreign-exchange program in my senior year of college, I was told surreptitiously of Edward's lust for the bottle and women. This family secret—perhaps better termed a cultural myth—reflects a national narrative that eroticizes the land as well as the women of South Africa. The image of South Africa as seductive temptress is based on the notion that the land has qualities associated with the female body. As Spurr points out, however, what we see in such narratives is how "the traditions of colonialist and phallocentric discourses coincide" (Spurr, 170). This narrative of sexual desire is also about colonial conquest and imperial aggression. The family's construction of this "secret" mirrors a national sexual anxiety and the eroticization of the colonized, and invokes larger cultural anxieties and fantasies of seduction. That this narrative is framed as a secret or myth and my retelling as a betrayal of family privacy is an example of the cultural coding of disloyalty. Annette Kuhn puts it this way: "Secrets haunt our memory-stories, giving them pattern and shape. Family secrets are the other side of the family's public face, of the stories families tell themselves, and the world, about themselves" (2).

The photograph not only represents a discourse on the imperial "progress" of a nation but it also situates the white male as the father at the head of the "global family." The photograph was taken at a time when social crises were reverberating throughout Britain and its colonies. For instance, Britain experienced crises in gender and race relations on both domestic and international fronts. White masculinity was being contested. Middle-class women were seeking better educations and the right for paid work, and working-class women were fighting for fair employment rights and conditions. In contrast to these social challenges and the weakening of gender, race, and class boundaries, the photograph suggests that history and "progress" belong to white European men. This rendition of *his*-story is also shaped by the way science constructed race, which the medium of photography captured; more particularly, by the discourses of evolution and Social Darwinism, wherein racial ranking was prolific and black people were deemed genetically inferior (see Harding, Stepan and Gilman). Interestingly, these visual and verbal narratives of biological and social superiority and competition parallel those that characterize the rise of autobiography as a genre, which is deeply connected to the historical evolution of Western male self-consciousness and the capitalist ideology of possessive individualism. For instance, early critics of the genre claimed that peoples of the "Third World" were "primitive," that they lacked autobiography and feared their images in the mirror. Gusdorf, for one, argued that "primitives" "lag[ged] behind the Western 'child of civilization' and . . . that they have not emerged from 'the mythic framework of traditional teachings . . . into the perilous domain of history'" (Gusdorf quoted in McClintock, 313). These patterns of objectification continue through Western mappings of the "other" and the consumption of testimonial literature of Third World women in the First World marketplace (see Grewal and Kaplan).

### How Far Have We Come?

The movement of the photograph from its prominent location in the family room to the basement of my parents' house is yet another rewriting of the progress narrative. The fact that this photograph of my great-grandfather was displayed in the family room of our newly purchased colonial home in a white, upper-middle-class New England suburb in the late 1970s confirms the family's status and upward mobility. The placement of the photograph carries an implicit message: "Look how far we've come from our humble beginnings."

The landscapes of my childhood and my family's geographical movement prompt questions about how I "encountered the other," how I did or did not acknowledge the presence of certain groups, and how what I experienced as home, my safe space, was secured on the basis of historical exclusions, violence, and omissions. I spent my childhood and early adolescence in a segregated suburb of Newark, New Jersey. Class and racial differences were geographically demarcated: the white working class and people of color, mostly African-American families, lived on the west banks of the Passaic River. Unlike the white residents on the Hill, who enjoyed a commanding view, people of color lived in a part of town known as the Valley. People on the Hill projected themselves onto people in the Valley: geographically, "whiteness" rose above and projected itself onto "blackness," or, as Ruth Frankenberg puts it, "Whiteness . . . comes to self-name, invents itself, by means of its declaration that it is *not* that which it projects as Other" (1996, 7). White middle-class families in my hometown were in a position of visual advantage, a location that presumably spared them from dealing with problems of race or class. We lived in a three-bedroom, stone-faced colonial house about midway up the Hill. Like most residents on the Hill, we defined ourselves by what we were not. Whiteness was "the invisible norm, the standard against which the dominant culture measures its own worth" constructed as both "everything and nothing" (McLaren 1995, 133). This monolithic construction of whiteness not only obscures ethnic and class differences among whites but also reinscribes the self-other binary; that is, we needed the "other" in order to see ourselves as unified subjects at the center. Like the gaze of my great-grandfather in the photograph, the spectatorial view from the hill functioned like a long chain of signifiers; the projection of blackness was construed as the necessary construct and counterpart for the establishment of whiteness. A social pecking order also existed among whites, particularly between first- and second-generation immigrants. Italian-American families lived along the crowded maple-lined streets, and a few Jewish families, mostly households headed by doctors and lawyers, dotted the larger lots on the corners. I grew up in a climate of anti-Semitism, which essentialized Jews as part of the white power structure, masked class differences among Jewish families in town, and erased historical memories of struggle.

Washington Street marked the racial boundary between the Valley and the Hill. Most small businesses were located here: an Italian grocer, a Jewish bakery. The border was not a place we inhabited, but a place we traveled through. Like clockwork, my father pulled into Meyer's Bakery after he picked my brother and me up from the Methodist Sunday school on the other side of the Passaic river; crumb buns and donuts would sweeten our return from what always struck me as an alienating experience. Although members of my extended family ran the church, as Sunday-school teachers and treasurer, and sang in the choir, I always felt as if I was just passing through; my presence was a symbolic way for me and my family to uphold an image of goodness. The only other time we stopped on Washington Street—the border—was for my mother to buy fruit and vegetables from an old Italian man, who ran his business from the back of a dilapidated truck. Our experiences of the border were defined by our purchasing power, consumption of ethnicity, and commodification of the "other."

Meanwhile, across the railroad tracks on the south border of town, racial uprisings devastated whole neighborhoods. If I had known that more than fifteen hundred people were injured during the 1967 racial uprisings in Newark, that there were more than three hundred fires, and that the town was under military occupation, I may have been frightened and certainly confused. But I felt nothing. My daily life went on as usual. The only time we went into Newark was to pick my father up at the trolley station on the edge of town. Unlike my friends' fathers, who were policemen, firemen, or truck drivers, my father was a white-collar suit-and-tie man who commuted into Manhattan daily. My little brother and I were proud of our father, and we waited anxiously in the backseat of the family car, eager to see his face appear in the cable-car window. If my childhood years can be defined through narratives of protection and control, my adolescent years revealed the paradoxes of these narratives. For example, the ethic of control and anxieties about dating and relationships led me to excessive concern over body image and dieting—an embodiment of this trope of control.

My family left our house on the Hill in New Jersey when my father's company transferred him from New York to Connecticut. At first, we all seemed happy to move to another state and buy a bigger house, which was our chance to differentiate ourselves from most of the working- and lower-middle-class residents in our New Jersey hometown. My English immigrant grandparents had to work hard to assimilate, whereas my family, born in America, displayed our class difference, as our crossing the border zones suggests, through our consumerism—our construction of market identities—and our mobility. There are compelling parallels between my family's economic and geographic mobility and my own mobility, represented by the position I held while gathering research for this book. For six years after completing graduate school, I was a visiting assistant professor of writing at a college far removed from the blue-collar destiny of many of my childhood friends. Working at an elite college meant learning to deal with the privileges and paradoxes of my position, this movement, and its pedagogical implications. Although I grew up in a privileged white, middle-class environment, at Oberlin I struggled with the sense of entitlement shared by many upper-class students. At this time, the continuation of my family's progress narrative was defined not so much by my economic stability as by my cultural and intellectual status as a college professor, albeit in a visiting position. My authority was tied to my advanced academic literacy, which continues to distance me from my family. I am the first woman in my immediate family to go to college and the only person in my family to obtain a doctorate. Now, as an assistant professor at Indiana University with the privilege of being a new homeowner and adoptive parent, I'm rewriting this personal and professional narrative yet again.

The theme of upward mobility was entangled with another cultural narrative about a presumed lack of what might be called "ethnicity." As English immigrants, my family was not visibly or, because they quickly lost their accents, audibly "other." One might think, as I did as a child, that Anglo-British customs were not alive in America—except for certain foods, like the Cornish pasties and saffron buns my grandmother made. To me, these customs, class, and patterns of communication were invisible, naturalized. My family members had the privilege of situating themselves beyond forms of ethnic signification. As the photograph of my maternal great-grandfather suggests, we occupied the position of the privileging signifier. For instance, Italian-American life was "other" to us, as were the lives of Latinos, Jewish-Americans, South Asians, and African-Americans. But because as an adolescent most of my friends were Italian-Americans, I was comfortable with the Italian-American culture. I craved what seemed like exotic foods: chicken savoy (marinated in vinegar, olive oil, and oregano), cavatelli with ricotta, tiramisu, and red table wine. I yearned for animated conversations at dinnertime and elaborate Catholic rituals and ceremonies, for incense and ornate altars. I always wanted to escape what I saw as the "sterility" of my own family heritage. My desire for the "other"—Argerio, Basto, de Angelo, de Giordano, Donatello, Esposito, Giovanni, Santantonio, Rizzo, Zanfini—was defined by the privilege of not being "other," of knowing the likeness would never be complete. Perhaps in my desire for the "other," the legacy of my great-grandfather's privilege and the self-other binary of imperial subjectivity played out most vividly. As Fredric Jameson puts it, this desire for and impulse to impersonate the "other" are inextricably bound with the historical treatment of ethnic groups as objects of prejudice (146). In fact, these two impulses reinforce each other; a single and centered subject (image of my great-grandfather) needs the self-other, subject-object binary for its formation (Grewal, 234). Reading this photograph and my family's reception of it involves not only the historical contextualization of the colonial gaze and photographic conventions but also a recognition of the cultural narratives of immigration, ethnicity, and upward mobility and of how the material history and shifting categories of the "other" are subsumed within these narratives. My yearning for the Italian-American "other" was, in some sense, a continuation of the historical impulse to impersonate the "other" and construct friendship narratives that erase privilege.

Throughout the 1980s, the photograph, part of a collection of portraits on the mantel, was an accepted part of the family history. But in the early 1990s, when attention to race relations in the United States increased, the photograph disappeared to the basement, where things go if they're out of style or on their way to the Salvation Army or a rummage sale. The deauthorization of the photograph as a family heirloom is telling. It suggests a growing awareness about the historical context of our privilege, albeit an awareness manifested by rendering invisible our most visible yet unspoken secret—our white privilege. Paradoxically, the removal of the photograph to the basement at once represents an awareness of our privilege yet constitutes that privilege as an absence: the family can't bear to witness itself as a negative presence. This denial is tinged, of course, with white guilt about our role within the colonial situation and the historical process of othering. It is also a narrative, like the friendship narrative, that seeks to avoid the problems of white privilege by foregrounding other things—for example, that we can put such experiences aside. The movement of the photograph to the basement, one might argue, is a way of maintaining order and of not "losing face." My adolescent yearning for the Italian-American "other" was also a narrative with whiteness at the center, as the defining core. My reach toward the "other" could thus be interpreted as a reinscription of the white Anglo-American identity that it set out to displace.

The process of reframing these stories imposes new narrative trajectories and autobiographical scripts onto the photograph. Two implied narrative lines in my reconstruction include a redemptive narrative that emphasizes the recuperation of lost memories and the transformation of personal consciousness. The transformation narrative is embedded in a larger narrative about the academy as a radicalizing agent. Although neither narrative is about a triumph over adversity per se, each refers to an increased level of critical consciousness. My reframing of the family photograph and its narratives might be read as emblematic of the movement through Freirean levels of consciousness—that is, the move from "intransitive thought" (where the individual experiences a lack of agency) to "semi-transitive" (a state wherein one claims a sense of agency yet continues to isolate and individualize social problems) to "critical transitivity" (a stage wherein one thinks about one's condition holistically and critically) (Shor 1993, 32). One could argue, for instance, that my reading of the family photograph reflects a certain level of critical transitivity; the constructed analytical narratives go beneath the impressions of the photographic surface to challenge the consequences of representation. However, as the storyteller, I cannot escape the contours of the framing apparatuses or their historical impulses.

Freirean principles encourage critical educators to create pedagogical narratives and forums for sharing and engaging stories of struggle and hope with an awareness of "how, as subjects, we have become disproportionately constituted within dominative regimes of discourses and social practices through race, class, and gender identities" (McLaren and Tadeu da Silva, 68). However, in our creation of these public narratives and spaces, we must be careful not to position ourselves as saviors (enlightened beings) and students as mere victims to be saved; not only does this pedagogical narrative uncritically project a state of false consciousness onto our students, but it also fails to acknowledge the "invisible" or masked literacies and levels of critical consciousness that students readily practice and claim both inside and outside the classroom.

This brings me to the second implied narrative trajectory of the academy as a radicalizing agent. It was within the academy, a site of relative privilege and entitlement that sanctions and legitimates middle-class values, that I was first exposed to Freire.[2] That the process of re-education has taken place, and continues to take place, within the structures of the academy suggests that the academy is a place conducive to such growth and transformation. This narrative, of course, is idealistic. But it is a pedagogical narrative of *hope* that I refuse to resign, a narrative that nonetheless must account for the fact that the academy is not an equally accessible or safe place for everyone to articulate social struggles or social dreaming. Thus, we must constantly work to comprehend our own and our students' social and political locations and how institutional relations are shaped by historical understandings and personal and generational biographies.

## Historical Contact Zones: Facing the Defacement of Autobiography

> The search for a more perfect self, for a truer, . . . a more authentic "I" too often represents a refusal to account for the position from which we speak, to ground ourselves materially and historically, to acknowledge and be vigilant of our own limitations and our own differences. (Martin, 15)

My reading of this photograph demonstrates that autobiographical acts are not isolated events; instead, they represent ongoing negotiations among historical conceptions and contradictory discourses of the self, family, and community. I am less interested in looking at autobiography as a contract between reader and writer or speaker and listener that testifies to or ensures its truthfulness (the traditional view) than I am in understanding how autobiographical acts are culturally, historically, and discursively mediated. What the photograph and my reading of it suggest is that "personal history is always embedded in social forms"; in other words, family history and personal identity are themselves contested terrains where various individuals take up subject positions that are part of the cultural present but which "always owe an ideological debt—whether good or bad—to the past" (McLaren and Tadeau da Silva, 55). My reading affirms that language does not reveal an "essential and unified historical subject. . . . [But] a subject historically situated and positioned in multiple and contradictory discourses" and contact zones (Bergland, 131).

The conception of autobiography that I bring to this study contrasts sharply with the views of early critics of the genre, who assumed there was a "true" self—a private, hidden, timeless, and unchanging self captured by the act of writing. Like the image of my great-grandfather, the autobiographer was positioned as a transcendental voyeur of life (Gunn, 7). In addition to the focus on the *bios* of the public white male autobiographer, early critics of the genre assumed that language was a transparent medium through which life-experience could be perceived—undistorted (Brodzki and Schenck, 1). It was this mimetic understanding of the relations between language and experience, and concepts of the self as a coherent and unified producer of truth, that led Georg Misch and others to view autobiography as a subcategory of biography. "The autobiographer was expected to subordinate imagination to the attempt to communicate trustworthy, verifiable, subjective messages" (Stone, 100).[3]

A later generation of critics turned their attention to the *autos* (the "I"), a shift corresponding with advancements in sociology and psychoanalysis (Gusdorf). Like their predecessors, they maintained that autobiography was a reliable source of self-knowledge and that language was a transparent medium through which life could be perceived undistorted. Many early scholars of the genre had confidence in autobiographers to represent their bios; therefore, they legitimatized an ideology that privileged autonomy, objectivity, and individuality and that was grounded in the metaphysical notion of an essential self. Critics who conformed to these normative prescriptions rarely attended to the autobiographical works of women because women's life experiences were deemed culturally insignificant by white androcentric criteria and paradigms of self-representation (Smith 1987, 8–9). As Rita Felski points out, these normative criteria "are of little relevance in discussing the tradition of women's autobiography, which typically focuses on the details of domestic and personal life and is fragmented, episodic, and repetitive, lacking the unifying linear structure imposed upon a life by the pursuit of a public career" (86). Moreover, as Sidonie Smith persuasively argues, according to "the degree to which critics assume a transparency of language as well as its ideological neutrality, they ignore the implications for women autobiographers of moving from the margins of culture toward the center in order to engage in a 'master narrative' that defines the speaking subject as [white and] male" (1987, 9).

By contrast, a third generation of critics, influenced by structuralism and poststructuralism, focused on the *graphy*—language and the act of writing. For instance, Barthes and de Man challenged the notion of referentiality that defined earlier critical moments and suggested that the *auto* "structured by linguistic configurations beyond any single mind, may be nothing more, and certainly nothing less, than a convention of time and space" (Smith, 5). In his 1968 essay "Death of an Author," Barthes, like de Man, responded to nineteenth-century biographical positivism and criticism that glorified the author as an "author-god" by arguing for the removal of the author and deconstruction of the principle of representation. Numerous contemporary critics contend it is de Man, not Barthes, who "mounts a frontal attack on the assumption that autobiography belongs to a 'mode of referentiality'" (Eakin, 185). De Man claims "the aspiration of autobiography to move beyond its own text to a knowledge of the self and its world is founded in illusion":

> "The specular model of cognition," in which "the author declares himself the subject of his own understanding," is not primarily a situation or an event that can be located in history, but . . . the manifestation, on the level of the referent, of a linguistic structure. (de Man quoted in Eakin, 185–86)

Here, the autobiographical act is no longer constructed as an act of retrieval of an already existing and complete self (the traditional view) but, rather, a linguistic act through which the self is created in the process of the telling. De Man refers to the autobiographical process of moving from life *(bios)* to text *(graphe)* as de-facement. In his essay "Autobiography As De-facement," de Man claims that autobiography "deals with the giving and taking away of faces, with face and deface, *figure*, figuration and disfiguration" (926).

The view of autobiography that I endorse—understanding autobiographical acts at their historical and cultural moments of production and reception—is a direct response to what I perceive as the limitations of the three generations of critics discussed above—namely, their inattention to the material body, the complex discursive nature of individual and collective agency, and how autobiography is bound up with cultural practices and principles of truth-telling, policing, and notions of authenticity and the "real." As Leigh Gilmore perceptively points out, autobiography has drawn its social authority from its proximity to culturally dominant truth-telling discourses, such as the confession, which itself is defined in relation to other discursive formations— for example, religion (spiritual confessions), the law (legal confessions), and psychoanalysis (the "talking cure") (Gilmore, 108–9). Of course, truth-telling is "a ritual that unfolds within a power relationship" and as a cultural process offers varying rewards; sometimes it is embraced, sometimes resisted, and sometimes it can be a form of punishment or an effort to stave off punishment (Foucault quoted in Gilmore, 112). The discourse of truth-telling is historically marked by notions of gender and race; consider how the white male is most often positioned as the judge.[4] Historically, autobiographical works that did not reflect certain "truths" or reproduce dominant ideologies of identity (namely, the values of individualism central to the patriarchal Eurocentric literary canon) were not even characterized as autobiographies and were considered unworthy of serious study (Gilmore, 41).[5] When studying autobiography, we should consider the textual, performative, and institutional frameworks that shape and authorize certain expressions of the self. We must ask: Who is authorized to tell the truth? Whose truth is being told and to whom?

This is not to imply that these theoretical traditions of autobiography did not themselves arise out of contact zones conditioned by historical, institutional, and sociocultural contexts but rather that their theoretical premises are not entirely conducive to an analysis of material production and reception of autobiographical acts. In fact, one of the great ironies of de Man's work is what is disguised, defaced, in his own writing. Although defacement (to mar the face of, to disfigure) may be the premise of de Man's theory of autobiography, effacement (to wipe out, obliterate) is the result. Indeed, the transformation of the material self into a text sets the stage for later theories about the disappearance and/or death of the author. Paradoxically, the author as we knew it is killed by critics such as de Man and Barthes, only to reappear in another form.[6] Insistent as de Man was in denying the relationship between the writer's life and the writer's creative output, today his works are usually read as autobiography. Seán Burke observes that "the de Manian legacy . . . shows how the principle of the author most powerfully reasserts itself when it is thought absent" (6). For instance, de Man's readings of the autobiographical works of others and his theoretical premises are shaped by his own silences, notably about his controversial work on a Belgian propaganda newspaper during World War II. "Between 1940 and 1942, the young intellectual [de Man] wrote 170 articles for the collaborationist Belgian newspaper Le Soir, a certain number of which express anti-Semitic and pro-Nazi sentiments" (1). Implicit in de Man's concept of autobiography is a significant effacement of his own position, a masking of his own dominating interests. De Man and

Barthes may have provoked self-reflexivity about issues of identity, author-ship, readership, subjectivity, and language, but, paradoxically, these par-ticular critical gestures also introduced new forms of historical and social amnesia.

One could also argue that historically marginalized groups share with critics like Barthes and de Man a nonrepresentative, displaced sense of sub-jectivity. While comparisons like these may have a certain allure, as Biddy Martin points out in "Lesbian Identity and Autobiographical Difference[s]," in actuality they "constitute a certain danger, given the institutional privileges enjoyed by those who can afford to disavow 'identity' and its 'limits' over against those for whom such disavowals reproduce their invisibility" (1988b, 78). Barthes's conception of the "death of the author" and the author's in-evitable return may have deconstructed the concept of referentiality and views of the reader and writer as static fixed entities. The contemporary ef-facement of European white male critics is not, however, equivalent to the historical and literary *absence* of women or men of color. One might argue, then, that the image of disappearance put forth by Barthes and de Man reifies a dominant white Western male space; although the author has disappeared and may be invisible, it is a privileged and thus superior invisibility. In de Man's "Autobiography As De-facement" and Barthes's "The Death of the Author," the "master subject" plays his usual disappearing tricks. What nei-ther de Man nor Barthes considers in these essays is how the "making of his-tory is tied up with the makings of a *silence*" (Felman 1992, 184). In fact, for many women and men of color, writing often feels like emerging from a kind of social death or confinement, in the sense that they have been culturally si-lenced or regarded as an absence (Bronfen, 404).

In writing about the problems of autobiography for women, Shoshana Felman suggests, in *What Does a Woman Want? Reading and Sexual Differ-ences*, that "*none of us, as women, has as yet, precisely, an autobiography*" (1993, 14). She continues, "Trained to see ourselves as objects and to be positioned as the Other, estranged to ourselves, we have a story that by definition can-not be self-present to us, a story that, in other words, is not a story, but *must become* a story" (14). Felman reads women's autobiographies as "missing." The metaphor of missing points most clearly to those stories that narrate the absence of a story. Felman's notion of the absence of women's autobiogra-phies is quite different from de Man's autobiography as defacement or Barthes's "death of the author." While women and men of color struggle for literary presence, Barthes and de Man lament their own self-imposed absence.

Lucy Grealy's memoir, *Autobiography of a Face,* is a compelling example

of the cultural significance and anxiety about the material body in the autobiographical reading moment. Grealy challenges the disembodiment of the
autobiographical moment associated with traditional male autobiographies
and deconstruction as she testifies to her own struggles to become a subject.
With these struggles comes a remapping of the relationship between the body
that is written and the body that writes. The title suggests that this is a book
about a face, that part of a person that metaphorically stands for the whole, at
least in Western culture. For Grealy, who as a young girl had cancer of the jaw,
her face became synonymous with her identity.

> This singularity of meaning—I *was* my face, I *was* ugliness—though
> sometimes unbearable, also offered a possible point of escape. It became
> a launching pad from which to lift off, the one immediately recogniz-
> able place to point to when asked what was wrong with my life. Every-
> thing led to it, everything receded from it—my face as personal vanish-
> ing point. (7)

For much of Grealy's life, she felt either invisible or painfully visible. Like the
black youth in the family photograph, for Grealy visibility was a trap. The
notion of visibility is, as I suggested, central to the formation of the self as
subject in Western culture. Grealy's memoir explores the problem of self-
representation by examining who defines what is seen. Her narrative points
out how medical technology has shaped the practice of visualization. It is precisely the visual apparatuses and ideologies of looking that interest me. Grealy
does not camouflage or efface the practices that shape her face and organize
her subjectivity; in fact, she describes how she became so self-conscious that
acts of reflection were honed into a "torture device" (6). She looked at her face
in the mirror and scrutinized it against the "normal":

> I was bald . . . I had buck teeth. . . . My teeth were ugly . . . they were
> made worse by the fact that my chin seemed so small. . . . how had my
> face sunk in like that? I didn't understand. Was it possible I'd looked this
> way for a while and was only just noticing it . . . More than the ugliness
> I felt, I was suddenly appalled at the notion that I'd been walking
> around unaware of something that was apparent to everyone else. A
> profound sense of shame consumed me. (111–12)

Grealy was not always revolted by the transformations of her face and the series of medical procedures; possible future operations gave her a glimmer of
hope. Her face was unfinished, a work in progress; "Yet each time I was
wheeled down to the surgical wing, high on drugs, I'd think to myself, *Now,
now I can start my life, just as soon as I wake up from this operation.* And no mat-

ter how disappointed I felt when I woke up and looked in the mirror, I'd simply postpone happiness until the next operation" (187).

What we see in *Autobiography of a Face* is a developing dual consciousness (common in autobiographies produced by individuals from historically marginalized groups), a self that recognizes itself as culturally defined yet continues to long for an identity that meets these cultural prescriptions. Her preoccupation with imagining an "'original' face . . . free from all deviation, all error," underlies the culture's revulsion by and dread of facial damage or deformity. This is particularly true for women, for whom moral judgments about beauty and desire focus on the face. As Sandra Lee Bartky points out in "Foucault, Femininity, and Patriarchal Power," already operative in Western culture is the idea that women's faces are defective; "The technologies of femininity are taken up and practiced by women against the background of a pervasive sense of bodily deficiency" (71).

*Autobiography of a Face* offers a view from the body, as opposed to the view from above or the view from nowhere associated with the death and/or effacement of the author in the early works of Barthes and de Man. As Elisabeth Bronfen puts it in *Over Her Dead Body*, "writing . . . presupposes the life of the author, a signature and a position in culture" (404). Sidonie Smith makes a similar claim in *Subjectivity, Identity, and the Body* when she argues, "When a specific woman approaches the scene of writing and the autobiographical 'I,' she not only engages the discourses of subjectivity through which the universal human subject has been culturally secured; she also engages the complexities of her cultural assignment to an absorbing embodiment" (22). It is precisely the alienation and disfigurement that result from living under oppressive conditions that prompt and motivate many women to write autobiography. Here again is a compelling irony: On the one hand, women are culturally assigned as equal to their bodies and their bodies are objectified; on the other, women struggle to claim a different body, to represent their own bodies. Women are simultaneously represented as a bodily presence and as an absence.

In a later work, *Camera Lucida*, Barthes explores the links between visual memory and self-identity and the relationship between life and death in ways that are explicitly gendered. Here, Barthes contemplates his mother's death and the inevitability of his own mortality while looking at a photograph of his mother as a little girl, which he calls the Winter Garden Photograph. This photograph gives him a sense of his "mother's being and grief at her death" (70). *Camera Lucida* thus can be read as an "elegiac autobiographical narrative" that laments the death of his mother (M. Hirsch, 5–6) and, I would argue, as an allegory of the gendering of the specter (ghost) of deconstruction (the "death of the author") in familial and deeply gendered networks of looking.

One can argue that in *Camera Lucida* the figure of the author (the lost referent) returns to lament his own death. We can read this nostalgic return through Barthes's description of the process of posing and being photographed. Barthes writes, "Once I feel myself observed by the lens, everything changes: I constitute myself in the process of 'posing,' I instantaneously make another body for myself, I transform myself in advance into an image. The transformation is an active one: I feel that the Photograph creates my body or mortifies it, according to its caprice" (10–11). Barthes attributes agency to the photograph and laments the loss of the self through the whimsical, impulsive, unpredictable, objectifying, and even freakish process of photographic representation.

> The Photograph . . . represents the very subtle moment when, to tell the truth, I am neither subject nor object but a subject who feels he is becoming an object: I then experience a micro-version of death (of parenthesis): I am truly becoming a specter. The Photographer knows this very well, and himself fears . . . this death in which his gesture will embalm me. . . . but when I discover myself in the product of this operation, what I see is that I have become Total-Image, which is to say, Death in person; others—the Other—do not dispossess me of myself, they turn me, ferociously, into an object, they put me at their mercy, at their disposal, classified in a file, ready for the subtlest deceptions. (14)

Barthes describes the process of self-construction and the act of posing and being photographed as a traumatic biographical process—that is, as a process of loss through which one becomes a ghost of oneself. Likewise, in the process of looking at photographs of others, it is the photographic referent (that is both there and not there) that haunts him. For Barthes, the trauma of representation—the loss of the self and the lost referent—is engendered through a narrative in which he laments his own childlessness and embodies the figure of the mother.

> Ultimately I experienced her, strong as she had been, my inner law, as my feminine child. Which was my way of resolving Death. . . . if after having been reproduced as other than himself, the individual dies, having thereby denied and transcended himself, I who had not procreated, I had, in her very illness, engendered my mother . . . My particularity could never again universalize itself (unless, utopically, by writing, whose project henceforth would become the unique goal of my life). From now on I could do no more than await my total, undialectical death. (72)

Marianne Hirsch argues that through the technology of imagining Barthes gives birth to his mother, "displacing her own maternity . . . [And] shaping a masculine maternity or a paternal form of generativity, a techno-birth" (170–71). Not only does the camera become the womb and the photographer both the creator and taker of life, but language and the act of writing and reading are construed as life-giving and, therefore, as also potentially murderous. That is, both the writer and reader, like the mother/photographer, have "the power to kill," to transform beings into "one-dimensional figures, immobilized at a given instant, made into icons or fetishes" (Hirsch, 175). Thus, Barthes "bestows on the maternal look [and the author] some of the disturbing characteristics and qualities of an all-seeing, dominating gaze" (155). What complicates Barthes's familial looking in *Camera Lucida* is that "his desire is to recognize not only his mother but himself, not only to recognize but to be recognized by her"(Hirsch, 9). As Hirsch rightly points out, "The familial look, then, is not the look of a subject looking at an object, but a mutual look of a subject looking at an object who is a subject looking (back) at an object" (9). It is precisely the mutuality of identification and discovery of self in relation to others that prompts one to read *Camera Lucida* as an "allegory of the autobiographical act" (Jay, 194). The reciprocal structure of looking foregrounds the process of self-construction and the reader's/viewer's projection of particular cultural scripts onto the autobiographical subject (Slater, 134). Likewise, as I look at the family photograph, I am looked at. Readers will project cultural narratives, myths, and ideologies onto my reading. For instance, family members may code my reading as a kind of betrayal, a narrative of contesting loyalties. I, like Barthes, am haunted by the photograph and the recognition of my narrative within the familial network of looking.

Barthes reconstitutes the loss of his mother and the fantasy of the mother's returned gaze in the cultural space of looking. While Barthes may long for the authenticity of the lost referent (in this case, his mother), ultimately he "turns [authenticity] into a kind of simulacrum in which the subject cannot stop 'imitating' himself. . . . The authentic self, in Barthes's terms, is finally an impossibility, for it would be a self freed from the process of becoming an object" (Jay, 194–95). This is, Jay argues, "the specter of the death of the subject (195)." Barthes writes:

> What I want, in short, is that my (mobile) image, buffeted among a thousand shifting photographs, altering with situation and age, should always coincide with my (profound) "self": but it is the contrary that must be said: "myself" never coincides with my image; for it is the

image which is heavy, motionless, stubborn (which is why society sustains it), and "myself" which is light, divided, dispersed; . . . if only Photography could give me a neutral, anatomic body, a body which signifies nothing! . . . In front of the lens, I am at the same time: the one I think I am, the one I want others to think I am, the one the photographer thinks I am, and the one he makes use of to exhibit his art. In other words, a strange action: I do not stop imitating myself, and because of this, each time I am (or let myself be) photographed, I invariably suffer from a sensation of inauthenticity, sometimes of imposture. (12–13)

Barthes denies the possibility of the self and, at the same time, retains the desire for the authentic subject—the self separate from the apparti of its conditioning. Finally, Barthes's formulation keeps in play the Self-Other, Subject-Object, Authentic-Posed binaries.

Many feminists have challenged such binaries and the concept of the "death of the author." For instance, Barbara Christian, in "The Race for Theory," argues that deconstruction occurred historically at a time when the literature of people of color became more visible (340). Lois McNay makes a similar point in *Foucault and Feminism*. She claims that many feminists are opposed to the convergence of feminism and postmodernism because the deconstruction of categories such as subjectivity and identity and the concept of the "death of the author" directly conflict with emancipatory feminist projects, in that they "den[y] women the chance of articulating and analyzing their experiences, just as they are beginning to realize the possibility of overcoming their marginalization" (6).

While I am sympathetic to this critique, like McNay, I think we need to challenge the "schematized terms of the modern/postmodern debate" (126). Moreover, I find problematic the conflation of the deconstruction of the subject with the erasure of human agency. Indeed, the deconstruction of the subject prompts a refiguration of human agency, not a nostalgic return to concepts of agency based on notions of stable, authentic self. As I have suggested, a materialist rhetorical analysis opens up the critical space to frame the writing body (both the material body that writes and the written body) as sites of cultural contestation, and to recognize how agency emerges from negotiations of conflicting positions and discourses (Bergland, 233–34).

The image of my great-grandfather as captured in the 1910 portrait can be seen as a metaphor for the positions of the Western imperial subject overseeing the terrain of representation. The photographer represents the critic capturing, sanctifying, and documenting this position from afar—that is, beyond the visual field. One might argue that my reframing of autobiography replaces the traditional author-god, which deconstructionists sought to disrupt, with an all-powerful reader. I hope, however, that my reading of the family photograph demonstrates that reading need not function as a colonizing authorial gesture that resecures a dominating, transcendent, or expansive sensibility. In fact, to reframe autobiography in pedagogical terms as social moments of negotiating meaning opens up the space for critical reflection on issues of agency and for the re-entrance of the materiality of experience and the body as sites of cultural contestation.

## Pedagogical Gazes and the Politics of Social Memory

The oppositional, yet dependent, tropes of detachment and control, self and other, and visibility and invisibility circulate in the highly charged pedagogical spaces of the academy. Indeed, the detached, yet privileged, pose that my great-grandfather assumes is a visual prototype for certain pedagogical as well as theoretical gestures. The photograph and my reading of the narratives that frame both its production and reception provide a schema for understanding the institutionalization of certain pedagogical postures and subject positions, traditional and progressive. The trope of making the invisible visible (that is, the experiences, writing, and art of marginalized groups), for instance, was common in early Women's Studies pedagogy and continues to inform multicultural pedagogy. But as I suggested in the Introduction, such pedagogies too often simply amount to curricular add-ons, revisions that do not fundamentally alter the superstructures of the academy or the ways that texts get read or how certain voices get integrated into the curriculum and become institutionalized. These pedagogical narratives of "otherness" projected onto the works of historically marginalized groups fail to consider the reciprocal nature of looking and how the reader and writer, like the photographer and viewer, collaborate in the reproduction of cultural ideologies. As a result, the framing apparatuses are not confronted. Nor are the following questions examined: How does the inclusion of texts by historically marginalized groups challenge dominant reading or writing practices? How are binary categories of the oppressed and oppressor reinscribed or fractured through cross-cultural reading practices? Are certain familial gazes (maternal, paternal) projected onto the pedagogical screen? What narratives of identity are institutionally sanctioned through reading and writing practices? Some of the same problems I discussed in my critique of autobiographical theory in the previous section are relevant here, particularly the idea that pedagogies of inclusion reify the self-other binary and see the reclamation of the heretofore invisible self as the critical goal. Likewise, the photograph of my great-grandfather with his black servant can be seen as a kind of allegory for what happens when we uncritically endorse a pedagogy of inclusion based on visibility politics, the self-other binary, and the logic of imperial spectatorship. Generations of Western scholars, teachers, and administrators have re-created the conquering and controlling gaze of the colonizer—a gaze that does not account for its own privilege but that relies upon traditional conventions to assert its power and authority and to position students, particularly female students and students of color, as spectacles. The pedagogical challenge in increasingly multicultural classrooms is to avoid replicating these binaries, to expose how they work, and to discourage situating the "cultural other" as a spectacle of a dominating, voyeuristic gaze. Andrew Lakritz puts it this way: "If we are . . . to find a productive way to address otherness in critical analysis, it must be first by a self-reflexive glance at the very optical machine that gives access to the other in the first place, that actually constructs the other as other" (17). For example, in traditional pedagogy, students are positioned as passive recipients (others), mere containers to be filled.

Paulo Freire refers to this approach to teaching as banking education. The autobiographical scripts institutionalized through banking models are those that position the teacher as the sole bearer of knowledge. When literatures of historically marginalized groups are incorporated into banking pedagogies in an effort to expand the canon, the "cultural other" becomes yet another commodity for consumption. Moreover, the burden of these texts becomes enormous, because they are meant to stand in for cultural diversity, to represent the experience of entire groups. Because banking pedagogies presume a one-way transfer of knowledge, the pedagogical dynamics and problematics of cross-racial and cross-cultural reading practices are ignored. The sense of community and civility that characterizes banking models has been based on the moral and political values of Eurocentric traditions. This pedagogically crafted homogeneity not only represses heterogeneity and silences relations as they occur in the contact zones of educational institutions but it also creates stable and fixed notions of difference. Such approaches to difference, as Lawrence Goldberg suggests, are the equivalent of a modern masquerade; in reality, the prevailing human social condition is movement and migration.

American educational institutions, as apparatuses of cultural production, play a major role in encouraging or hindering these movements and in defining what constitutes a "culture." For example, debates over what constitutes "American" identity and culture persist, as do battles for institutional support for programs that give voice to the experiences of groups historically marginalized in the United States, such as Asian-American Studies, African-American Studies, Latin American Studies, and Women's Studies. Many composition programs, especially those that move beyond the narrow call for the standardization of academic discourse and universal concepts of knowledge and language at the expense of multiple literacies, are immersed in similar struggles, although debate over what constitutes American culture and identity in composition is often disguised as debate over what constitutes proper "academic" writing. As I discuss in chapter 3, many traditional educators and administrators have argued that the only role of composition programs is to teach students the basics, by which they mean standard English and "objective" academic language and conventions. The inherent elitism in the call for a standard, homogeneous language is exacerbated in the academy by the existence of a distinct group of non-tenure-track faculty, many of whom are graduate students teaching in writing programs and most of whom are women (Holbrook), so that what we see in many English departments nationwide is marginalized labor teaching the standards of access (Schnell). I find these patterns profoundly disturbing; not only do they contribute to the exploitation of graduate students but they also institutionalize cultural and linguistic hierarchies.

Rather than imagining or striving for homogeneous writing cultures or discourse communities, I urge faculty and administrators to recognize the academy as comprised of contending and overlapping linguistic and cultural contact zones. Moreover, we need to situate the pedagogical goal of enabling all students access and facility with standard academic discourse in a larger social and materialist analysis, which fosters an awareness of how language and knowledge shape and are shaped by institutional contexts, disciplinary constraints, and existing power relations. The tensions between experience and language are particularly vivid for "basic" writers, whose struggles are compounded institutionally through the uncritical perpetuation of dominant ideologies of academic literacy. Colleges are not homogeneous monolingual sites connected by one competence and grammar shared equally among its members, nor are they equally conducive and accessible to all student groups and populations. In fact, student populations that historically have been marginalized often are forced to cross cultural-linguistic terrains defined by dominant forms of expression. Students often must abandon their cultural and linguistic origins and adapt to the dominant discourse and culture of the academy. Students who speak in Black English Vernacular and students for whom English is their second language, for example, are often viewed as inferior, even through these students often demonstrate greater rhetorical flexibility because they must learn to speak and write in many codes simply to survive. One challenge of teaching writing today is developing pedagogical strategies that expose dominant language and its conventions, consider how these conventions can be used for interventionist purposes, and that recognize that the linguistic field of the classroom is unstable and flexible.

Monoculturalism and the preoccupation with the establishment of common cultural literacies date back to the nineteenth century, when the concept of universality shaped intellectual traditions. By the late twentieth century, monoculturalism reflected the Eurocentric attitudes and demarcations initiated by U.S. immigration policy. In this sense, monoculturalism was contemporaneous with melting-pot assimilation (Gardner and Newfield, 4–5). Cold War rhetoric and the construction of the Third World for Euro-American and Russian interests also reinforced monoculturalism. In reaction to monocultural and banking models, a generation of teachers has promoted more integrated models of education, which emerged from the countercultural movements of the 1960s, and attempted to let all voices and experiences be heard.[7] While pedagogies of integration may strive for inclusivity by giving voice to cultural expressions at the sociocultural margins—like the photograph of my great-grandfather that represented the black youth but basically positioned him as a spectacle—the center often continues to be defined monoculturally.

Contrary to monocultural and banking models of education is the Freirean model of problem-posing education espoused by numerous feminists and critical educators, including Giroux, Gore, hooks, Luke, Shor, Simon, and Weiler, among others. Problem-posing approaches attempt to enable students to become active subjects in the learning process. The goal of problem-posing education is not to focus on individual salvation or self-esteem (though these may be by-products) but to enable learners to develop a critical consciousness. Critical consciousness involves: drawing connections between knowledge and power; becoming both self-reflective and socially reflective; developing analytic habits of thinking, reading, and writing that foreground the historical nature and context of knowledge and that challenge myths and values learned in mass culture; and taking part in and initiating social change (Shor, 32–33). Problem-posing approaches to education are often described as participatory, dialogic, democratic, multicultural, situated, and activist (34–35).

At its best, critical pedagogy does not play into reductive visibility politics, but even critical pedagogies are vulnerable to essentializing tactics. Moreover, appropriations of the Freirean model, particularly in North American institutions, pose specific challenges. For instance, teachers who focus solely on the *methods* of learning associated with problem-posing education and who do not engage the emancipatory politics of the Freirean model or its historical specificity often reproduce a form of philosophical and pedagogical liberalism, a stance not primarily concerned with redistributing power and knowledge. One challenge of situating problem-posing education in the Western context is recognizing how a pedagogy that emerged from literacy work with the underclass in Latin America gets translated into American schools. Henry Giroux and other critical educators have responded to the systematic appropriation and depoliticization of Freirean pedagogy in the West by encouraging teachers to engage Freire as an anticolonial and postcolonial thinker. Giroux advises them to explore how their location as Western teachers shapes their reading of Freire, to challenge practices that erase the voice of the "other," and to examine the cultural, theoretical, and ideological borders they are enclosed within and/or protected by (1994a, 142).

Freirean pedagogy is anticolonialist in its recognition of the historical and institutional structures that privilege and exclude particular voices, its repudiation of domination and oppression, and its call for the decentering of monolithic and imperial forms of authority (Giroux 1994a, 150; McLaren and Tadeu da Silva, 84). I share Giroux's concern over the appropriation of Freire's work and ask those who draw upon Freirean pedagogy to recognize the politics and limits of their own critical and pedagogical positions. However, I'm less enthusiastic about labeling problem-posing education, whether practiced in First- or Third-World contexts, as postcolonial. As McClintock suggests, the term *postcolonial* is "prematurely celebratory"; it obfuscates the continuities of language, power, and neocolonialism that shape the legacies of colonial empires (12). Indeed, for groups such as Native American peoples in the United States, Palestinian inhabitants of Israeli Occupied Territories, and Catholic residents of British-occupied Northern Ireland, there is nothing at all "post" about colonialism. The term is particularly misleading with respect to women; as McClintock points out, "No postcolonial state anywhere has granted women and men equal access to the rights and resources of the nation state" (13–14).

To describe Western classrooms as postcolonial spaces inadvertently privileges the social location of certain learners over others. Consequently, we must ask, "For whom is the academy a postcolonial site?" The academy, as a major component of a capitalist society, safeguards the futures of certain populations and nations. The American educational system provides a means for stratifying individuals. For example, the gap between upper-income and lower-income educational levels in this country is gradually widening. Small liberal arts colleges such as Oberlin excel at educating the well-prepared but are less successful at recruiting and retaining students at risk. Part of the problem is that many small colleges and universities have cut support services and programs designed to address the needs of particular groups of students. Moreover, for many first-generation college students, women and men of color, working-class people, and minorities, entering the academy is akin to crossing a border into different cultural spheres and circles of uncertainty.

The academy does not always recognize or accommodate such issues and struggles.

Even in classrooms where teachers and students examine these struggles through problem-posing methods, historical inequalities cannot be suspended. While it is important to develop learning environments that enable dialogue among students from various cultural backgrounds, to conceptualize classrooms as unequivocally "safe spaces" is to ignore the intractable differences among students and/or between students and their teachers. Moreover, as the rise of incidents of sexual assault and hate crimes on our nation's campuses indicates, colleges and universities are not equally safe spaces for all students.[8] According to Mary Louise Pratt, "safe houses" are "social and intellectual spaces where groups can constitute themselves as horizontal, homogenous, sovereign communities with high degrees of trust, shared understanding, temporary protection from legacies of oppression" (455). However, very few spaces on campus (or anywhere in our society for that matter) can offer the advantages Pratt proposes. First of all, even "safe houses" constructed to counter dominating relations within the larger community are seldom homogeneous. In fact, members of "safe houses" often seek to protect diversity. In addition, dominant groups can violate "safe houses." Consider, for example, the experiences of women living in Baldwin Cottage, the women's collective on the Oberlin College campus. During the fall of 1995, the words "I hate Baldwin women" and "Donated with hatred to all you desperate, fat, disgusting Baldwin dykes" were written on the residents' community message board, and a copy of a *Penthouse* video with additional remarks was left on a windowsill. Although Baldwin Cottage exists as a place where women can retreat from the Oberlin College contact zones, this incident demonstrates that the space is not unconditionally safe.

My personal living space on the Oberlin campus could be seen as yet another example of the problematic nature of "safe houses." For four of the six years I taught at the college, I lived in the college-owned Monroe-Bosworth house, which is located near several campus "safe houses"—the African Heritage House, La Casa Española, the German and Russian House, the Third World House, and Baldwin Cottage. James Monroe, an Oberlin College graduate (1844), was an abolitionist and antislavery politician who sheltered fugitive slaves, served in the state legislature, and accepted a position at the college as professor of rhetoric and belle lettres in 1849 (Blue, 285–89). Monroe bought the house from the college with the understanding that he would honor Oberlin's credo of "labor and learning" by employing students in manual labor. In 1862, he sold the house and moved to Rio de Janeiro to serve as U.S. consul during the Civil War. Edward Bosworth, a professor of religion and dean of the school of theology, and his family owned the house from the turn of the century until 1956 (Blodgett 1985, 78). The house is one of many in Oberlin that functioned as "safe houses" for escaped black slaves on the Underground Railroad. Knowing that "safe houses" are not unequivocally safe, it would be more accurate to describe locations on the Underground Railroad as contact zones; they were sites marked by the languages and experiences of their abolitionist occupants as well as by the struggles, experiences, and languages of black slaves from the south. I often think about the movement of the oppressed into the homes of the privileged and contemplate the terms of interaction between white abolitionists and black slaves and the historical narratives that shape our understanding of these interactions. Abolitionists may have opposed slavery as an institution, but not all white abolitionists were antiracists. For example, many were motivated by religious and moral sentiments to protest slavery but did not want to destroy the racial hierarchy (hooks 1981, 124).

There are compelling rhetorical parallels between the constructed pedagogical relationships of black slaves and white abolitionists in abolitionist discourse and white educators and students from marginalized groups in critical pedagogy. Peter McLaren in *Critical Pedagogy and Predatory Culture*, for example, envisions a pedagogy of solidarity with the powerless as a position of "cosuffering with the oppressed as they struggle both to transcend and transform the circumstances of their disempowerment" (23). While the concept of cosuffering suggests that we speak *with* the oppressed, we should remember that pedagogical stances created out of empathy for others and those that emerge from marginalized peoples themselves are not historically equivalent and, therefore, are not interchangeable. Because the pedagogical construction of a state of cosuffering may very well inhibit social analysis, a teacher's privilege in relation to the student must be examined. We have to consider, for example, how identification can be used to re-establish authority and hierarchical relations, as well as what identifications remain submerged or repressed. As Lakritz cautions, "The very structure of authority that allows us to identify and empathize inserts us back into the structure of inequality the identification would dismantle" (12).

In *Thinking Through: Essays on Feminism, Marxism, and Anti-Racism*, Himani Bannerji discusses the challenges of developing antiracist pedagogies and coalition building in the academy and makes a point about how the empathy of friendship often stands in for transformative action (116). She focuses on her own experiences and professional relations as a woman of color with white colleagues in Canadian academic settings.

Why do they [whites] only talk about racism, as understanding us, doing good to "us"? Why don't they move from the experiences of sharing our pain, to narrating the experience of afflicting it on us? Why do they not question their own cultures, childhood, upbringings, and ask how they could live so "naturally" in this "white" environment, never noticing that fact until we brought it home to them? (117)

According to Bannerji, empathy may be a starting point, but it is not enough. Although experiences of gender oppression may lead me to identify and empathize with the plight of the black youth in the photograph discussed earlier, my experiences of oppression cannot be conflated with his. Like most white women, I have been denied equal participation with white men; nevertheless, I share the privilege of whiteness with my great-grandfather and have greater access to white man's culture than do people of color. As critical educators and scholars, we must not presume an unmediated exchange of experiences or domesticate difference through the nonreflective and uncritical sharing of personal experience. Problem-posing pedagogies and pedagogies of liberation may be created out of empathy for others and reflect critical linkages between dominant and minority forms of cultural expression, but these linkages must not conflate the social positions or the stories of the privileged and the oppressed. While acts of solidarity with oppressed peoples are certainly part of the struggle for transformative pedagogies, solidarity is not the same as cosuffering. Distinctions must be drawn between acts of solidarity (where people from geographical and historically segregated groups come into contact with one another and work toward a common goal) and the notion of a uniformly constant and universally empathic antioppression stance. My goal is not to rank oppressions or to delimit the importance of empathy but to point out the contradictory nature of agency and the difference between cosuffering and acts of solidarity in order to mobilize these contradictions and differences toward liberating ends.

These distinctions raise important pedagogical questions about how we understand teacher-student relations and cross-cultural reading and writing practices in our classrooms. Pedagogies of inclusion often honor modes of reading akin to identification. Multicultural pedagogies that simply add more material endorse a conception of reading in which the writer and reader presumably determine each other by mutual substitution or identification. Problematically, this conception of reading ignores how language conventions and narratives are not shared equally among readers and writers—and fails to acknowledge the social identities and cultural and familial narratives that shape a reader's interpretive process, not to mention the structural and economic issues of access. We have to recognize that people in different positions in the contact zones of our classrooms read texts differently. While it is possible to construct counter-narratives and resistant stances as acts of solidarity with oppressed peoples, we must be skeptical of the historical tendency of white culture to reposition itself at the center of what initially may seem to be a transformative multicultural pedagogy. This does not mean that members of privileged classes cannot work with those who are marginalized in struggling against injustices, but rather that those of us who have cultural capital in the academy use our privileges to work against the historic impulse to assume the identity of the "other" or to impersonate the "other" by stating a shared victimization (M. B. Pratt, 40). For instance, the narrative of friendship that lives on in my family's reading of the photograph could be seen from a pedagogical standpoint as a "provisional effect of 'institutionally produced redemption discourses'" (Roman 1997, 272). My family's perspective on the photograph of my great-grandfather is layered with the rhetoric of empire, immigration, upward mobility, and so on; as such, it reveals the shifting and situational nature of the family's identity and shows how the material context alters the family's interpretation. Moreover, my analysis of the various readings of this photograph suggests that the "production of identification (or disidentification) with an imagined or fantasized 'other' involves crucial, complex, and contradictory relations of power" (Roman, 1997, 272).

This reading posits several pedagogical implications. First, it calls for a pedagogy that foregrounds the cultural and material production and reception of autobiographical acts. Second, it suggests the need for a pedagogy that distinguishes among multiple registers of spectatorship and that interrogates the ways that teachers and students have been disciplined and stylized to produce certain narratives of the self. Third, it urges teachers to consider the transformative potential of a pedagogy of multiplicity, which introduces narratives that enact new forms of location—that is, those that fracture the self-other binary and put forth multiple identities, oppositional yet nonessentialist identities, cross-cultural and plural subjectivities (Grewal, 234). Finally, it suggests that pedagogies of autobiography must not simply be about having students integrate the personal into traditional classroom discourse; they must be about exploring with our students how identities are negotiated among conflicting and multiple discourses and how power is constituted and claimed rhetorically. In order for the oppressed to become agents of their own liberation, teachers and education scholars must fuse the knowledge accessible to them because of their social position with the knowledge of the people. In other words, "intellectuals must . . . share the power over knowledge, [and] share the power to shape the future" (Aronowitz 1993, 21).

Essentially, I advocate the critical integration of autobiography as part of the development of what Mary Louise Pratt calls "the pedagogical arts of the contact zone."[9] I propose that both teachers and students become reflective of the cultural narratives that shape their relations to each other and the historical contact zones and historical sites of conflict and growth that give these narratives their form.[10] *Framing Identities* is as concerned with dominant and resistant expressions of power as it is with how these binary categories become solidified or fractured in certain pedagogical contexts.

## 2

## AUTOBIOGRAPHY AND

## FEMINIST WRITING PEDAGOGY

Picture a New England schoolhouse in the late seventeenth century. Rows of young white boys sit in wooden chairs facing the teacher's podium, black slates resting in their laps. In the rear of the room, young white girls stand behind a curtain far from the warmth of the iron stove, eavesdropping on the boys' recitations. The only reason the girls are tolerated at all is because the town neglected to specify their exclusion from the school when it was first established (Kendall, 12). These young girls are simultaneously "inside" and "outside" the public sphere; the curtain confines them to a camouflaged zone. This vignette provides a vivid example of how spatial contexts and gender relations are entwined in American education. And it illustrates how gender, race, and class differences influence notions of the private and public spheres.

Despite the entrance of women into coeducational institutions in the nineteenth century, traditional ideologies of gender and white middle-class concepts of the private and public sphere continued to shape American education. For example, when white women and African-Americans were admitted to degree programs in 1833 and 1835, respectively, the segregated spatial and curricular arrangements of earlier periods persisted. Oberlin College, one of the first to open its doors to students regardless of race or sex, had policies that relegated women to their separate sphere. The segregation of women was based upon nineteenth-century models of womanhood designed for upper- and middle-class white women. As one historian put it, the "Oberlin co-eds were being prepared for intelligent motherhood and a properly subservient wifehood": "Washing the men's clothes, caring for their rooms, serving them at table, listening to their orations, but themselves remaining respectfully silent in public assemblages" (Flexner quoted in Spain, 156). As Daphne Spain points out, "This division of labor was patterned after family relationships in which the man was the head of the household" (156).

Oberlin College is an example of a nineteenth-century academy that imagined itself as a public space within which "'private persons' [namely white men] deliberated about 'public matters'" pertaining to the "common good" (Fraser, 70). Men were schooled in formalized languages and the public art of rhetoric and persuasion—the "I" was a public "I" claimed by public men—and women were schooled in the private art of conversation. Oberlin offered one of the first coeducational courses in rhetoric, but many women were hesitant to speak among the men in class because they had been taught public silence for so long. That women were even trained in the art of conversation reflects their subordination and the denial of their equal participation in public discourse with white men. The opening image of this chapter is a metaphor for the position of upper- and middle-class white women in relation to upper- and middle-class white men. White women are positioned as spectators; they are exposed to white man's culture but their exposure is limited. Not incidentally, the rhetoric course ended when several women asked to return to separate classes (Solomon, 28). Some formed their own literary societies in which to debate current events and to share personal experiences, and many contested the traditional divisions of labor.

Although young white girls are no longer forced to sit outside classrooms listening in on boys' debates or relegated behind a curtain in the back of the schoolroom, American schools, colleges, and universities remain spaces not equally conducive to and tolerant of all forms of cultural and linguistic expression. The presence of white women and people of color in spaces traditionally defined as white and male has not solved inequalities in social power. Among the responses to the perpetuation of inequities on American campuses has been the call from feminist educators for more inclusive curricula and the creation of "safe spaces" in the form of housing and support networks for white women and people of color. These so-called safe spaces are not entirely free of hierarchical relations, but because they exist as responses to dominant-subordinate social and spatial relations within the academy, they allow for the possibility of resistance and provide spaces for healing and strategizing (Fraser). Paradoxically, however, such spaces often reinscribe the same gender distinctions and ways of thinking about race from which white women and people of color have struggled to free themselves.

Like the image of the young white Protestant girls standing behind the curtain in the seventeenth-century schoolhouse, an echo of traditional gender ideologies, accompanied by white middle- and upper-class notions of the public and private, can be found in contemporary feminist pedagogical projects. Indeed, one might argue that this image represents the constructed notion of the private and public spheres in early feminist theory, namely white feminism. The public/private distinction marks the history of the white feminist movement in the United States. For example, in consciousness-raising groups of the 1960s, women gained political consciousness by examining and sharing personal experiences, thus giving rise to the feminist slogan "The personal is political." While these groups were inspired by the Black Power movement in the United States, they downplayed race and class in pursuit of women's common oppression. The "personal is political" concept challenges the public/private distinction, insisting that politics shape the personal. But, as Aída Hurtado points out, the public/private distinction "is relevant only for the white middle and upper classes since historically the American state has intervened constantly in the private lives and domestic arrangements of the working class. Women of color have not had the benefit of the economic conditions that underlie the private/public distinction" (849). In some sense, then, the opening image can be said to reflect "differences in women's [and men's of color] relational position to white men" (850). In this image, there are no girls of color behind the curtain or, for that matter, boys of color in the classroom.

Contemporary feminists often invoke the personal-is-political slogan in curricular-revision projects calling for greater visibility of women's personal experiences and representation of women's accomplishments. Yet these approaches frequently fail to take into account how these experiences have been shaped by regimes of domination and exploitation. Moreover, many such projects, based upon notions of the personal as political or of making the private public, do not account for class, race, and sexual differences among women or for differences among urban, suburban, and rural living conditions. Patricia Hill Collins forcefully argues that the private/public dichotomy is not a useful distinction for interpreting African-American communities, for which the private often refers to community spaces outside the home.

Many feminists in composition studies reinforce liberal middle-class notions of the family and its distinctions between private and public spheres. They do this in two ways: by invoking expressionist pedagogies of autobiography, which stress self-discovery and individual growth, and by imagining the feminist teacher as a nonconflictual maternal figure. Recent feminist pedagogical work in composition challenges these expressionist pedagogies and white middle-class liberal notions of gender and the family. In the late twentieth century, when our classrooms are becoming increasingly diverse, white middle-class notions of the private and public spheres and expressionist conceptions of autobiography are no longer pedagogically feasible. Instead, a new conception of autobiography and its pedagogical role in the academy, particularly in feminist classrooms, is required to salvage its potential as oppositional discourse. Through the use of spatial concepts such as borderlands, contact zones, and coalition building, feminists challenge rigid class-based notions of the private and public spheres and explore the paradoxical nature of doing autobiographical work in the academy; feminist-writing classrooms, situated in spaces made available by larger patriarchal structures, are themselves paradoxical. The following survey of various conceptions of autobiography in feminist-writing pedagogy over the last decade will, I hope, demonstrate why autobiographical acts are important in the academic environment and clarify their potential and risks. Two key questions inform my exploration. How have feminist teachers in composition within the last decade used autobiographical spaces to challenge traditional pedagogies? How has the genre of autobiography become feminized in writing pedagogy? In seeking answers, I focus on both the strategic uses of autobiography and its limitations and on the recent interest in autobiography in multicultural-writing pedagogies.

## Pedagogical "Blind Spots"

One of the first anthologies to attempt to define a feminist approach to composition was *Teaching Writing: Pedagogy, Gender, and Equity* (1987), edited by Cynthia L. Caywood and Gillian R. Overing. Many contributors to *Teaching Writing* position the personal voices of women and the genre of autobiography as alternatives to traditionally and institutionally imposed masculine voices and genres. For example, Olivia Frey argues in "Equity and Peace in the New Writing Class," "The teacher no longer has the Truth about writing. The student has the truth as she makes the writing her own" (97). Frey continues:

> The new writing class encourages a woman to develop her inner resources. She must make choices, discover her purpose as a writer, shape her writing according to her own needs. . . . As the student makes small choices, then important ones, she discovers her rhetorical voice along with her personal female voice. . . . the new writing class recovers the authority of the writer's own experience. . . . in this case prescriptive rhetoric and grammar, no longer "intervene between herself and herself," between the image in the mirror that society has created, and the genuine self behind the mask (101–2)

The pedagogical assumption here is that if women would only write about their own experiences, then patriarchal constraints of the academy will gradually cease to intervene. The female self is depicted as a "'natural' being imprisoned in the system and needing to free itself from . . . institutional restraint" (Hill, 124). The autobiographical subject is constructed as if she were a fixed referent, as if social prescriptions and discourses could somehow be transcended and the "genuine self behind the mask" revealed. Sexual difference is presented as a given, and the relationship between representation and identity is construed as mimetic, as if language were a mirror of reality. It is significant that the autobiographical subject is repositioned in a way that disrupts the bourgeois male subject by redefining, this subject as female and giving her qualities historically awarded to men, including the ability to discover a unified core essence or true self. In Frey's repositioning of women's voices, however, she reinscribes an oppositional logic based upon liberal notions of gender and space, where "masculine" is associated with the political and public and "feminine" with the personal and private. I am not suggesting that it is false to recognize that women are silenced by the academy or that some women have been confined to the private sphere. I am, rather, arguing that a pedagogy that focuses solely on making women's voices present without framing these voices as socially produced and situated within the structural and literary parameters of the academy will not enable women to confront the system and its discourses or to recognize asymmetrical power relations among themselves.

Numerous feminists in composition invoke maternal metaphors for reconceptualizing relations between students and teachers and cultivate abilities in women students that researchers such as Carol Gilligan (1982) and Mary Field Belenky et al. (1986) have found characteristic of "women's ways of knowing." In "Sexual Politics of the One-to-One Tutorial Approach and Collaborative Learning," another example from *Teaching Writing*, Carol Stranger argues for a pedagogy that privileges collaboration and consensus building. Drawing upon Nancy Chodorow's theory of pre-Oedipal development in *The Reproduction of Mothering*, Stranger proposes that "successful collaboration in the classroom" can create "oceanic feeling[s]" in women writers and reproduce "a perfect sense of oneness" associated with the primary identification with the mother (40). "In the sense that collaborative learning taps learners' early experiences with their mothers," she claims, "it is a feminist pedagogy" (40). This image-metaphor of the feminist teacher as maternal figure, and the projection of a holistic unified nonconflictual self, does not, however, account for political struggles in the "private" sphere, the experiences of students who are also mothers, or provide a full picture of the complexities of motherhood. The projection of autobiographical scripts and ideologies of motherhood works toward creating classroom climates that maximize the comfort level for white upper- and middle-class women by buffering critical intrusions from white working-class women and women of color, but it does not expose the fragmenting qualities of most middle-class white women's lives. To define the maternal and the feminine as private, harmonic, and nonconflictual can reinforce traditional gender distinctions and a discourse of class- and color-blindness.

Maternal metaphors can, however, assume a subversive function. Indeed, a fundamental claim in pedagogical appropriations of French feminist discourse has been the link between the maternal and the subversive (Worsham 1991), between the feminine and experimental writing (Bridwell-Bowles). Maternal metaphors of female empowerment may ultimately silence women by rendering some women invisible. The problem is not so much that cooperative and nurturing relations are privileged over conflict but that these relations are rooted in a logic that associates them with the bodies of white heterosexual women. Another troubling aspect of the invocation of the feminine as a metaphor for resistant language is that language of resistance is often linked to the experimental discourses of the modernist literary avant-garde—a movement not necessarily synonymous with the social marginalization of women (Felski, 5). The interruption of dominant discourses and the affirmation of unofficial discourses are important aspects of feminist approaches to writing. But simply to associate the genre of autobiography only with the private or feminine is to remain trapped in a model with intrinsic limitations—namely, that the experiences of white middle-class women stand for the whole. Although metaphorical reformations have significantly influenced feminist pedagogy, I remain concerned about their capacity to assign women to limiting categories of gender and confine them to traditional roles by reinscribing polarities such as passion/reason, personal/political, private/public, and body/mind.

Feminist research on autobiography in composition has not fully challenged the primacy of gender analysis over other modes of difference. For example, in "Composing As a Woman," Elizabeth Flynn uses Carol Gilligan's theory about gender differences in moral and intellectual development to interpret patterns in the autobiographical narratives of four first-year college men and women. Flynn found that the narratives of the men stressed separation over connection, whereas the women wrote stories of connection or frustrated connection (428–29). While both Flynn and Gilligan acknowledge that these patterns are socially constructed, both researchers tend to universalize gender differences. In "Women's Ways of Knowing/Women's Ways of Composing," Janis Tedesco wisely points out that the findings of Belenky et al. and Gilligan are descriptive; that is, they are mediated through the speaker's languages. She argues that these works "summarize how women themselves perceive their experiences and attitudes" (253). While Tedesco acknowledges that language shapes identity, neither she nor Flynn questions the naturalizing power of women's descriptions or considers how gender is discursively displayed, displaced, and/or essentialized. Neither theorist fully accounts for the fluidity of identity categories themselves or the complexities of women's and men's discursive and spatial movement between and among them. The problem with pedagogical appropriations of the work of Belenky et al., Chodorow, and Gilligan to date lies in many feminists' resistance to account sufficiently for ways that both women and men negotiate cultural scripts and how they challenge developmental schemes by constructing multiple speaking positions as they move from one context and genre to another. Flynn has critically revisited the issue of essentialism in illuminating ways in her 1995 essay "Review: Feminist Theories/Feminist Composition."[1]

A more recent pedagogical piece that centrally positions autobiography but fails to acknowledge how writers struggle with inherited narratives of the self is Maxine Hairston's controversial essay "Diversity, Ideology, and Teaching Writing." Hairston, a self-described liberal, positions herself in an adversarial relationship to a generation of composition teachers-scholars who, informed by social constructionism, put "ideology and radical politics at the center of their teaching" (180). According to Hairston, the cultural left has taken over; deconstruction, poststructuralism, and Marxist theory have "trickled down to the lower floors of English departments where freshman English dwells" (183). Interestingly, Hairston recognizes the spatial segregation of composition programs through verticality metaphors and an image of leaky basement plumbing, yet she reinforces this marginalized position by associating English departments with the theoretical and composition programs with the pedagogical. Not only does Hairston refuse to acknowledge the political nature of all pedagogical situations, but she also strategically dismisses or ignores altogether the scholarly work of writing teachers who focus precisely on the ways that inequities are pedagogically inscribed and structurally reinforced. Recognizing the increasing linguistic and cultural diversity of the student population in American higher education, Hairston argues that students are our "greatest multicultural resource" (190). "Real diversity," she claims, "emerges from the students themselves and flourishes in a collaborative classroom" (191). She continues:

> The beauty of such an approach is that it's *organic*. It grows out of resources available in each classroom, and it allows students to make choices . . . This approach makes the teacher a midwife, an agent for change rather than a transmitter of fixed knowledge. (191–92)

I agree with Hairston that writing courses should be student-centered, but I do not find her description of student-centered approaches as "organic" (as in *natural* or *apolitical*) accurate; these approaches are just as political as any other. Equally problematic is Hairston's idealistic portrayal of the writing classroom as a safe space for the "free exchange of ideas" (188). Hairston construes this room to be a neutral public site wherein autobiographical experiences can be shared without invoking differences shaped by gender, race, or social position. The assumption here is that all students present are equally empowered. Hairston falsely assumes that the mere presence of writers from diverse cultural backgrounds will foster greater understanding of social differences. Additionally, she does not consider how inequities can be reproduced through writing and reading, particularly cross-cultural readings. As Nina Chordas points out in "Classrooms, Pedagogies, and the Rhetoric of Equality," "The blind spots in pedagogies that presume open and equitable writing spaces derive partly from idealistic notions about the unconditioned individual and myths about America as a classless egalitarian society" (217–23).[2]

I don't quarrel with the feminist hope for developing pedagogies that recognize the shared struggles of college women or for student-centered multicultural pedagogies; *Teaching Writing*, "Composing As a Woman," and "Women's Ways of Knowing/Women's Ways of Composing" have successfully challenged patriarchal academic conventions and traditions. But pedagogical projects that do not enable both women and men to recognize how societal structures have shaped their voices can actually reinforce the status quo. The pedagogical positions of autobiography discussed thus far tend to privatize and depoliticize the personal voice and, in so doing, uncritically reproduce cultural values that reinforce inequities in the academy. Feminists must step outside such narrow definitions of autobiography. We must remove the curtain that perpetuates the illusion that private and public spheres are fundamentally separate and applicable across different populations. We must expose the ideology of selfhood associated with the genre of autobiography, which in Western societies has been defined as a universal, disembodied subject marked as masculine (Smith 1993, 5–11). It is not a question of rejecting the autobiographical but, rather, of locating it in a different theoretical and pedagogical context. As bell hooks suggests, the discourse of memory can be used to "shift the focus away from the mere naming of one's experience . . . to talk about identity in relation to culture, history, and politics" (1989b, 110). Autobiography can no longer be positioned in feminist-writing pedagogy simply in terms of gender differences. The privileging of gender analysis over other forms of difference has been challenged by the diverse experiences of working-class women, lesbians, gay men, and people of color, who argue that social relations shaped by sexuality, class, and race are experienced simultaneously. In order to acknowledge the power of dominant discourse in shaping a writer's voice and to recognize the possibility of resisting these shaping forces, feminists must better understand the paradoxical nature of doing autobiographical work in the academy and the paradoxical qualities of feminist-writing spaces.

## Paradoxical Writing Spaces

Riot grrrl 'zines—"homemade" publications (copied and stapled or sewn together) that offer a discursive space for young women to express themselves without using tools of the mainstream media—are interesting to study as paradoxical feminist writing spaces.[3] They serve a function similar to that of nineteenth-century women's literary societies, except that the exchanges among women are in print. The term *grrrls* is used strategically by creators of 'zines and their contributors to deny identification with the "adult" academic and patriarchal worlds of status, hierarchies, and standards. Although riot grrrl press offers some young women a "safe space" in which to share personal experiences, to express anger against the academy, and to critique mainstream patriarchal society and technology, as Irene Chien points out, they are also exclusionary. Produced by women at private high schools and elite colleges, many 'zines reinforce the privileges of the white upper middle classes even as they challenge other conventions and boundaries. What I find particularly interesting about riot grrrl 'zines is the way their contributors negotiate with and appropriate the discourses of dominant culture and liberal feminism. Consider the enactment of the social spaces of writing and gender in the following excerpt written in 1993 by an Oberlin student for the Ohio feminist riot grrrls 'zine *Real Hot Spit.*

> I am in a cafe. There are tables here, where I am, and more outside, under an awning, with a glass wall in between. Two longhaired older men are outside at tables, watching me write. They make me nervous. Every time I look up to see if they are still watching, I meet their gaze. This, of course, encourages them. I feel very self-conscious. Maybe I should do something. Make a sign. "STOP WATCHING ME" but that would probably make them or one of them come over. Any excuse to say something to me. If I look to check if they're still watching, they'll take it as a come on. Go away! I can feel eyes on me now. I hate feeling self-conscious. . . . I've written the sign. Big letters in the back of my notebook. I wonder what would happen if I held it up for them to see. Perhaps we'll see. I held it up. They laughed. Why do people not realize the power they have? My heart is thumping but at least I let them know.

I don't need to share my feelings with them—someone's tapping on the glass. I'm not looking up. I showed them that I didn't want them to watch me anymore, so now they shouldn't be. I don't have to check. More tapping. Someone comes up to me, "excuse me, those guys over there want you to look at them." I'm sure they do. Should I? I look up to see, written on a napkin held up to the window: ENTRAPMENT! . . . Does that mean that in order not to be watched I must put on a sweater? Leave the room? Why the hell is it MY goddamn responsibility? What do I have to do NOT to "entrap"? What did I do to lead them on? It's not all for me to think about—shouldn't they have to? They don't *have* to because there's no danger involved. For me, as a grrrl, my status (according to American culture) DEPENDS on those looks. They are supposed to vindicate me as feminine, fill—temporarily—the void of insecurity that the fashion and "beauty" industry has ripped open in me. Part of being "feminine" is being seductive, entrapping. But if a man rapes me, then femininity becomes incrimination. LA

What fascinates me about this piece of prose is how the writer articulates her feelings about the paradox of watching her watchers. As she literally watches herself being watched, the writer is aware of her position as "other." Although she is separated from her onlookers by a pane of glass—a transparent curtain divides the "outside" public from the "enclosed" public—the glass does not protect her. In an attempt to interrupt the male gaze and its threatening presence, she holds up a sign that says, "STOP WATCHING ME," which assures the two men that she is paying attention. Instead of breaking the male gaze or claiming a sense of agency, her action reinforces the men's prerogative. She becomes even more self-conscious of her position as one who is watched. What power she claims is constantly challenged: the men laugh at her, they continue to watch, they even engage in her "game" of sign writing. She recognizes the impossibility of staying completely outside of or escaping the power of the male gaze and the way it positions her as other: "What can I do not to entrap?" she asks. "In order not to be watched [must I] put on a sweater?" Unable to reverse the power of the male gaze, she detours through it to see herself. She is forced to concede that, at least in part, her status "DEPENDS on those looks." Clearly, power lies with the one who looks. The image of the writer displayed here is not only the subjectivity of the woman seen but the desire of the men looking. The gaze will not let go, not even of her text. Since the writer cannot free herself from the language of the gaze, she writes from within it. In this sense, she is literally and figuratively caught inside the space from which she writes. The writer's agency is not the reporting of the event but her ability to situate herself as a medium of the testimony, her self-consciousness about how she has internalized the male gaze psychologically and discursively. Moreover, she claims a sense of narrative agency through the strategy of reversal, which makes a spectacle of the male looker. She recognizes her position as object and uses this recognition to claim her status as a subject.

While women's personal testimonies may disrupt traditional values, genres, and discursive conventions of the academy, they do not automatically result in alterations of dominant ways of organizing and understanding identity and difference. As this 'zine excerpt demonstrates, the writer may be aware of how dominant discourses shape her identity, but she ends up reinforcing them by perpetuating some of their essential binaries. She does this by presenting unified discursive identity categories—women and men—unmarked by race or class. Although race and class do not figure explicitly in the written text, two images are superimposed over it. One is of a woman of color in a skimpy bodysuit, and the other is of a white male in a business suit. Here, femininity and masculinity are explicitly racialized. One might also argue that these images enact cultural stereotypes by depicting white men as predators and controllers of black women's sexuality. Whether the author created these images or an editor added them later is unknown. What is clear, however, is that the way these images and the text depict race is linked to larger social trends toward relying upon visible differences. As Ruth Frankenberg points out, "Skin has been and remains the foremost signifier of racial difference" (144). When differences are based solely upon the color of one's skin, ethnic, sexual, and class differences within the white population and among people of color are ignored.

I can imagine this text and its particular feminism emerging from a pedagogy that does not focus on women's agency or on how writers claim agency through negotiations with dominant narratives and cultural scripts but from one that locates women, unmarked by difference, solely as passive victims of patriarchal structures and discourses. The pedagogical challenge that this 'zine excerpt poses to feminist teachers is to find ways for students to recognize how their constructions of self are shaped by feminist discourses and ideologies, and to enable them to consciously engage these discourses. If, as feminist writing teachers, we are to transform pedagogies of domination and the essentializing differences that some feminist pedagogies produce, then we must critique the struggles and invisibilities within our own and our students' work. This means listening for the silences, as well as recognizing how what was previously unspoken is newly encoded. As hooks puts it, "'The politics of location' necessarily calls those of us who would participate in the formation of counterhegemonic cultural practice to identify the spaces where we begin the process of revision" (1990, 145). Unlike the feminism displayed in the 'zine excerpt, which frames difference through an us/them, male/female construction of power, imagining oneself in a counterhegemonic autobiographical space is much more complex. The 'zine excerpt provides a pedagogical opportunity to consider how feminist autobiographical spaces are critical sites for the construction of social identities and how they may be marked paradoxically by the interplay of dominant and counterhegemonic discourses as they shift from one context to another.

The concept of paradoxical spaces has been put forth by numerous feminists, namely feminists of color and lesbian critics whose notions of location imply "contradictory spatialities" and "heterogeneous geometries" (G. Rose, 140–41). For example, Aída Hurtado, in "Relating to Privilege: Seduction and Rejection in the Subordination of White Women and Women of Color" (1989), profoundly challenges the spatial division of the world into a male public and female private. She suggests that the autobiographical work of women of color is not so much a projection of the private into the public but, rather, an enactment of how the "public is personally political" (849). Patricia Hill Collins also articulates the paradoxical positions of working-class black women in American culture; she describes the position of black domestic women workers in white homes as an "outsider within-stance" (quoted in Rose, 152). Diana Fuss suggests a similar dual position common to lesbians and gay men who may be simultaneously inside and outside: "To be out, in common gay parlance . . . is really to be in—inside the realm of the visible, the speakable, the culturally intelligible . . . [but] to come out can also work not to situate one on the inside but to jettison one from it" (Fuss quoted in Rose, 151).

Additionally, numerous feminists contest and blur the boundaries between the public and private by mapping the terrain of autobiography differently and by explicitly bringing autobiography into their scholarship (e.g., Anzaldúa, Bannerji et al., Behar, N. Miller, and Williams, among others). In her discussion of feminist autobiographical manifestos, Sidonie Smith shows how such texts challenge the hegemony of white liberal feminism and nostalgia for the pastoral tradition, wherein the speaker leaves the metropolis for a more "natural" space that promises "reinvigoration" and access to "truer selves" (170). Autobiographical manifestos, according to Smith, unqualifiedly assert "the politicization of the private and the personalization of the public, effectively troubling the binary complacencies of the *ancien regime* of selfhood with its easy dichotomization of private and public" (160). In her analysis of Gloria Anzaldúa's *Borderlands/La Frontera: The New Mestiza,* for example, Smith points out that the "topography of the borderland is simultaneously the suturing space of multiple oppressions and the potentially liberatory space through which to migrate toward a new subject position" (169). Anzaldúa embraces this paradox by adopting multiple positions in her negotiations with the predominant cultural and linguistic identities of her borderlands experience: "I will no longer be made to feel ashamed of existing. I will have my voice: Indian, Spanish, white. I will have my serpent's tongue—my woman's voice, my sexual voice, my poet's voice. I will overcome the tradition of silence" (59). The concept of borderlands moves between centers and margins, dismantling traditional notions of singular selves and stable places of origin. Border residents are fluid, neither completely inside nor powerlessly outside dominant cultures. However, we must be careful not to romanticize such fluidity; after all, it reflects a deeply geographical and social history of exploitative migrant labor and forced movements.

One might argue that the meta-narratives that divide the world into male public and female private are in decline, replaced with an awareness of heterogeneous differences, contradictory spatialities, and movements. Although the inadequacies of expressionist feminist projects are becoming clear, it is important to recognize the perpetuation of binaries and essentializing practices in public institutions and their presence as structuring devices in feminist pedagogy and our students' writing.[4] With few exceptions, namely the work of Laura Brady, Susan Jarratt, Min-Zhan Lu, and Lynn Worsham, feminist-composition teachers-scholars have not fully explored these contrary impulses and paradoxical positions.[5] In "Writing against Writing: The Predicament of Ecriture Feminine in Composition Studies," Worsham, for example, questions the uses and limitations of experimental feminist discourse in the academy. She warns feminists who incorporate, or are thinking about using, *écriture feminine* in their writing course that, if resistant discourse is simply appropriated, it may become neutralized within the very "ideological space that it resists and refuses" (94). Jarratt in "Feminism and Composition: The Case for Conflict" maps out feminist adaptations of expressionist approaches to composition and offers an alternative feminist pedagogy that recognizes conflict as a source of inquiry. While Jarratt does not specifically focus on the position of autobiography in feminist pedagogy, her work has significant implications for feminists working on integrating autobiography into their writing classrooms in more productive ways. She claims, for example, that teachers need to help "students to locate personal experience in historical and social contexts" and to design courses that enable "students to see how differences emerging from their texts and discussions have more to do with those contexts than they do with an essential and unarguable individuality" (121). What I find particularly striking about Lu's pedagogy scholarship is that she blurs disciplinary boundaries and blends auto-biographical and academic discourse in ways that highlight negotiations among them. She approaches composition pedagogy dialogically, by placing "different orders of experience—each of whose languages claims authority on the basis of its ability to exclude others—into dialogue with each other" (Holquist, 87).

### Crossing Borders: Pedagogical Tourism or Coalition Building?

In "Conflict and Struggle," Lu applies Gloria Anzaldúa's metaphorical concept of borderlands to composition in order to emphasize the complexities of social, personal, and textual relations among students and teachers. When describing her teaching methods, she alludes to "language as a site of cultural struggle and conflict" and suggests that teachers "draw upon students' perceptions of conflict as a constructive resource" (905, 889). While the concept of borderlands and its attention to the heterogeneous nature of spatial and discursive positions offer feminists new ways to conceptualize the dynamics of autobiographical discourse, one has to consider whether a writer has chosen to reposition herself on the borderlands or whether such repositioning has been imposed on, or chosen for, her. For example, not all students and teachers in the United States have the same freedom to cross into or out of the borderlands. Moreover, shifting geographical locations are not always about play (tourism) or pilgrimage (journey, search for origins); for many populations, such movement is about vulnerability, displacement, exile, and so on. As Puar points out, the discourse of "'travel' remains captured, by its historical legacy, as a concept within whiteness, of luxury, leisure, and privilege, embodied and embedded as an extension of empire, of imperialism, and of colonialism" (88). Since many students and teachers have not been cast out of their home or language, as have Anzaldúa and Lu (1987), is their movement into the borderlands or margins a form of pedagogical tourism? Who is envisioned as a traveler? What kinds of traveling subjects are we?

Caren Kaplan cautions First World white feminists like myself to ask such questions in her essay "Deterritorializations: The Rewriting of Home and Exile in Western Feminist Discourse" (1987).

> For the first world feminist critic, therefore, the challenge at this particular time is to develop a discourse that responds to the power relations of the world system, that is, to examine her location in the dynamic of centers and margins. Any other strategy merely consolidates the illusion of marginality while glossing over or refusing to acknowledge centralities. Thus, the first world feminist critic may be marginal *vis-à-vis* the literary establishment or the academy that employs her, yet she may also

be more closely linked to these institutions than a non-western or third world feminist critic. (189)

I invoke Kaplan's warning precisely because of the apparent reluctance on the part of liberal feminists in composition to contextualize their identity positions and theoretical appropriations of, and alliances with, the borderlands. Kaplan points out, "Oppositional consciousness can not simply be put on like a cloak, it is shaped by experiences of oppression" (191). There is a danger inherent in moving from one cultural space to another, a potential for a reenactment of domination—a kind of representational colonialism that seems to grant the feminist teacher-scholar a panoramic worldview and an ability to move through historical geographical terrains unnoticed.

I am particularly concerned about the potential of metaphoric reconfigurations within multicultural pedagogies that position feminist teachers as innocent wanderers or neutral cartographers of the experiences of the oppressed. Lu refers to this pedagogical tendency as "cultural tourism": "Teachers and students approach cultural diversity by assuming that they themselves are somehow outside of rather than implicated in the cultures *about* which they read and write" (1994, 1–2). Like Lu, I believe it would be far more useful for feminists to think about writing classrooms as potential "contact zones" (Pratt's concept). Framing the feminist-writing classroom as a contact zone challenges utopian notions of it being a "safe space," notions that often ignore differences among students and teachers. This is not to suggest that we don't need to create spaces where students are comfortable to disagree or challenge each other's assumptions but, rather, that we interrogate feminist pedagogies that invoke notions of safety while masking inequalities of power (Kozol, forthcoming). Declaring the feminist classroom a potential contact zone can help us understand the perils and paradoxes of writing autobiography and doing feminist work in the academy.

One result of this view of the feminist classroom as a potential contact zone is the reconceptualization of the relationship between the self and language. As Lu suggests, "Instead of affirming the belief that there is some kind of stable essence within each of us . . . the concept of the contact zone teaches us to perceive one's self . . . as made and changed through interaction with others, in the process of negotiating with those with less as well as more privilege than oneself" (1994, 6). This is not to diminish the very real oppressions that composition teachers face, particularly women, but rather to ask ourselves if and when we have concealed our own privileges and mobility.

It is not my intention to turn the metaphor of the contact zone into a commodity. The concept may not apply equally to all institutions and contexts, particularly those where the student body is relatively homogeneous. Nevertheless, we must recognize that gender and racial differences are not the only factors that define conflicts and inequities of contact zones; differences of class, culture, language, sexuality, and geopolitical location must also be taken into account. Instead, I suggest that as a conceptual model it enables us to understand the power of language as action and to recognize how autobiography and the social languages and conventions that a writer uses to construct the self may reproduce, as the 'zine excerpt demonstrates, the very conditions that subjugate the writer in the first place and/or obstruct the writer's ability to focus on his or her own position and power relations. The writer of the 'zine excerpt literally wrote *in* the contact zone, using a language that was trying to overcome itself; she questioned the male gaze by invoking the very language and values that it privileged. Writers from border cultures also challenge conventional constructions of identity as fixed and unified. Indeed, what we often see in such texts, as well as in theoretical works that give voice to border identities, is reference to "code switching, cultural mixing, and linguistic sharing"—a process that has been referred to as cultural "bricolage" (George Lipsitz), "cultural fusion" (Lynell George), and transformations (Stuart Hall) (quoted in Wellman, 36). As David Wellman aptly puts it in "Red and Black in White America: Discovering Cross-Border Identities and Other Subversive Activities,"

> Border cultures produce identities that are neither singular or static. In these locations, multiple cultural identities are invented, and people slip in and out of them without being called upon to renounce their initial identifiers. . . . Border peoples trying on new and different identities learn that identities can be changed. They find out that one is not completely bound by bloodlines, nationality, or occupation. . . . They learn how to be culturally competent actors in multiple cultural contexts. Border cultures therefore contradict conventional sociological wisdom. They fracture received categories. (37)

The feminist repositioning of autobiography demands the creation of writing and reading spaces where subjectivities can be examined with respect to their historical, cultural, geopolitical, and rhetorical configurations. We must be able to "hear the multiplicity of discourses within a single language" (Hicks, xxvi). Moreover, we must consider these questions: Who is crossing what borders? Who is in the position to create border identities? Are border crossers forced into such acts, or are such movements and crossings of their own choosing? After all, the boundaries that define communities are freighted with radical inequalities and forms of domination. So while it is possible to construct border identities as acts of solidarity with oppressed peoples as part of the struggle for a transformative critical pedagogy, it is necessary to be skeptical of the historical tendency of white-culture representatives to position themselves as border guards or to ally themselves with a consumerist ethic that makes imperialist spaces of borders (McLaren 1995, 109). My warning echoes that of Peter McLaren, who argues that border identities are "different for the exile, for the metropolitan 'professional' intellectual, and for the tourist" (113). Likewise, international students, students of color, first-generation college students, working-class students, and differently abled students experience their entrance into the academy in different ways.

While the concept of the contact zone allows us to consider the negotiations of identities and borders in the academy and deconstructs the pedagogical fantasy of discourse utopias and universal sisterhoods associated with expressionist feminist pedagogies, there is potential for misuse. As feminist teachers embrace the paradigm of conflict and its critiques of liberal strategies such as collaboration and classroom decentering, we must be careful not to construct new pedagogical situations that silence students who are uncomfortable writing about personal experiences or who are less "intellectually combative."[6] A pedagogy based on the contact-zone concept does not demand the creation of combative or confessional classrooms but, rather, requires the construction of writing and reading spaces that enable writers to experiment with a wider range of viewpoints (Lu 1994, 7). This will involve challenging students' ideas about autobiography and questioning the kind of self-making marked by slogans such as "Just do it" or "Become whatever you want to be," which treat autobiographical positions as if they were simply a matter of individual choice.

As long as we remain aware of the pitfalls of both self-representation and representing others, there is hope for the transformative use of autobiography in feminist-writing instruction and research. The challenge, as I see it, is the constant struggle to situate oneself in the position of a questioning subject—to develop an antagonism in oneself. As Paulo Freire suggests, this involves identifying with positions that allow one to critique one's "own" subject position (JanMohamed, 246). Unlearning one's "own" position does not, however, result in the attainment of a historically transcendent point of view but, rather, involves repositioning oneself within the cultural production of knowledge (Spivak, 42). The concept of the contact zone can help us recognize how various groups in the academy "delineate their discursive boundaries, name and expel the Other, express and reinforce their bonds, their sense of being 'at home' with each other" (Altman, 504). As critical educators, we must "explore the zones of cultural difference by moving in and out of the resources, histories, and narratives that provide different students with a sense of identity, place, and possibility" (Giroux 1994b, 341). In this sense, the metaphor of the contact zone may also help us understand the difficulties involved in building coalitions across differences. The metaphor captures well the complex position of autobiography within feminist-writing pedagogy—a pedagogical terrain of contesting social languages, histories, and identities that are heterogeneous, contradictory, and in process.

# 3

## WRITING IDENTITIES:
## THE "ESSENCE" OF DIFFERENCE

*I didn't want the white kids at my school to see me as black. I feared that they would associate me with negative images of Blacks. I began to listen to white music and to dress as the white girls did. . . . I began to "talk" white, "act" white, and I even tried to disassociate myself from my culture as much as possible. . . . I strongly believe that if the curriculum was structured so that it was an Afrocentric curriculum, then black students would do just as well as their counterparts, because they will see the value in their culture. (Nicole)*

*In reading Adrienne Rich's "When We Dead Awaken," I found myself in a familiar position. Her goal in writing the essay was directed towards women, and I did not feel right reading it. The essay takes a stand in which, as I interpreted it, I was the aggressor, the one at fault. I felt responsible for the acts of men before me and felt obliged to feel guilty. At once, my response was revulsion and embarrassment, and a residue of those emotions stays with me with each rereading. Yet, I no longer feel that Rich was utilizing male readers as targets, but seeking to have them see differently. (Gary)*

These two excerpts from autobiographical texts of first-year college writers depict some of the ways students negotiate their identities within the contact zone of the multicultural classroom. Students write both with and against the social discourses of academe. They write *with* the academic grain by using language that embodies the academy's conventions and expectations, and they write *against* it by constructing disruptive subject-positions and discourses that challenge and displace the academy's authority. That they write both with and against the grain signifies the contradictions of writing autobiography in academic settings, where teachers traditionally reward students for writing texts that preserve myths of objectivity and the impartiality of scholarship. As these students' texts suggest, autobiographical writing involves the complex negotiation of identities, which are themselves affected by language and are in a constant state of struggle.

In this chapter, I argue for the primacy of students' autobiographical texts in a feminist multicultural writing curriculum, and I urge writing teachers to recognize the identity negotiations and interplay of social discourses articulated through the processes of writing and reading autobiography. My readings of students' texts are intended to show the complications inherent in using autobiography in multicultural settings and to offer a way of teaching that recognizes these complications. The social-dialogic method of reading that I propose challenges expressionist readings of autobiography, which have long dominated the field of composition and which assume that the personal voice can be achieved apart from the individual's participation in social-material realities. My approach to reading and teaching autobiography is informed by the social-dialogic theories of language, resistant postmodernist and materialist theories of identity and experience, and Freirean critical pedagogy, which insists that teachers start with the experiences of learners and engage in an ideological critique of the experiential (Bakhtin, Knoblauch). Basically, it presumes that there is no true, private, hidden, or unchanging self or essence that writing or reading autobiography makes visible. To declare that the true self or the personal voice lurks somewhere deep within, as the expressionists do, is to ignore how discourse communities define which voices are the most personal or real (Henning, 680). (In the following sections, I discuss how discourse communities in the academy delimit the personal voice.) If we do not recognize how students must negotiate their identities in response to perceived power relations and teacher expectations, we run the risk of dismissing the complexities and struggles involved in writing autobiography within the academy.[1]

By focusing on a critique of students' constructions of readers and of themselves as writing subjects, I am not suggesting that teachers don't have to revise their curricula to include voices subsumed within or repressed by the traditional canon. But there is danger in thinking that new content in and of itself is liberating for all students. Curricular-reform initiatives that are preoccupied with integrating new material (namely, the published auto-biographies of writers from diverse backgrounds) may universalize students as readers and writers and cultivate simplistic pluralist notions of voice and free expression without openly acknowledging principles of power, access, and privilege operative in the classroom. Indeed, pluralist principles often neutralize opposition and can lead to classroom practices that may actually regulate diversity; in simply pluralizing voices, as Elizabeth Ellsworth points out, one "loses sight of the contradicting and partial nature of all voices" (312). The add-more-spices-and-stir approach to multicultural education also has racist connotations in that it tends to exoticize difference. If we are to take seriously the status of students as writing subjects without simply positioning them as objects in a pedagogical situation, then we must look beyond the idea that multiculturalism is a set of plans or content to be implemented. Our efforts toward curricular transformation are more worthwhile if we also focus on the discourses of our students, who have been virtually absent from most institutional conversations designed to support multiculturalism. The interplay of social discourses in the two student excerpts above illustrates some of the ways students negotiate their identities discursively and claim authority.

Nicole (all students' names are fictitious), an eighteen-year-old African-American woman in my introductory writing course, wrote about her experiences at a private, predominantly white high school. The assignment Nicole responded to encouraged students to recognize the partiality of their voices and to explore how the forces of culture and history have shaped their education. In "Up by What Bootstraps?," Nicole constructs difference by pointing to the reproduction of white privilege in her select high school. But as a high-school student, the excerpt suggests, she attempts to conceal racial differences through accommodation. In response to contradictory social messages (she was both an insider and an outsider at her school), she began to "talk" and "act" white. Although Nicole becomes part of the community because of her class privilege, as an African-American woman she is alienated by the institution because of race's role in the construction of knowledge and power. She exposes institutional racism and examines how the language of race expressed at the level of group consciousness can serve the voice of black liberation.

Nicole's text suggests how the language of race can function as what Mikhail Bakhtin calls a double-voiced discourse. Bakhtin claims, "The word in language is half someone else's. It becomes 'one's own' only when the speaker populates it with his own intention, his own accent, when he appropriates the word, adapting it to his own semantic and expressive intention" (quoted in Higginbotham, 267). Nicole underscores the complexities denied by expressionist constructions of difference by acknowledging race as a shifting cultural sign that has historically served the voices of black oppression and black liberation (267). The essence of difference in Nicole's text is not a result of "natural" forces, as it is often constructed in expressionist pedagogies of autobiography, but an effect of social and linguistic struggle.

Gary, a nineteen-year-old white European-American, is responding to an assignment that encouraged students to explore their processes of interpreting Adrienne Rich's essay "When We Dead Awaken: Writing As Revision" and their positions as readers. Here, he reveals his preoccupation with what he interprets as Rich's positioning of the male reader. "I found myself in a familiar position," he writes. "I was the aggressor, the one at fault." He said he was "obliged to feel guilty." Not surprisingly, Gary bases his response solely on an understanding of difference as "difference between," a conception that invokes sexual difference as the primary category of analysis; after all, Rich constructs difference similarly in her essay. One could argue, for example, that Rich essentializes gender difference through the construction of women as a universal and stable category. By the final paragraph, however, Gary has convinced himself that since he is not the intended audience, the best he can do is to try to put himself in Rich's shoes and "read as a woman":

> I do not delude myself into thinking that the essay was written to me; I have to make myself a part of it by restructuring my thinking toward it. . . . Many factors come into play for me in finding my natural aversion to the essay. In trying to read what she says from the point of view of a female poet, I may be able to get a sense of what she declares to be true.

Operative here is the deconstruction of readership through the simultaneous displacement and redeployment of essence. Gary deconstructs himself as a male reader by hypothesizing himself as a female reader. But what does it mean for Gary to read like a woman? What kind of woman reader is he? Does his hypothesis allow him to forego his responsibility to consider how he is implicated in all this? Is Gary's reconstruction of himself as a female reader another kind of essentialism? Is Gary's reconstruction merely a linguistic convenience? Is it a response to a struggle with me, because I, as a self-defined feminist, might expect him, as Rich does, to see differently? Unlike Nicole, who recognizes existing power relations and her own disempowered position and who attempts to enter the predominantly white discourse community by adjusting her language and behavior, Gary attempts to enter a feminist discourse community by erasing his historically empowered position.

## Dialogism and Diversity in Composition

I reviewed these two student texts (and numerous others) in the summer of 1992 while revising a class called Gender, Race, and Language; my goal was to address more adequately issues of authority and power within academic-discourse communities. The class is an elective special-topic writing course cross-listed in women's studies that counts toward the college's newly legislated cultural-diversity requirement. In order to graduate, entering students must complete at least nine hours of course work dealing with social and cultural diversity, including courses that emphasize methods of analyzing and interpreting cultural differences. One of my primary goals in the course is to engage students in an analysis of discursive constructions of identity and difference through writing, reading, and analyzing autobiographical texts.

The curriculum includes readings that address social constructions of race, gender, ethnicity, and sexuality, including *The Woman Warrior,* by Maxine Hong Kingston; *Yours in Struggle,* by Elly Bulkin, Minnie Bruce Pratt, and Barbara Smith; *Talking Back,* by bell hooks; and *Hunger of Memory,* by Richard Rodriguez, and documentary films such as Marlon Riggs's *Tongues Untied.* I encouraged students to read the autobiographical works and the theoretical in a number of ways. I asked them, for example, to think about their positions as readers and viewers and to consider these questions: What roles does each writer or filmmaker seem to construct for you as a reader or viewer? How does your position as a reader or viewer manifest a partial view? How does each writer define the relationship between identity and voice? What are the various components of each writer's understanding of personal positioning that recognize how identifying factors such as gender, race, class, and sexual orientation affect an individual's prerogatives and privileges? How does each writer frame relations among people across differences?

Early in the semester, students wrote autobiographical texts that concern the role of storytelling in their families and described their histories as readers and writers. At the end of the semester, they interrogated their constructions of themselves as autobiographical subjects, after recognizing the complex ways they negotiated their identities as writing subjects in earlier pieces. I encourage students to use their writing as data, to use course readings as theoretical and methodological filters, and to consider questions such as the following: How are gender, race, class, ethnicity, or sexuality embodied in your writing? Did you construct difference as difference between men and women or between whites and blacks? If your construction of difference is not predicated on such binaries, how would you define it? Each time students reread their autobiographical texts or reflected on the process of writing them, they reexamined, to some degree, the autobiographical self or selves. In short, metatexts enable students to investigate the social forces that shape their personal voices and further the possibility that experience is open to contradictory and conflicting interpretations. In fact, what I learned after analyzing numerous student autobiographies and reading students' reflective texts about themselves as writing subjects is that students move quite readily among contradictory social discourses and subject positions and, in so doing, complicate expressionist notions about unified selfhood. One way they do so is by constructing autobiographical works of multivoiced elements that can be read as "historically or imaginatively [situated] in a field of other persons' utterances" (Bialostosky quoted in G. Clark, 16).

Bakhtin's concept of dialogism helps us understand the interplay of social struggles and discourses invoked by autobiographical transactions in the multicultural classroom. According to Bakhtin, "Meaning is formed in a dialogically agitated and tension-filled environment . . . where competing ideologies, languages and values are operative" (*Marxism,* 276). Bakhtin describes this diversity of social languages as "heteroglossia," or "verbal-ideological points of view."Although composition teachers often seek to achieve a unified literary discourse (which serves to shelter some cultural groups from the full force of dialogism and to repress the perspectives of many unofficial discourses), multicultural education is about teaching students how to investigate those official and unofficial discourses and the power relations they enact. Multicultural literacy is not about initiating students into the logic of dominant discourses or simply celebrating a diversity of voices, as some recent multicultural composition textbooks imply (McLaren 1991, 156). Writing pedagogies designed to promote multicultural literacy should not be based on appeals to an uncritical mass of differences. Rather, they should help students recognize the limits of their self-positionings and worldviews, practice critical citizenship, and develop critical awareness of the power of discourse instead of being subsumed by it (Giroux 1992).

To meet these goals, teachers of writing across the curriculum should focus on how language shapes identity and knowledge. It is particularly important that the pedagogical process enables students to explore the self as a discursive and cultural construct in courses that rely on autobiographical experiences. Just because the self is seen as socially constructed, however, does not mean that it has no agency. Indeed, as Judith Butler observes, "to be *constituted* by discourse" is not "to be *determined* by discourse, where determination forecloses the possibility of agency" (1990, 143) (emphasis in original). The writing subject in all his or her multiplicity can construct subject positions, however transitory, that can subvert, diffuse, or dislocate expressionist concepts of selfhood (notions of the self as static and fixed) and dominant forms of social discourse. Although feminist perspectives that foreground relations between the discursive and the material and that recognize the fracturing of postmodern identity in the writings of the disempowered have emerged in composition, pedagogies of autobiography are steeped in expressionist rhetoric. For example, in relying on the bifurcation of expressive (private) and social discourse (public), the former associated with the feminine and the latter the masculine, a number of feminist scholars have created pedagogies predicated on assumed differences between the discourses of men and women. While I recognize the importance of their work in contesting patriarchal views of teaching and in legitimizing autobiographical discourse, I contend that a feminist counter-pedagogy that simply shifts the terms of engagement and alliance cannot meet the objectives of multicultural education at the turn of the century. A countermodel that privileges gender differences over other differences will misrepresent the complexity of autobiographical transactions between writers and readers in the multicultural classroom.[2]

I'm not suggesting that we abandon gender as an identity category but, rather, that we understand identity categories and concepts of difference as culturally, politically, and pedagogically shifting. We don't have to assume that the category "women" has a natural composition. As Fuss observes, it can be understood as a sign that is "historically contingent and constantly subject to change and to redefinition" (20). Identity can be understood as "a story, a history. Something constructed, told, spoken, not simply found" (Hall quoted in Giroux 1992, 128). Even though a writer might construct the self as moving from one stage of development to another, she or he is not passively transmitting an earlier self but, rather, constituting it in language. The autobiographical writing process can be construed, then, as intrinsically dialogic, and the autobiographical subject can be read as always in the process of becoming. I call for a multicultural pedagogy that focuses primarily on social aspects of language and identity construction to expose the inequalities that disempower and marginalize writers and to build classroom communities that enable students to construct positions of resistance. Thus, multicultural literacy is not simply a facility with multiple discourses but an awareness of how certain literacies are institutionally legitimated and others negatively coded.

## The Politics of Difference and Essence in Pedagogical Terms

To formulate a pedagogy of autobiography that meets the needs of multicultural education, we must openly acknowledge essentializing practices. When used strategically, the intriguing double-voiced discourse that essentialism creates signifies the potential power of resistance, and can disguise differences or privilege certain identities. Feminists have long wrestled with the politics and interplay of essence and difference. Fuss, for example, advances a theory about the essence of difference that attempts to give agency to individuals at the same time it places them within discursive configurations. Like several postmodernist feminists, Fuss argues against a naive essentialism—an appeal to pure or original femininity that universalizes women's experience—and instead constructs essence as an effect of discursive practices and cultural systems of representation. One might argue that Fuss does not counter essentialism so much as displace it. She recognizes that the disempowered in particular "need both to theorize essentialist spaces from which to speak and, simultaneously, to deconstruct these spaces to keep them from solidifying." "Such a double gesture," Fuss continues, involves "the responsibility to historicize, to examine each deployment of essence, . . . each claim to identity in the complicated contextual frame in which it is made" (118).

While Fuss recognizes, theoretically at least, the double discourse of essentialism (how it can be used strategically by marginalized groups and how it can be used to gloss over differences among groups), she has been criticized from a pedagogical standpoint for using marginalized voices to expose the negative effects of essentialism in the classroom. Fuss claims that essence can silence students when, for example, they claim that only women can speak for the feminine experience. When used this way, she argues, essence circulates as a privileged signifier that often depoliticizes oppressions, blinds students to other modes of difference, provokes confusion, and dead-ends class discussions (116–17). In "Essentialism and Experience," hooks criticizes Fuss for constructing the marginalized other as the essentialist and not sufficiently addressing how systems of domination are already in place in classrooms— namely, how teachers and students espouse expressions and critiques of essentialism from locations of privilege. hooks's response to Fuss raises important pedagogical questions: How is essentialism expressed from locations of privilege in multicultural settings? How is the other constructed? How do marginalized groups put essentialism to use strategically? How do students conceal, display, or displace essentializing practices?

I have noticed that students new to feminist concepts or multicultural curricula are often enthusiastic essentialists who appear to shift from narrow-fixed essentialist positions to strategic essentialist positions as the semester progresses; I also have observed, however, that these are not clear-cut developmental shifts. Any given expression of identity or essence may be embedded within conflicting subject positions and discourses. I am, therefore, less interested here in tracking developmental shifts than in interrogating the interlacing subject positions and essences negotiated within particular student texts. While some postmodern feminists might claim that my invocation of the concept of essence is a political-pedagogical faux pas because of the term's strong associations with expressionist views of identity, I believe that critical educators, particularly writing teachers, should explore the uses and limits of essentialism through its contradictory, strategic, and ironic positions within language, not to mention social movements.[3] Indeed, I argue that the autobiographical subject cannot be written as a fundamental essence (text equals body); it can only be written as a strategic positioning.

With these theoretical concerns as a descriptive device and the above pedagogical questions as guidance, I turn to the autobiographical texts of three college students. My analysis of these texts is intended to strengthen the links between resistant postmodern feminist theories of identity and a social-dialogic practice of reading and teaching autobiography, not to provide a universalized or prescriptive pedagogy or method. Although my examples come from three first-year female students of color, my intent is not to advocate pedagogy that places students of color in the roles of educators of difference. Nor do I mean to suggest that critiques of essentialism should be explored only in relation to women's writing; as my opening analysis suggests, discourses of essence certainly interpolate the texts of college men. I focus on the three texts because they offer compelling responses to some of the pedagogical questions raised earlier and because they demonstrate that the student positioned as the marginalized other and newly introduced to a feminist multicultural curriculum does not necessarily construct a naive essentialist (or expressionist) position. In contrast to Fuss's pedagogical observations, I have found that invoking autobiographical experiences can lead to productive class discussions if students directly critique their constructions of audience and voice and consider the material consequences of particular concepts of identity and difference.

## Autobiography and the Language of Location

Students are invited to investigate how identities and differences are negotiated and produced in their everyday lives on campus for a unit I call The Politics of Location and Experience. Before writing their essays about the results of their investigations, students read Ruth Perry's "A Short History of the Term *Politically Correct*" and other essays on the politics of language. Maria, an eighteen-year-old student from Puerto Rico, wrote about the essentializing practices of political correctness permeating certain discourse communities on the Oberlin College campus. The writing option to which Maria chose to respond invited her to consider the conditions under which she first heard the term *p.c. language* and whether her understanding of it had changed since then. She also examined who enforces politically correct language at the college and explored its effects on her and the community. The title of her essay, "Here I Stand" (which invokes the political oratory of Martin Luther King Jr.), affirms Fuss's observation and Spivak's claim that the "clearing of a subject-position in order to speak or write is unavoidable" (Spivak quoted in Fuss, 32). This clearing does not, however, result in the construction of a fixed self but, rather, provides a context for the textual staging of the negotiation of several subject positions. In fact, Maria's essay allowed the class to discuss the strategic use of essentialism and illustrates how students staged essences and negotiated differences in their autobiographical texts.

## "Here I Stand": The Staging of Essence

Early in her narrative, Maria writes about how essentializing practices of political correctness contribute to the censoring of her voice and simultaneously alienate her from her peers and her culture.

> I have lived quietly these past few months at [college] standing silently in a corner, absorbing, listening, admiring yet not being able to speak. . . .
> "Maria, your culture is so oppressive."
> "Why do you wear make-up? Men don't . . ."
> "Don't say freshman."
> "I feel sorry for your sister. Why did she have to stop working when she gave birth to the baby? Why didn't her husband stop working instead of her? So disgusting, such a backward country. I feel pity for the women."
> I didn't have the courage to respond and defend my Puerto Rican pride, my own culture, my own self. Now I want to stand up and do more than just listen. I want to scream and make everyone realize that I am not an ignorant marionette sitting in a corner. I want them to hear what I've got to say and understand for once that my ideas are as important as their own. . . . Do they have any idea about how they make me feel, of the times I cry myself to sleep thinking of the ways to make myself less ignorant, less Puerto Rican, more like them? . . . How could I be expected to rebuild all that which I have been constructing all my life. I don't want to change at this point in my life where I need my true self more than ever. I need it for courage, strength, and assurance and for everything they try to take away from me.

In this passage, Maria reports having been subjected to essentializing assumptions that include the construction of Puerto Rico as a "backward country" and preemptory assumptions about gender relations. One of her first responses to this criticism is a desire to assimilate: "I cry myself to sleep thinking of the ways to make myself less ignorant, less Puerto Rican, more like them." Later, she counteracts her desire to assimilate by claiming, "I don't want to change at this point in my life where I need my true self more than ever." Maria reacts to the essentializing practices of others by essentializing herself; however, instead of undermining the concept of essence, she uses it to her benefit.

> Now I sit here and contemplate my thoughts once more . . . I feel stronger and with all I've got at this moment I break the strings which held me down to that infernal corner. I move away from it and declare myself free. I won't let anyone ridicule, ignore, or shush me anymore. . . . I won't feel pressured or suffocated anymore for I am going to take control of my life. Now, tell me, with all I've got, "Ain't I a woman!"

By appropriating the title "Ain't I a Woman?" from Sojourner Truth's speech at a women's rights convention in Akron, Ohio, in 1851, Maria essentializes her own experience as a woman of color by glossing over important historical, geographic, and cultural differences between herself and Truth. Even though her use of Truth's language partially erases differences among women of color, she draws from a speech that revealed how whiteness hides its partiality, exposed the racialized configuration of gender, and subverted the essentializing practices of white middle-class feminist activists who universalized women's needs on the basis of their own experience.

Maria does not invoke the Black English Vernacular of Truth's speech as recorded by Frances Gage (the version that the class read), which would further subvert this universalization by exposing sociolinguistic differences. But by situating her words historically in the field of Truth's utterance, Maria implicitly invokes the double-discourse of essentializing practices. When expressed from locations of privilege, essentializing practices can serve not as a strategic response to domination but as a silencing force; this suggests that the double-discourse of essentialism lies in recognizing the motivation behind its invocation (Spivak and Rooney, esp. 3–13). Truth's language functions for Maria as an enabling constraint: as internally persuasive discourse, "it is '*open*' in each of the new contexts that dialogize it, [and thus] this discourse is able to reveal ever newer *ways to mean*" (Bakhtin, 346). This is true, of course, for all the voices invoked in this chapter; none is static and all shift as they "enter into interanimating relationships with new contexts" (Bakhtin, 345-46). On the one hand, we could read Maria's textual staging of essence as a strategic response, the assumption of a position of resistance. On the other, we could read it as an act of appropriation that decontextualizes the original intent of

Truth's words. Either way, Maria's text reveals how essence, difference, and agency exist in particular historical and discursive contexts.

### "A Change in My Textual Voice": The Autobiographer As Agent

Angela, an eighteen-year-old African-American woman, uses race and gender as analytical categories in her autobiographical essay, "A Change in My Textual Voice." She examines the shifts and nuances of her academic voice, focusing on a paper she wrote about Charlotte Perkins Gilman's "The Yellow Wallpaper" for another English class, in which she reiterated her professor's interpretation instead of developing her own. The professor, a white male, asked her to critique the short story using a psychoanalytic approach, which made her feel uncomfortable. According to Angela, her professor interpreted Gilman's nameless narrator as a passive victim and the "woman" in the wallpaper as Freud's internal partner, or thought monitor. But Angela instead inscribed the narrator herself as agent and the "woman" in the wallpaper as a victim.

> My professor believed that the narrator wanted so bad to get out of the room that she began to believe that the "woman" in the wallpaper was there to help her, not hurt her. But I thought the "woman" in the wallpaper represented her desperateness to escape. By helping the trapped "woman" get out of the wallpaper she would be helping herself escape.

The subtle transfer of agency here is important, for the "woman" in the wallpaper is now read as an expression of the entrapment of the narrator in a male "text," not as a projection of the narrator's madness or the internalized other. The following passage further displays Angela's awareness of the consequences of one man's reading of a fictional text:

> It bothers me that we live in a male dominating world, not only that they're males . . . but white males. . . . I'm not a feminist or a world renowned writer, but I shouldn't have to censor my writing to get by. Because voicing our opinion threatens the power that men have over us . . . we cannot go outside the realm of expected "womanness.". . . Writing to please someone else not only hinders your writing in terms of style, language and creativity, but it also destroys your self-esteem.

The irony, of course, is that even though Angela did not manage to read against her professor's text in her English paper, she now places him as an antagonist in her own text. Writing her autobiography is an act of resistance.

Later in the piece, Angela broadens her analysis of her reading and writing situation: "These views that men have about how women should write are not only expected from male audiences, but trickle down to the expectations of female audiences." Consequently, she continues, "writing for female audiences becomes just as hard as writing for male audiences because the expectations are the same but for different reasons." For Angela to write with authority, she must not only construct a stance oppositional to white men but also, because of asymmeterical race relations already operative in the classroom and educational institutions, deliberately negotiate her relation to other white women. How then am I, a thirty-five-year-old, middle-class Anglo-American woman, implicated in Angela's construction of otherness? The same question can be asked in connection with all my students' texts: Is my otherness—in terms of racial identity, age, class, or gender—an enabling constraint? How am I constructed as a reader of texts? Am I perceived as a trustworthy audience? Are these students speaking directly to me? Am I perceived as giving voice to them? If I am perceived this way, what does this suggest about my position as a white feminist? Does it suggest that I may have to work harder not to position myself as a white savior? In other words, that I have to work against such essentializing positions?

One way to work against essentializing teacherly positions is to recognize how we negotiate identities with students and to consider how one's position may shift from writer to writer, from text to text. Like the students in the class, I am not free of internalized oppressions and social discourses about race and gender. Not only must I continually reflect on my internalized discourses but I must also realize that pedagogically I can function as an enabling reader who bears witness to a writer's struggle. I can serve as a point of counteridentification, or I can function entirely as a constraint. Angela struggled in my class to negotiate her identity as a writer against the grain of both dominant and subdominant discourses appropriated by the other (that is, by me, as well as other white women in academia). She is forced to be other to those who are others themselves, or as Michelle Wallace would put it, she is "the 'other' of the 'other' in public discourse" (53). This situation is complicated, of course, by the fact that writers are always made other to themselves through writing. It is the simultaneity of her struggles with the hegemonies of dominant and subdominant discourses, however, that characterizes the identity negotiations and dialogic nature of her autobiography.[4]

## "Another Look at My Faith": Strategies in Context

Students of color often use the categories of gender, race, and ethnicity in analyzing their struggles as writers; white students less readily address their whiteness as a contributing factor. But rarely do students consciously consider the category of class. Many students at Oberlin are, in economic terms, from upper-middle-class families, yet they tend to identify themselves as middle-class, which leaves certain assumptions about class and culture un-challenged. Constructs common to upper- and middle-class experiences and ideology do surface, however, in their writing. Many students construct the private and public as two distinctly different spheres, constructs that are fur-ther complicated by cultural differences.

A nineteen-year-old Chinese Malaysian student named Kim, for exam-ple, initially expressed difficulty with the autobiographical focus of the course. She said that because she came "from a culture that clearly distinguishes the private and public," she felt uncomfortable revealing such "personal material" to "outsiders, least of all strangers in a classroom." She continued, "Perhaps part of my reluctance is also due to the view that I have of a classroom—a for-mal setting where 'academic' knowledge is passed on from teacher to student." These excerpts not only reveal how cultural ideology structures students' as-sumptions about autobiography but they also suggest some of the tensions in-herent in using autobiography in multicultural settings.

The excerpts suggest that even well-intended pedagogical practices may silence and alienate some students while privileging others and that appeals to identity and its way of shaping social discourse are not universally favored critical acts. In short, autobiography cannot simply be exported from one cul-ture or institution to another. As teachers working in multicultural class-rooms, we must be careful not to become imperialists in search of universaliz-ing practices. Rather, we should acknowledge struggles with and differences within the pedagogical situation itself. At the same time that Kim reinscribes a private-public dichotomy, she also complicates expressionists' longstanding claims for authenticity in the genre when she suggests she will have to invent herself, to engage in what some postmodernists have termed the inevitability of fiction in writing the self (see S. Smith 1987, 47).

Kim decided to stay in the course even though she was "not sure what would come out of it" and knew that writing autobiographies would proba-bly make her "feel sad [and] homesick ," as she felt during her first year of col-lege. A central theme of Kim's work was mediating her "dual identity." Her writing for the entire semester focused on competing languages and discourse communities in her life; she speaks English and Malay fluently and can con-verse in several Chinese dialects. In her final paper, "Another Look at My Faith" (an assignment proposed by the students themselves), she experiments with the dialogic nature of autobiography in ways that challenge the conven-tional linear, reflective, and progressive autobiographical form. From the be-ginning, tensions among discursive postures emerge, including the persona of the reflective autobiographers, the autobiographer as poet speaking to God, the "official" language of religion appropriated by the writer, and the writer's unconventional presence, which serves as a disrupting force. In the following excerpt, Kim disrupts her prior unconditional allegiance to the authoritative discourse of patriarchal religion by positioning a section of I Corinthians among contradictory voices.

> The church elders gave us a simplified version. They said that when we gather to worship, the angels are looking down from heaven on us. How can we show them that the glory of God, man, is equal to the glory of man, woman? As such women in church have to cover their heads; it is *because of the angels* and not because we are not equal to men. But notice the language used, *man did not come from woman, but woman from man; neither was man created for woman but woman for man . . . the woman ought to have a sight of authority over her head.* All these verses insinuate that the woman can only find fulfillment in a man, because she is *created for him.* She is also to be submissive and subservient to him as he has *authority over her.* Her relationship to God is second-rated as she is only the *glory of man* and not the *glory of God.* Also, she has to direct her questions to her husband (indicating that she has to have one) and not to God as she cannot speak directly to him while in church. She has no voice in church.

The juxtaposition of these discourses defies the scripture's insistence that the word not be taken in vain. Kim plays with the borders of this authoritative discourse by using different frames and contextualization, breaking it apart and using typographic cues to objectify it even further. Here, the conscious embedding of narrative utterance—the interfacing of official and unofficial discourses and the representation of contesting literacies—establishes the writer's authority and agency.

Another central feature of Kim's autobiography is its critique of the totality of cultural metanarratives—namely, the common representation of Asian women as silent and docile. Kim battles for female subjectivity by confronting this stereotype and by creating a position of resistance within a culturally specific context, the church. Through the language of autobiography, she constructs herself as a moving site of opposition and contestation and situates her textual self within, alongside, and against oppressive and totalizing discursive social practices. In the following passage, she directly challenges dominant ideologies of the "orient" and the authoritarianism of patriarchal religious discourse, both of which reduce Asian women to an idealized essence.

> I forgot to bring my veil to church today. *I refused to wear my veil in church today.* I feel scared, I know that I'm going to get into trouble, especially since I am a youth group leader. *I can feel them watching me—*

*"she has been Americanized."* My head feels so bare . . . *It feels good to stand before God.* I was right, here comes Mr. Daniel . . . "as a youth leader you should be setting the example for the younger ones". . . *I am.*

For Kim, as for all the students discussed here, her sense of narrative authority and agency lies in her movement among institutionalized discourses, subject positions, and autobiographical scripts in the subversion and diffusion of hegemonic forms of social discourse and in the construction of positions of resistance, which, however transitory, are "strategies in context" (Ellsworth 1989, 317).

If differences exist within particular social and discursive configurations, then writing identities in the multicultural classroom is not about finding a true essence or writing a real self; it is about recognizing that these autobiographical essences and selves do not originate with the subject alone. Instead, as Norma Alarcón suggests, these voicings of the self can be seen as social "discourses that transverse consciousness and which the subject must struggle with constantly" (365).

Autobiography, if framed dialogically, can help students and teachers address diversity in ways that do not merely celebrate or appropriate differences but that recognize each student's complex identity negotiations and discursive positions. It is precisely the embedding of multiple social discourses and interlacing subject positions that make autobiography so promising a catalyst for multicultural literacy, especially if students are brought into the process of critique. If students become engaged in a cultural and historical analysis of their autobiographical texts, they too can begin to discover "mutual implication"—that is, the relation "between the self and the cultural heritage within which selfhood has meaning" (Spellmeyer, 269). To make such reflexive acts and exchanges part of the multicultural classroom is to enable students and, I hope, teachers recognize how they locate themselves discursively and help them participate more critically in the exchanges that determine and maintain these locations.

# 4

"YE ARE WITNESSES": AUTOBIOGRAPHY
AND COMMEMORATIVE PRACTICES

In 1903, the American Board of Commissioners for Foreign Missions of the Congregational Church erected the Memorial Arch on the Oberlin College campus to commemorate the American missionaries who died in the 1899 Boxer Rebellion in the Shandong Province in north China. Oberlin College was a particularly suitable site for this memorial, having a tradition of religious and political reform and missionary zeal since its founding in 1833. Ninety years after the erection of the arch, in the fall of 1993, the inside of its semicircle was spraypainted with the words "Death to Chinks Memorial." On the outside of the crescent sides were the words "Dead chinks, good chinks" (Oberlin 1995, 1). These graffiti appeared in a climate of racial tensions. In the space of a few weeks, anti-Muslim graffiti were found on the door of the Muslim Student Association, graffiti against blacks appeared in the men's room in the college gym, and two wooden crosses were burned in front of one of the student-housing co-ops. The combination and proximity of these incidents on the small, insular, and politically liberal Oberlin campus created an atmosphere of tension and concern.

At first, local newspapers referred to the graffiti on the arch as a defacement. The assumption was that a member of the white community had committed an anti-Asian hate crime. But when the college newspaper, the *Oberlin Review*, published an anonymous letter by a self-identified Asian-American student who claimed responsibility for the graffiti, the defacement began to be seen in a different light. Its purpose, according to the letter writer, was to draw attention to the politics of commemorative practices and to the racial politics on campus. The graffitist argued that the arch "glorified white accomplishments" and made no mention of the "thousands of Chinese who were killed or raped." But instead of unifying the community in the fight against institutional racism and the monumentalism of Western imperialism, the fact that the graffiti artist was an Asian-American unsettled existing conceptions and elicited conflicting claims of authority and authenticity from different communities. Many white students felt they had been unfairly positioned as perpetrators of the hate crime. Several Asian-American students felt that the graffiti reinforced essentialist racial politics by generalizing the Asian-American standpoint. A number of feminists sympathized with the graffitist's antiracist position, but they thought that by concealing her gender identity (in the letter, she did not identify herself as a woman), she had missed an opportunity to reimage Asian-American women as activists and thereby challenge their stereotype as docile and subservient. Finally, some people felt that the graffiti were insensitive to the sacrifices of Oberlin missionaries who died in the rebellion and to the grief of family members still in the community.

The graffitist's disclosure of identity and the responses to it raise critical questions about the relationship between the pedagogy and politics of identity and the writing of history. Who has the authority to interpret the graffiti? Who has the authority to construct whose history? Is one group's interpretation more authentic than another's? Is each group obliged to have its own historians and critics? How can feminists and critical educators acknowledge and respect the experiences, values, and culture of different communities while still envisioning forms and pedagogies of commonality?

For a long time, feminists have analyzed women's struggles for voice in the academy. But the graffiti prompt us to consider how intersections of gender, race, and national identity shape those struggles. If feminism is to remain an active and vital force in the academy, feminists must acknowledge the political and cultural boundaries that distinguish forms of protest from crimes of hate, and must see how the slippage between these opposed discourses shapes teachers' and students' struggles for power and a sense of place. We must also investigate further the relationship between cultural and political activism. Beyond the specific concerns of one small campus, the arch incident shows that the interrogation of past events and their representation are imbued with questions of autobiography and notions of authenticity. Moreover, this incident prompts us to consider how autobiographical acts exceed the moment of their articulation.

At Oberlin, the incident prompted certain groups to solidify their identity positions. The graffitist's disclosure of identity reinforced for many white males a sense of victimization and self-righteousness. The sad irony is that her graffiti reified a racial position—white defensiveness—that the graffitist hoped to dislodge. In an era defined by myriad conflicts related to identity; by the blurring of national, cultural, and disciplinary boundaries; and by backlash against reforms that benefit women and men of color (e.g., affirmative action), it seems especially crucial to focus on the performative nature of language and how social differences intersect and are mobilized in campus politics and to examine the consequences of that intersection and that mobilization for particular communities.

Mary Louise Pratt's notion of the contact zone helps us understand the dynamics of autobiography in student activism and cultural politics in the academy and how historically oppressed groups negotiate power and authority, rhetorically protest inequities, and imagine communities in the context of institutional power relations. Student activism and responses to student activism from the faculty and administration can be seen as contact zones wherein narratives of identity and autobiographical scripts collide and the contradictions of power, politics of representation, and construction of historical memory are made visible. In this chapter, I consider how autobiography and identity-based discourse figured in student activism on the Oberlin campus during the fall of 1993 and their pedagogical consequences. What I propose in this chapter is a self-reflexive pedagogy of action. Toward that end, I ask teachers-researchers to investigate the dynamics of campus activism and to bear witness to and keep alive the vitality of intervention in their classrooms and pedagogy scholarship. Student activism is a form of knowledge-making that has pedagogical investments. Like many feminists (Brodkey and Fine, Ellsworth, Flannery 1991, Jarratt 1991, Kirsch, Lu), I have tried to bridge the divisions between classroom and community and to engage questions of agency and conflict in my teaching and research. But not until the fall of 1993, when I was teaching an introductory writing course titled Gender, Race, and Language, did I discover the potential of feminist teaching as a form of activism and the role that a rhetorical and cultural materialist analysis of campus politics and student activism could play in the writing classroom.

My reading strategy of the events on the Oberlin campus and of the narratives, both written and spoken, that emerged during and immediately after the cross-burning and arch incidents is shaped by encounters with materialist feminism and postmodern theories of subjectivity and language. Having already reviewed these theoretical frameworks in earlier chapters, my purpose here is to highlight the theoretical aspects that are most important for understanding my analysis of student activism, commemorative practices, and the framing of agency and resistance in the academy.

Materialist feminism emerged in the late 1970s from feminist critiques of Marxism and its inability to sufficiently address women's oppression. Early materialist feminists, focusing on women's oppression and patriarchal economic social arrangements, "search for central commonalties" among women (Nancy Hartsock quoted in Crosby, 133). Materialist feminists of the 1990s continue to focus on women's economic and social oppression, but they also engage questions of difference and acknowledge the exclusivity of the idea that women share a collective oppression (Crosby, 135). Postmodern theories of subjectivity and language have provided materialist feminists with useful frameworks to critique the totalizing category of women and the racist imperialism in mainstream Western feminism.[1] Significantly, critiques of white feminists' exclusions have not led materialist feminists to abandon politics or the notion of human agency. Materialist feminists' rethinking of the concept of agency is particularly important for understanding the dynamics of autobiography in student activism and with what pedagogical consequences the social signification of the self is shaped by institutional contexts and histories. Materialist feminists of the 1990s and postcolonial feminists, whose work is often associated with materialist feminism, see agency in terms of how it is shaped by historical practices, positions, and discourses. Chandra Talpade Mohanty reads the autobiographical subject in ways that demonstrate how experience and social action are mediated by institutional systems, historical frameworks, and material relations (1990, 146). Materialist feminists see individual subjects not as determined by forms of social mediation and, therefore, lacking agency but as complex and often contradictory sites of representation and struggle over power and resources (Newton, 8–9). Rather than view women's oppression and resistance as founded on universal principles, we should view them as social phenomena formed by the contested histories of nationality, race, and gender identity. The arch incident at Oberlin College exemplifies materialist-feminist arguments about how language and narratives of identity encode social relations of power and how cultural representations of identity mobilize competing and often irreconcilable interests.

My interest in representations of power and resistance in the academy and in how a rhetorical and cultural analysis of student activism can enrich feminist teaching and pedagogy scholarship on autobiography prompts a return to and reinterpretation of the activist roots of feminism. The history of women's activism in the United States is fraught with contradictions and significant absences. For instance, the women's-rights movement in the mid to late nineteenth century was organized by college-educated middle- and upper-class white women, many of whom opposed slavery as an institution but did not challenge directly the hierarchical relations of race and class in

American society (hooks 1981, 124). Although some white women's-rights advocates were antiracist, many supported racial segregation and advanced their cause at the expense of blacks. For instance, some used slavery as a metaphor for their own oppression, a tactic that deflected attention away from their privileged race and class. Similar patterns characterized white feminism through the 1970s and 1980s, much of it failing to address differences among women and the simultaneity of oppressions based on race, gender, class, sexual orientation, and national identity. As in the original women's-rights movement, the category of woman was synonymous with white woman (Crosby; Davis; hooks 1981; Lorde).

Given the exclusivism of the women's-rights movement and the limiting concept of a universal feminist standpoint, academic feminists today might wonder what can be gained from retracing their activist roots. Indeed, why should we look back at all? First, to reject outright feminism's activist roots is to ignore the important role that the women's-rights movement played in developing gender consciousness and empowering women (even if mostly middle-class white women) to see themselves as agents capable of organized resistance. Second, to forget feminism's white-centered roots is to ignore how they were contested historically, how women whose interests were not reflected in that movement carved out new narratives of identity and new spaces from which to speak. Academic feminists can learn from the failures of early feminist activism. Just as activism is imbued with certain narratives of identity, so too are the narratives that we construct about its history. My goal in this chapter is to engage the narratives of identity that shape student activism and to consider how certain identities and histories are discounted or discredited in campus discourse (Friedman 1995b, 18). The women's-rights movement and critiques of its exclusivism can provide powerful tools to examine critically campus activism and narratives of resistance and to recognize how privilege finds "ever deeper places to hide" (Spelman quoted in Newton, 163). I suggest that we look for the teachable moments in student activism and campus conflicts and encourage students to reflect on how their actions are mediated historically, so they too can become more active in writing the history of the institution and its transformation.

## Framing Institutional Memory: The Hidden Transcript

The Memorial Arch is a granite, semicircular colonnade standing at one of the entrances to the town square (see figure 4). Inscribed on the face of the archway in the center are the words "Ye Are Witnesses," and on one of the crescent-shaped sides, are these: "The Blood Of Martyrs The Seed Of The Church." A person walking through the arch can see bronze plaques embedded in the

Figure 4. The Memorial Arch, Tappan Square, Oberlin, Ohio (1903). Used by permission of Oberlin College Archives, Oberlin, Ohio.

granite wall to the right and left. These plaques list the names of the Christian missionaries from Oberlin killed in the Boxer Rebellion in Shandong Province. The Boxers, wanting to drive foreign influence from their land, first rose against their neighboring Chinese Christian converts and then against the foreigners. Approximately thirty thousand Chinese Christians were killed; the number of non-Christian Chinese who perished is unknown (Jacobson).[2]

If we interpret the graffiti on the Memorial Arch as a historical and ideological phenomenon, we must recognize how language shapes historical memory and how national politics and religious discourse anchor the kind of witness that the monument announces. Whose history does the monument represent? Who has access to the monument and its particular history? What role do particular witnesses play in generating certain historical memories? How do these memories shift according to the way witnesses define themselves? To deconstruct the arch's imagined audience, viewers must first read through the expectations of its designers and the values the arch celebrates. They must acknowledge the Western declaration that the killed missionaries were martyrs. The phrase "Ye Are Witnesses," a declaration and an exhortation, refers to both the martyrs and the present viewers as witnesses. Martyrdom means "to witness," "to testify that Jesus is the Son of God," and "to refuse to renounce one's faith in the face of persecution and death" (Hevia, 319–20). Since missionary discourse on the Boxer Rebellion maintains that the missionaries in China had "suffered and borne witness to their belief and had all led pious and exemplary lives" (320–21), those who died could be considered martyrs from various Protestant vantage points. The New Testament Christian narrative of suffering, death, and resurrection is expressed on the crescent sides of the arch in the proverb mentioned above, "The Blood Of Martyrs The Seed Of The Church," and in three other inscriptions: "If We Died With Him We Shall Also Live With Him," "More Than Conquerors Through Him That Loved Us," and "Neither Count I My Life Dear Unto Myself."

In the early twentieth century, missionaries often portrayed the Chinese subject as uncivilized, barbaric, and believing in magic, which was how the Christians characterized the Boxers' polytheistic religious beliefs. This view of the Chinese draws on an essentialist rhetoric of race that conflates skin color with intellectual capacity and character (Frankenberg, 14). Many American missionaries saw the Chinese as people capable of becoming civilized if converted to Christianity. To the Boxers, missionary imperatives were imperialistic acts that reduced Chinese cultural space and made Asia coextensive with the United States.[3] Neither reading is completely accurate because each suppresses important cultural and historical contradictions. First, the Memorial Arch at Oberlin does not reflect the range of American sentiments toward either missionary work or China. Second, missionary work is complicated by the contradictions between religious universalisms and national particularities. Third, the feudalism of the Qing dynasty certainly marginalized the peasants by denying them access to social wealth, but the anti-imperialist and anti-Christian struggles among the Chinese were not necessarily directed against that feudalism. The Boxer slogan "Uphold the Qing; exterminate the foreigners" was not logical; "supporting the Qing could never mean getting rid of the foreigners" (Jikui, 110). The Qing dynasty itself "had become the complete slave of imperialism" (Minghan, 38). Ding Minghan writes that "in those days when China occupied a semicolonial status, and the Qing dynasty had become the tool of imperialists who controlled China, it was impossible to attack imperialism without also attacking feudal rule" (34). If the arch represented an uncontested history, the graffiti initiated a reinvestigation of the constructed nature of that history and its contradictions.

The arch was spray-painted on Sunday morning, November 7. As reported by John Rafter in the college newspaper, the *Oberlin Review,* the college building-and-grounds maintenance crews were alerted that afternoon and quickly covered the graffiti with brown paper. They weren't able to remove the paint from the arch, because they lacked the staff and because the cleaning chemicals were ineffective in the cold. The act of covering up the graffiti foreshadowed the responses of the administration and of some faculty, who considered the graffiti vandalism. At a general faculty meeting, a tenured white male called it an act of lawlessness and urged the college to reevaluate its vandalism policy. A tenured woman of color said that this response showed indifference to the struggles of subordinate groups and minimized the graffiti's political challenge as a form of activism.

Graffiti are almost always a coded version of what James Scott calls the "hidden transcript" (14). He defines this term as nonhegemonic, subversive discourse generated by subordinate groups and concealed from certain dominant others. Hidden transcripts are usually presented so they will not jeopardize the speaker or actor (14). Graffiti are mostly a medium of the urban black male subculture (Warner, 397). Urban graffiti are largely personal signatures, identifiable as trademarks or monograms only to the initiated (398). The graffiti on the arch, unlike typical urban graffiti, were not accompanied by a personal signature. The phrase "death to Chinks memorial" refers to the lives that the monument fails to remember and to the consequences of the meanings that the monument generates. The graffiti on the arch were a hidden transcript made public, a subversive act generated by a member of a subordinate group. But initially they were generally interpreted as an anti-Asian hate crime. The community's lack of understanding or dismissal of the graffiti's potential as counterhegemonic discourse shows the ineffectiveness of the use of this medium for protest, the slippage between injurious and insurrectionary speech acts, and how even critical discourse on racist speech can become an instrument of its perpetuation. In other words, despite the intention to resignify racist speech—"Dead Chinks, Good Chinks"—its recirculation reproduced pain and trauma. In addition, the graffiti, like the original inscriptions on the arch, are coded by national rhetoric and national boundaries. The word *Chink* is a racial slur that some Westerners use to refer to Asians. Both the graffiti and the original inscription assume a Western audience.

The arch had previously provoked protests when, during commencement processions, several Oberlin students and faculty members had walked around the structure instead of under it to demonstrate their disapproval of its exclusions. But this was the first time the college community's interpretation of the memories generated by the arch became part of the memorial itself. A gift from the class of 1994 to the college was a pair of plaques dedicated—in both English and Chinese—to the Chinese who died in the Boxer Rebellion. The English translation of the inscribed poem by Du Fu reads: "I am Grieved by the War / and have not Slept. / Who has the Strength to Right

Heaven and Earth?" Reactions to the plaques varied. Some students and alumni said the gift was "a token concession," an "effort to appease concern regarding unequal representation" and to "silence voices expressing their rejection of imperialism which is linked to expansion of capitalism and the perpetuation of racism." Others expressed "dismay that the people involved in killing the Oberlin missionaries now share the monument with their victims" (Oberlin Shansi Memorial Association Newsletter, 2). In short, the Oberlin community continues to struggle over the meanings of the arch and its construction and over its mediation of historical memory. During the spring semester of 1995, the Oberlin Memorial Shansi Association organized a symposium to educate the community about the Boxer Rebellion and the interventionist aspects of making history. The symposium and the struggles on the Oberlin campus demonstrate that "the shape of memory cannot be divorced from the actions taken in its behalf." If we were "to remain unchanged by the recollective act," as James Young observes, "it could be said that we have not remembered at all" (1993, 13–15).

The Memorial Arch graffiti followed other racist incidents on campus. A week earlier, two wooden crosses were found burning in front of the Harkness student-housing co-op. According to residents, scarecrows on the crosses were burned in anticipation of Halloween and the yearly Bike Derby (Rafter, 1). Regardless of its intent, the act had racist meanings. That co-op members allowed the cross burnings to continue revealed their cultural insensitivity to the historical significance of the sign and to its potential harmful effects on certain groups on campus and in town. Many students and faculty members perceived the cross burnings as part of a historical totality, in contrast to their response to the words "death to Chinks memorial." But those who witnessed the graffiti and those who witnessed the burning crosses were both engaged in reading history's narrative in the process of rearticulation formulated around issues of cultural identity and notions of authenticity (Hennessy, 99).

## Imaging the Academy As a Public Space

The arch graffiti, the cross burnings, and the general increase of racial epithets on campus prompted four hundred students to hold a rally to protest institutional racism, to create support for a hate-crimes policy, and to urge the administration to address the situation immediately. "Oberlin in the long run is about changing attitudes, ending racist mentalities. It's about making you accountable for your actions. You write 'chink' on the wall, you are accountable for that," one student at the rally said. "We didn't pay all that [tuition] to be called niggers and chinks," another student commented. Organizers of the demonstration, primarily women of color, said it was an opportunity for students of color to voice their concerns. A few white students tried to join the list of scheduled speakers but reportedly were not permitted. At the rally, one of the leaders said, "Their voices have been heard. . . . Now it is our time to speak." "That is not acceptable," someone from the crowd yelled (Tryzelaar, Kearney, and Schneider, 7).

Afterward, a meeting was announced for "all people of color"; it was organized to develop a collective response to the rise in racial tension on campus. Several white students and a journalist attempting to attend the meeting were asked to leave, after being accused of antagonism and of trying to take control of the meeting. All but one student, a white male, left; after refusing several times to leave, the remaining student gagged himself with a bandanna. This student was reportedly removed from the meeting by a visiting professor, a man of color, and a fellow student. Although his actions may have been based upon an idealized image of Oberlin as a unified community where individuals equally share power, the students of color experienced his presence not as an act of unification but as one of control. The self-gagged white student failed to understand the legitimate need for students of color to create a space to voice experiences silenced by dominant groups in the academy. Using a tactic that oppressed groups have used in their struggle for freedom, he implied that he was himself a victim. This appropriation assumes a common humanity on white-centered terms and thus averts white eyes from the realities of power (Frankenberg, 143). Unlike the graffiti on the arch, his act contains no hidden transcript. On the contrary, the persistence of the white male's performance of silence is symbolic of the attempts of dominant groups to police and monitor the hidden transcript. His visible gesture symbolized free speech as the curtailment of his individual rights and renders invisible the forced segregation and silencing of people of color. The white male's symbolic self-gagging and his physical removal from the meeting bolstered reverse-racism arguments on campus, cast him as a martyred defender of free speech, and silenced other positions in the ongoing dialogue about race.

The next day, the white male student reported a fire in a garbage can outside his dorm room and the words "Racists must die" spray-painted on the wall with an arrow pointing to his door (Riccardi). These events prompted Frederick S. Starr, the president of the college at that time, to acknowledge heightened racial tensions on campus and to denounce the use of physical force. Starr's rhetoric, like the student's symbolic gesture, was color-blind. Basing his sense of community on the idea that all its members are historical equals, he argued for the "non-exclusion of individuals on the basis of race, versus feelings of solidarity" (Riccardi). In a letter addressed to the Oberlin College community, Starr wrote:

> Over the past ten days the Oberlin campus has witnessed a number of alarming examples of hateful graffiti and symbolic acts. . . . We all regret these recent examples of crude hatred and hurtful bigotry. We are all demeaned by such acts, but I want to extend a hand in particular to anyone who feels intimidated by these objectionable signs and to anyone in whom they arouse *fear*. For the foreseeable future, I authorize any such person to call Campus Security to be driven or accompanied by a campus security officer on or off campus as needed. (Starr)

This statement reduces the significance of institutional abuses of power by shifting the focus to individual acts of intimidation. By using the collective *we*, the president suggests that the entire Oberlin community has been demeaned. But the historical fact is that we are *not* all equally demeaned. Who constitutes the public community at Oberlin? Were the privileged injured, or were they horrified by the witnessing of injury?

In a letter from the president, Alfred Mackay, former dean of the college; and Patrick Penn, former dean of students, the administration stated, "Whatever the outcome of any judicial process [regarding incidents surrounding the removal of the white male student from the student-of-color meeting] it is important that the College at this time reaffirm its commitment to free speech, openness, mutual respect, and fairness." The administration said that the principles of free speech and nondiscriminatory practices can coexist—a laudable sentiment—but the administration did not look closely at the conflict between an unbending defense of the First Amendment and the college's goals of promoting equality, honoring diversity, and providing a safe environment for all students, faculty, and staff. The administration's idea of free speech was abstract and did not account for how, in certain contexts, freedom of speech can interfere with the rights of others, that in the case of hate speech the competing values of liberty and equality are jeopardized (Matsuda, 47). The administration's absolutist interpretation of the First Amendment erased the historical reality of racism and sexism at the college.[4] The administration failed to acknowledge how racist acts infringe upon the right of people of color to participate fully in the community and to recognize the institutional silencing of certain voices. Rather than focusing on the college's responsibility for creating a climate conducive to learning, the administration seemed to prioritize the freedoms of the perpetrators of hate speech.

During an open forum later that week, several faculty expressed opinions that contradicted letters from the administration. Professor Adrienne

Jones, characterizing the college, used *we* differently. She began her presentation with an autobiographical statement: "Today, I come to you not only as a faculty member but also as one of the precious few African-American faculty members on this campus, and even further as one of only three tenured African-American female persons in the *history* of this college" (Jones). She spoke of the "tyranny of Oberlin's liberal reputation," "the gap between the real Oberlin and the mythical Oberlin, and the barriers that African-Americans have faced and continue to face in the academy. She said:

> We are outraged that administrators, faculty, and a majority of students spend more time defending what we perceive to be racist acts, and denying our reality. . . . Solving issues of racism and oppression is *not* offering to talk with victims or providing escort services. . . . It is *not* sprinkling black students throughout a white campus like pepper dots to educate the majority about diversity and multiculturalism. . . . Whenever folks hear the name Oberlin College, the image of a sort of paradise of liberal thought, free speech, and multicultural existence is raised in a very positive way. . . . [This] mythology . . . functions as a mask behind which administration, faculty, and students hide. (Jones)

Unlike the self-gagged student's use of the symbolic silencing gesture of race to portray white males as collective victims of the politics of students of color, the professor's strategic use of *we* bears a relation to the graffiti on the arch. The Asian-American student used the phrase "dead Chinks, good Chinks" to point out the underlying nationalism, essentialist racism, and exclusionary rhetoric of the monument—how it commemorates only the deaths of the missionaries from Oberlin, not the 30,000 Christian and countless non-Christian Chinese who died in the Boxer Rebellion. Likewise, Jones's invocation of the collective "we" was mobilized to expose institutional patterns of racism against historically marginalized groups.

Another speaker at the open forum, Professor Clayton Koppes, a tenured white male, further questioned the administration's depiction of the academy as a neutral zone, a place where individuals and groups continually negotiate their identity and sense of community. This speaker grappled with the contradictory aspects of his own location and the fracturing of power in the institution.

> I speak as a gay man. Like so many people at Oberlin I am the victim and the beneficiary of multiple positions. I know the pain and the anxiety caused by discrimination. The kick-in-the-gut feeling of violation when my office door was spattered with homophobic epithets, and the sense of being alone with only a few friends to whom to turn. . . . But I

also speak as a member of the College Faculty Council and, in a very committed way, as a member of the beloved community of Oberlin. . . . Majority members of the community need to be especially aware that invocation of free speech—a basic human right—must be coupled with an awareness of how power and privilege may distort what is often taken to be a neutral right. (Koppes)[5]

These excerpts from faculty speeches at the open forum highlight the extent to which the dominant view of free speech at Oberlin inflects the image of the academy as a "fairness zone" (DeMott, 131).

Critical race theorists suggest that one way to respond to the increase of hate crimes on American campuses is to develop policies that narrowly define hate speech. For instance, speech that infringes on public order or that incites violence—so-called "fighting words"—is not covered by the First Amendment and thus is unlawful on college campuses. As Charles Lawrence III points out, the problem is that most college policies fail to recognize that racist speech does not always lead to violence. Targets of sexist, heterosexist, or racist speech often avoid escalating the conflict by internalizing the harm done them. According to Lawrence, the fighting-words doctrine also "presupposes an encounter with two persons of relatively equal power" and is, therefore, blind to the particular cultural experiences and discursive practices of women and men of color (69). Likewise, Mari Matsuda is careful to distinguish between the freedom to criticize institutions and hate speech directed against the least powerful in the community. Like other critical race theorists, she argues for a narrow definition of unlawful racist speech. Speech is racist, she argues, if a message of racial inferiority is directed against a historically oppressed group and if the message is persecutory, hateful, and degrading (36). Matsudi recognizes that there may be difficult cases. At the University of Michigan in the early nineties, there were more than twenty cases of whites charging blacks with racist speech; in one, a black student was punished for using the phrase "white trash" (Glasser, 8). Matsuda attempts to counter such measures with her narrow definition of hate speech and her focus on power relations and the specificity of the historical context. The intention of critical race theorists is not to avoid the larger issues of equality or to undermine the First Amendment but, rather, to ground the First Amendment in the experiences of victims of oppression.

A broad definition of hate speech might equate the graffiti on the Memorial Arch at Oberlin, particularly the phrase "death to Chinks memorial" (a criticism of the institution), with the burning crosses (a clear symbol of hatred to African-Americans). Rather than equate these acts, critical race theorists undoubtedly would consider the status of the target of the hate crime, the crime's historical context, and the amount of freedom the perpetrator enjoys. Critical race theorists view hate crimes as part of larger historical patterns, and they imagine the academy as a contact zone. From the perspective of critical race theorists, hate speech does not merely reflect relations of social domination but becomes the vehicle through which domination is enacted. Hate speech thus "acts upon its listener . . . [and] enjoins the subject to reoccupy a subordinate social position" (Butler, 18).

In *Excitable Speech: A Politics of the Performative*, Judith Butler points out that the rhetoric of wound and injury in critical race theory "suggests that language can act in ways that parallel the infliction of physical pain and injury" (4). I endorse critical race theorists' focus on language's historicity and contend that language can and does threaten the body, that language assists violence, and that language can wield its own violent force (as seen in statist censorship, exclusive acts of representation, and speech that incites violence). However, critical race theory does not account sufficiently for the fluidity of social positions, the unpredictability of language, or the slippage between injurious and insurrectionary speech acts. For example, the phrase "Dead Chinks, Good Chinks" was seen by some members of the Oberlin College community as an act of hate, while others interpreted it as an insurgent act that exploited hateful speech in order to undercut historical exclusions and injury.

Hate speech gains its power through repetition and its historical resonance; in this sense, its does not originate with the individual speaker. Rather, as Butler suggests, hate speech is a ritual that "exceeds the instance of its utterance"; however, as the Memorial Arch incident on the Oberlin College campus suggests, "excess is not fully capturable or identifiable (the past and future of the utterance cannot be narrated with any certainty)" (3). Moreover, what the arch incident foregrounds but which even narrowly defined hate speech codes do not seem to account for is how, despite the intentions of the speaker to counter hegemonic discourses, the resignification of hateful speech also can reproduce trauma and pain. What may be intended as critical discourse can become an instrument for the perpetration of hate merely through repetition. Thus, the arch incident on the Oberlin College campus elucidates the risks of the resignification of hateful speech as a strategy of resistance.

This is not to say that speech acts such as "Racists must die" and "Kill all Jews" are comparable signs of racial violence, as implied by Margaret Morrison in her response to an earlier published version of this chapter; to equate such speech acts is to deny the profoundly distinct embodied memories, pain, trauma, and historical resonance that they elicit. Morrison builds her argument against hate-speech codes, particularly as articulated by critical race theorists (a category under which she mistakenly situates my reading of the arch), by contemplating the logic of reversal and the ethics of strategic essentialism. She wonders if it would be ethical "to employ a strategic essentialism—to light fires in the garbage cans of straights and call for the death of all heterosexists ([a] call not in the narrow definition of hate speech), because [she] was fired from a job once for being out as a lesbian and because queers have been bashed in various ways for centuries?" (210). Morrison goes on to imply that strategic essentialism is "a trap that some marginalized groups fall into, a trap set by the very economy they think they are overturning when all that they are really doing is setting themselves up for a return to the master-slave relationship" (210). Her point is that such reversals do not get us very far but that they, in effect, "mimic the strategy of the oppressor instead of offering a different set of terms" (Butler quoted in Morrison, 210). I agree with Morrison that efforts to rein in speech may function in ways that reinforce essentialist categories and identity politics and, I would add, advance conservative political agendas, especially if we consider the inconsistencies in recent court decisions on hate speech.[6]

However, what Morrison fails to acknowledge in her characterization of strategic essentialism are the political gains that such acts have played historically and how strategic essentialism, like all uses of language, is contextually effective or limiting. Nevertheless, given the institutional resilience of racism, sexism, and heterosexism, we do need to seriously consider how hate-speech codes, even those that are narrowly defined to have restrictive jurisdiction only within the university, may end up reinforcing essentialist identities and social categories by projecting autobiographical scripts that force the subject to occupy a fixed social position and thereby reproduce hierarchical structural relations and static notions of power. In other words, in implementing such codes, there would need to be a legal recognition of identity categories and social positions to corroborate the historical narrative. How would these identities and social positions be defined and by whom? Critical race theorists have not accounted for how social positions and identities may be stratified and mobile, how social positions and power shift from one context to another, or how social-identity categories may be strategically claimed and even historically hateful speech resignified as a form of resistance.

There is perhaps a subtle distinction between my position and those of critical race theorists, but I believe it is an important one, which arises from the instability of language and its effects. Indeed, this is precisely why I do not endorse hate-speech codes that completely conflate speech with conduct. Although all speech acts are performative in one sense or another, as my analysis of incidents on the Oberlin campus suggests, the relation between speech and its effects is often incongruous. This is not to say that individuals should not be held responsible for the repetition of speech that leads to or causes injury—"fighting words"—but that the concrete effects must be shown. In other words, we need to distinguish between the consequences and effects of speech acts (their perlocutionary function) and the idea that speech acts perform the injury itself (illocutionary function) (Butler, 18). Speech acts function in both illocutionary and perlocutionary ways, and hate speech can *enact* domination. However, I do not think it is advisable to base legislation on speech's illocutionary function, because the claim that speech acts perform injury suggests that the projection of subordination onto the subject is effective and complete (Butler, 18). This formulation of hate speech denies the subject's agency and his or her ability to respond critically to such acts of hate. Furthermore, efforts to tighten the reins on individual speech acts and the legalistic focus on personal injury may silence the examination of broader institutional conditions that establish and support contexts of hate and violence and collapse political opposition into juridical discourse—for example, if the graffiti on the arch were coded as actionable hate speech.

I endorse the efforts of critical race theorists to replace liberalism's abstract formulation of free speech with legal recognition of injurious speech. However, I do not believe that we can with any certainty claim that all speech is an unequivocal form of conduct. While I am not against all forms of regulation, and while I believe language can wield its power in abusive and violent ways, the primary responsibility of the academy should be to provide safe pedagogical contexts for students to become critically aware of the pain and trauma that live on through language and to give them the tools to critically negotiate, resist, and interrogate the historical legacies of hate speech and the violence of representation. Finally, the way to ensure students' physical safety and freedom of critical inquiry is to endorse regulations that deter discriminatory conduct and recognize the perlocutionary functions of speech.

## Students Speak Out:
### The Pedagogical Implications of Personal Testimony

"I am a person of color and I am threatened on this campus."
"I am Asian American. I do not have the privilege of ignoring this. I am threatened."
"I am a black woman of color and a senior here and I feel very threatened."

These statements are transcripts of students' oral testimonies presented at Oberlin College during a speak-out held after graffiti appeared on the Memorial Arch and crosses were burned in front of a student co-op. More than six hundred students gathered in the evening in a dormitory dining room to exchange views about the racist incidents and the administration's handling of events and to explore ways people could work together toward institutional change. Few professors and administrators attended. Some students talked about the need for a hate-crime policy and for greater institutional support of students of color and of the Office of Multicultural Affairs. But most related personal experiences as political testimony. Their accounts reminded the community that the recent incidents occurred in a historical context of institutional racism; many students, particularly students of color, used the speak-out to make the hidden transcript public.

After several students of color had testified to feeling threatened on campus, a white male student stood up and said:

> This is not just about race. This is not just about color. This is about how people look at one another. . . . a lot of people look at one another through a very cloudy filter that shows only their skin colors: we look at each other as black, white, Asian, Latino. My filters are clean. I look at each person as individuals and see them as who they really are.

Putting forth the idea that all human beings are essentially the same, he was attempting to erase identity categories. According to him, it would be racist not to act in a color-blind fashion.

Insofar as students' testimonies gloss over differences within a racially defined group, they are essentialist. But essentialism practiced from a place of resistance is not equivalent to essentialism practiced by dominant groups. Whereas the self-gagged white male student positioned himself as representative of the victimization of white males, students of color used essentialist tactics to reveal racist practices. The particularity of their testimonials exposed the falseness of the neutralizing rhetoric of the administration and others in dominant positions. Later that evening, an Asian-Indian male student invoked the dominant discourse of essentialist racism (the view that natives of Africa, Asia, and the Americas are biologically inferior) to show how it could be used against whites. "The only people who have been threatened and harassed this past week have been white," he said. "What kind of animal do you think this white person is?" he asked, to a chorus of hisses. This student used the language of the colonizers to write the discourse of reverse racism.

The color-blind rhetoric of the administration and the reverse-racism standpoint expressed by the self-gagged student both contrast with calls for white students to recognize their privilege and to work toward institutional change. An African-American female at the speak-out exclaimed, "It's time that your white comfort be threatened. It's time that your class privilege (whatever color it is) be threatened. It's time that your apathy and inaction be threatened." Then a white female student approached the microphone and urged listeners to consider the inadequacy of essentialist analyses of white power and privilege.

> I am a white student and I feel threatened on this campus. . . . [The] hate towards white people [is] just as frightening and abhorrent as the words written on the arch against Asians. . . . I am a descendant of one of the few survivors in my family who had not been tortured, or tortured and murdered, robbed or degraded, or been the recipient of one of the horrors of the sadistic mind conjured during the persistent elimination of the Jews during World War II. Yet, a generation later, I still bear the insults: a swastika being painted on my house, of having my mailbox blown up, as well as having the windows of my house smashed in on a regular basis. I am certainly not a stranger to the hurt and anger that comes along with anti-Semitism, and I am personally involved in searching for a place which will lead to all forms of future human harmony.

Her articulation of cultural identity suggested that the dominant class views her as an outsider at the borders of whiteness (Frankenberg, 230). She had pointed out the limitations of a black-and-white analysis of cultural marginalization now and historically.

Students spoke for two hours. Although it might be argued that their personal testimonies overshadowed their analysis of social inequalities, the public staging and their repetition of identity positions had an important pedagogical impact on the community. Student use of personal testimonies challenged and made visible the unacknowledged positions of dominant groups. In contrast to the president's "I," which spoke on behalf of a presumed collectivity, the "I" of the student testimonials expressed social affinities and recognized its outsider status among privileged discourses (Nichols, 183). Much as the graffiti presumed a witness, the amplifying resonance of testifying turned both speakers and listeners into witnesses: speakers witnessed themselves and their position in the academy, and listeners witnessed the speakers' witnessing. The word *testimony* derives from the Latin *testi* (witness). As Young points out, "To testify is literally 'to make witness'—an etymological reminder that as witness and testimony are made, so is knowledge" (1988, 19). The graffiti incident and the speak-out taught students the power of language to shape action. Their testimonials, many of which functioned in strategically essentialist ways, a creation of the contact zone, connected autobiography with political resistance (Pratt, 35).[7]

## Linking the Classroom and Community
## through a Pedagogy of Witnessing

The politics of language and identity highlighted in my analysis of the fall 1993 events on the Oberlin campus yields a range of pedagogical discourses. The color-blind and power-concealing rhetoric that the president and self-gagged white male student adopted (e.g., "We are all the same blood") translates into writing pedagogies and literacy projects that do not recognize power imbalances in communities and writing cultures. Pedagogies that conceptualize difference only as a matter of individual choice are based on the principles of cultural assimilation and personal responsibility, both of which are basic tenets of classical liberalism.[8] Standpoints that ignore inequality can translate into far more conservative practices that regulate the curriculum through corrective measures and domesticate historically oppressed groups by constructing pedagogies of language control, standardization, and normalization.[9] For example, instead of grappling with the increasing cultural and linguistic diversity on our nation's campuses, the new right has called for a return to the "great books" of Western civilization and the establishment of a common culture (A. Bloom, H. Bloom, E. D. Hirsch). Many multicultural writing pedagogies say that their objective is to integrate the works of groups historically oppressed, but many reproduce the status quo, simply adding more voices to the curriculum while preserving the language and values of the dominant group. Similar patterns characterize early feminist pedagogies of writing, especially those that tried to validate women's experiences but ignored intersections of gender, race, class, sexuality, and national identity. Educators who seek to develop antisexist and antiracist pedagogies must reflect on the experiences and languages of traditionally oppressed groups and bear witness to the ways particular social constructions of differences shape reader-writer and student-teacher relations. I urge critical educators and feminists to develop activism-oriented pedagogies that recognize the intersections of social differences and the links between classroom and community rhetorics and that locate teachers and students at those intersections as cultural agents who negotiate power and extend and revise the practices of democracy. Teachers and students need to better understand how institutions function so they can be more active in the history and transformation of those institutions. Moreover, they must recognize how power and resistance are historically and discursively constructed at the crossroads of social differences and must use this knowledge to develop more critically reflective and democratic learning communities.

During and immediately after the arch incident and the cross burnings, many students said they had lost precious study time and experienced severe emotional stress. I invited students in my two introductory writing courses—Gender, Race, and Language and Basic Composition—to integrate their experiences into their course work. I encouraged them to examine how different theories of race, gender, and ethnicity and contesting narratives of community shaped the campus debates over free speech, hate speech, and institutional racism. I wanted to create a pedagogy that framed the classroom and the campus as places of learning and rhetorical analysis, as places that made them reflect on their assumptions and positions in the community. To enlarge, as Henry Giroux puts it, on "the range of cultural significations that can be taken up as classroom texts" (1994a, 119), I had my students examine campus events as textual and material phenomena. They clipped articles, letters, and editorials from campus publications and listened to tapes of the speak-out and forums. Some students worked with Mary Louise Pratt's essay "Arts of the Contact Zone" to investigate the contesting rhetorics and power relations enacted in those spaces. Ruth Frankenberg's *White Women, Race Matters: The Social Construction of Whiteness* was particularly useful in getting my white students to move beyond guilt and toward an understanding of whiteness that acknowledged ethnic differences, historical privileges, or struggles and achievement.

One of the difficulties I encountered was white defensiveness expressed by students in both oral and written exchanges. Leslie Roman defines white defensiveness as "the relativistic assertion that whites, like 'people of color,' are history's oppressed subjects of racism" (71). One student—I'll call him Stan—in my introductory writing class that semester said during a class discussion that he felt he was a victim of reverse racism, excluded and unfairly positioned by students of color as the white male enemy.[10] Stan decided to write an essay about this experience and share an early draft of his paper, "White Middle-Class Heterosexual and Republican Good-for-Nothing Male," with the class, which included only one other white male but a range of other cultural backgrounds—African-American, Asian-American, Latin American, Indian, and Afghan. In his first draft, Stan wrote, "White heterosexual males have a unique burden, to carry the shame of their descendants." He said he felt "completely shunned out and alienated" during the rallies on campus and was "enraged" over the meeting designed specifically for students of color.

During a class workshop, students raised questions that further antagonized Stan. An Asian-American woman asked him what he had done to prove that he wasn't a stereotypical white male. I tried to guide the class to move beyond personal criticism and look more closely at the principles and experiences informing Stan's position, to use the conceptual frameworks I had introduced earlier in the course. We discussed Stan's conflation of ethnic identity with race, a position that denies his whiteness. Pertinent to this discussion are personal psychological issues that informed Stan's observations about race and that triggered feelings of alienation. For instance, Stan writes about his experiences as an adopted child with no knowledge of his own cultural heritage: "I have no history and thus feel alienated when it comes to race." After class, Stan told me that his classmates had convinced him that his argument was weak and his claims unsubstantiated, but he seemed even more defensive. I realized that his defensiveness might increase along with his awareness. I suggested that he talk with other students about their perceptions of or experiences as white men at Oberlin. The problem, as I saw it, was that Stan had essentialized himself as the enemy and assumed the passivity of a victim. My objective was to get him to examine his defensiveness and also to realize that he was generalizing the white male experience. Stan seized the pedagogical opportunity and decided to interview other male students at Oberlin about their responses to the recent debates and racist incidents on campus and to revise his paper, now titled "Perceptions of the White Heterosexual Male at Oberlin College." Thus, what started as a paper in which the student claimed authority through self-denigration and humor was recoded in more standard academic terms. After Stan interviewed twenty or so students, seven of whom he identified as white heterosexual males, his conception of the white male community seemed to harden. One white male interviewee claimed that people at Oberlin expected him to be ashamed of who he was. According to this student, whom I'll call Ben, "Somehow, it was my responsibility to constantly feel apologetic for the foolishness of long since dead whites and the racist whites found throughout the world." Ben's testimony led Stan to conclude that such "outside pressure" was responsible and that it justified Ben's indifference to the plight of minorities. The biological frame-up that Stan responds to is one that imposes a condensed historicity of privilege onto the white male body.

Stan's analysis of the evidence he gathered was not consistent and reflects, I believe, his own process of identity negotiation. He reported that a gay black student, whom I'll call Derek, felt that "we are all subject to the society that the white heterosexual male has created—a society in which white heterosexual males are privileged because of their race, sexuality, and gender." After providing examples of what Derek called the "destructiveness" of white heterosexual males, Stan made the following statement: Derek "doesn't believe we should blame individuals. He believes in educating individuals. . . . He doesn't believe in revenge or oppressing the white male. I agree, but he is still making negative generalizations of the white male as the greedy oppressor." Stan seems to agree with Derek's call for the education of individuals, yet he characterizes Derek's historical grouping of white men as unfair. The identity narrative that emerged was one of blame and responsibility. Stan focuses more on the individual, and Derek seems to want to look at the larger picture.

I pointed out to Stan the gaps between Derek's concept of oppression and Stan's understanding of race. By focusing Stan's attention on his own narrative of whiteness, I hoped to enable him to move beyond the essentialist discourse of reverse racism and to recognize the historical inaccuracy of equating twentieth-century white male students' experiences of alienation with the silences imposed on historically oppressed groups. It was not my intention to invalidate Stan's feeling of alienation, but it was my pedagogical responsibility to encourage him to situate his claim of victimization within a historical framework. I wanted Stan and other students in the class to bear witness to the particularity of their struggles, privileges, and agency and to investigate historical events and experiences that may be dissonant cognitively and culturally. In hindsight, I can now see that Stan's sense of his fractured "insider" identity as an adopted child may have enabled him to question and witness his own racial constructs.

A pedagogy of witnessing can help develop students' abilities to interrogate those neutral legal principles and conceptualizations of the academy as a neutral zone and to see how identities and power are negotiated through speech acts. A writing course with that pedagogy can prepare students to respond to situations of conflict when they arise on campus and can shape and inform student activism. Instead of reducing institutional practices of racism, classism, heterosexism, and sexism to mere textual representations to deconstruct, I invite students to investigate language and its relation to the material realities and systemic patterns of subordination. A pedagogy of witnessing strives for both critical reflection and action; it works against "cultural monumentalism" (Giroux 1994a, 151) and calls for an interrogation of the past and the present as living history (Giroux 1994b, 340). As critical educators, we must both examine our histories and their legitimatization by institutions and enable our students to link historical memory with critical consciousness.

The challenge for faculty members is to recognize forms of institutional racism, sexism, ethnocentrism, and heterosexism at work in their classes and curricula. But curricular interrogation and revision alone cannot transform power relations and inequities in the academy; we must also reinforce pedagogical changes with institutional reforms that give groups full participation in the re-creation of democracy. The challenge for teachers and administrators is to look at hate crimes as part of a historical totality, to educate students about injurious and insurrectionary uses of language, and to provide oppor-tunities to break away from binary models of difference (black-white, male-female) that ignore the complexity of racial and gender politics in America and to use policy to liberate, not dominate or censor. And we must recognize when the categories of equality and free speech collapse. We must draw "links between movements for social justice and our pedagogical and scholarly en-deavors and [we must] expect and [demand] action from ourselves, our col-leagues, and our students at numerous levels" (Mohanty 1994, 62). What is at stake is not simply a struggle over words in the contact zone of the academy but also a struggle over a range of institutional practices and social relations.

5

THE RISKS OF AUTOBIOGRAPHY:

IDENTITY POLITICS, SEXUAL-OFFENSE

POLICIES, AND THE RHETORIC OF RIGHTS

"We're Gonna CRASH Your Policy" (October 1991); "Sexual Offense Policy Will Be Tabled Again" (September 4, 1992); "College Faculty Torn Over New Sexual Offense Policy" (September 18, 1992);" Faculty Amends Proposed Sexual Offense Policy" (December 4, 1992); "Sexual Offense Policy Called Inadequate" (March 12, 1993); "New Sexual Offense Proposal to Be Presented" (April 9, 1993); "GF Approves Sexual Offense Legislation" (May 13, 1993); "Sexual Offense Issues Consume Campus" (May 28, 1993). These headlines only hint at the level of intensity with which the Oberlin College community pursued the process of revising the college's sexual-offense policy. After countless general faculty meetings and with the help and hard work of an ad hoc committee formed in 1991 and persistent student and faculty lobbying, the general faculty adopted a revised policy in the spring of 1993.

Oberlin College's history of faculty governance presumes that policies concerning faculty and students (which have implications for administrators and staff) will be debated on the floor of the general faculty. The initial draft of the sexual offense policy that came to Oberlin's general faculty, which includes faculty from the College of Arts and Sciences and the Conservatory of Music, had a long history. In November 1990, students formed the Coalition against Rape, Sexual Assault, and Sexual Harassment (CRASH) in response to what they perceived as flaws in the college's 1982 policy. One of the problems they sought to remedy was the discrepancy between the number of sexual offenses reported and those that allegedly occurred but remained unreported.[1] Many students and faculty wanted to revise the policy so it would address the gender and power dynamics inherent in sexual offenses, create a centralized network and grievance procedure that would be more accessible for victims/survivors to work through, and add provisions for a more comprehensive educational program. One of the most critical changes that CRASH sought concerned the language of the policy and the absence of attention to questions of power and interlocking oppressions based on race, gender, and sexuality (Redick and Harris, 6). The administration, on the other hand, supported a revised policy in order to protect the college from lawsuits, a very different agenda from the more pedagogical and equity-framed needs expressed by many faculty and students, who wanted a policy that helped ensure safe learning environments. In other words, the administration positioned the institution as vulnerable and in need of protection from individuals, while policy supporters positioned it as responsible for the safety and protection of individuals.

As the sexual-offense debates demonstrate, general faculty meetings and, more specifically, policy making can be viewed as sites of learning, pedagogical contact zones defined by unequal power relations wherein competing autobiographical scripts and discourses collide. For instance, institutional narratives of identity (discourses of inequality, of individual freedom and liberty, of the law and the juridical person) are reproduced through disciplinary and bureaucratic processes, as well as through individual acts of self-representation. My goal in this chapter is not to provide a historical account of the sexual-offense policy at Oberlin College or to discuss the effectiveness of the policy or its implementation; it is, rather, to describe how autobiography and identity-based discourses became a site of struggle in the debates over the sexual-offense policy among the faculty. Autobiography is not an unequivocally empowering medium, but it does have the pedagogical potential of initiating critical reflexivity about self-positioning. Bureaucratic liberalism and individualism can, however, undermine its transformative potential. In the debates over the sexual-offense policy among the general faculty, autobiography becomes naturalized in the discourse of individual liberties and the law. Because the discourse of rights historically has privileged certain identities over others, it could be said to function as a kind of tacit autobiography. The autobiographical elements of the discourse of rights are compounded in a small rural liberal-arts college like Oberlin, where most discourse is heard as autobiographical, and identity-positions often become solidified; the community as a whole often recognizes particular experiences about which someone speaks.

Moreover, the institution imposes certain narratives of identity and "structures of legible subjectivity" (Smith and Watson 1996, 11). Within the context of general faculty meetings, which are conducted according to parliamentary procedure and usually chaired by the dean of Arts and Sciences, certain subject-positions are mapped out and discourses institutionalized.[2] While the aims of parliamentary procedures presumably are identical to the aims of democracy, based on equality of opportunity and majority rule, these procedures reinforce white male privilege and a paradigm of impersonal abstraction and hierarchy and prioritize a legalistic framing of issues. In contexts such as general faculty meetings, where certain groups are better represented than others and individuals are differently ranked, parliamentary procedures do not ensure that all individuals are equally free to participate or that all groups are equally represented. Parliamentary rules ignore how power differentials hinder speech. In a context where power is unevenly distributed, autobiography is used in ways that resecure rather than challenge existing power relations. Moreover, institutional needs (which themselves shift depending upon who defines them) promote certain readings of autobiographical acts and make certain subject-positions available. For example, most participants adopt ready-made communicative templates so that their speech fits the discursive framework of the imposed system. Parliamentary procedures dictate what kinds of exchanges are permissible and what kinds of stories will be heard.

The political stakes involved in unmasking how autobiographical discourse shapes policy debates and how certain narratives of identity are read in academia are significant. Most importantly, exposing these patterns may reveal how institutional and bureaucratic narratives of identity overpower what might be radically different perspectives. Defined by political and institutional struggles over representation, general faculty meetings provide a window through which we can see how identity-based discourses affect political and institutional subjection. The value and urgency in investigating the dynamics of autobiography in this pedagogical site are that they expose the authorized and authenticated discourses and realist strategies through which people negotiate contesting identities and claims to power, discursive and material.

Debates about sexual harassment and sexual assault on American campuses focus on the establishment of the "Real." People on all sides of the debates—lawyers, administrators, students, faculty—fight for the terrain of the "real," and they do so in the languages of autobiography and the law. What at first may seem to be oppositional discourses—namely, the languages of law (which typically draws its authority by abstracting the experiential) and of autobiography (which draws its authority by articulating the particularities of experience)—are actually both concerned with clarifying and establishing the "real." In the previous chapter, I focused on the academy as a social terrain where conflicts over the historical "real" occurred in debates about commemorative practices. Here, I consider whose stories are authorized as "real" or rendered authentic and how debates over the "real" intensified as power inequities became increasingly exposed through discussions about the sexual-offense policy. I examine how those in structural positions of power reconstruct dominant narratives about identity through the universalizing rhetoric of the law and particular uses of autobiography within public argumentation that recast those in power as victims. Implicit in the inverted victim narrative is the realization that behavior once permissible may now be considered harassment. This case study of the discursive process of revising the college's sexual-offense policy illustrates how identity-based discourses are "shot through with politics, with varying assumptions about power, privilege, and legitimacy" (Bernstein, 122). I use the case study of debates on the floor of the general faculty to engage the problematic conflation of autobiographical discourse with the "real" and uncritical endorsements of the genre as an empowering medium in order to articulate the risks of autobiography and reimagine its transformative and pedagogical potential in feminist politics and pedagogy in the academy. My critique should not be seen as a call for eliminating faculty governance but as an effort to further democratize governance. Given the current climate of faculty downsizing, efforts to eliminate faculty tenure, and so on, faculty participation in governance remains crucial.

## Autobiographical Scripts: Individual Rights and the Language of Consent

The general faculty meetings featured both tacit and explicit autobiographical scripts. Tacit autobiographical scripts are those acts of disclosure that are not presented as autobiography but that nevertheless privilege the social position and location of the speaker. In debates among general faculty, tacit uses of autobiography were disguised through the rhetoric of individual rights (particularly the rights of the accused) and through filibustering tactics that reinforced the positions of those in power. Explicit autobiographical scripts were often concealed in pedagogical arguments. These two scripts are interdependent and often reinforce each other. For example, in discussions of the consensual-relations clause of the policy, the prohibition of student-teacher relationships invited both tacit and explicit disclosures from several male faculty members; autobiographical disclosures referred back to the discourse of individual rights and privacy.

Discussions about the sexual-offense policy at the general faculty meetings were overwhelmed with legalistic questions and the discourse of rights, particularly faculty rights and the need for protection from unfair accusations.

Larger issues about community ethos and educational responsibilities were camouflaged by both tacit and explicit uses of autobiography by those in positions of power. Tacit uses of autobiography include utterances that are presumably not about the self but that privilege certain identities over others. More precisely, some of the most powerful members of the community— namely, tenured white men—focused on the "biased" nature of the policy and its procedures and on what they saw as its failure to secure fully the rights of the accused. The thrust of their argument was the fear of false testimony. These men shifted the discussion from gender inequality to individual freedom and liberty. They frequently positioned the law as a universal and objective system, whose neutrality is not considered an expression of gendered, racial, or class interests. Although the law often attempts to position itself "outside the social body," it nevertheless regulates the body and reflects certain values about gender, race, class, and sexuality (Smart, 12).[3] The illusory nature of this presumed neutrality became obvious as the general faculty meetings continued.

There are numerous reasons why legal discourse and digressions became ascendant, not the least of which are parliamentary procedures themselves, which prohibited discussion of larger issues unless the faculty suspended parliamentary process and opened the discussion up to the entire community. There were at least two other reasons why legal discourse impeded the progress of the meetings. First, the college's lawyers had warned the higher administration that it needed a revised sexual-offense policy to protect the college against lawsuits. Despite this charge, the administrators did not show strong leadership on this issue, and their vacillation facilitated the digressions and stalling tactics of a group of senior male faculty. Second, some faculty simply used the tradition of faculty governance at Oberlin to forestall passage of the policy and to show faculty power during the waning days of the administration.

The filibustering tactics functioned as a kind of tacit autobiography, because they enabled a particular group of senior male faculty to focus solely on individual rights. Autobiographical scripts were sometimes cloaked in pedagogical arguments. For instance, a senior white male explicitly talked about how the policy would affect his "aggressive and confrontational" teaching style; this disclosure reveals a lack of awareness of coercive power in the teaching profession. The fear articulated here is about the conflation of authoritarian teaching styles with sexual harassment. Despite my own disapproval of authoritarian pedagogies, the need to retain academic freedom is crucial, which is precisely why the policy contends that the creation of an unreasonably hostile, offensive, or intimidating environment needs to be proven in order for a claim of sexual harassment to hold any legal ground. Those in positions of power used pedagogical arguments and tacit and explicit auto-biographical scripts to shift the focus from a discussion of historical and insti-tutional inequalities and the need for safe learning spaces to one of faculty privileges and rights. These patterns were most obvious in discussions about the consensual-relations clause in the sexual-offense policy, which prohibited "consensual relations among faculty and the students they supervise and among supervisors and the employees they oversee" (Tryzelaar 1993b, 11). One implicit message of the consensual-relations clause is that "we can't change society, we can only change ourselves." In these meetings opposing re-sponses to the consensual-relations clause stayed at the level of interpersonal relations. Positions that politicized the personal were marginalized. And an-other kind of presumably depoliticized autobiography emerged, one predi-cated on a discourse of rights, privacy, and unacknowledged institutional power.

In one meeting, a visiting assistant professor in his early thirties disclosed that during the previous semester he had dated a female student three years his junior. "Does the college think this was unwise?" he asked the general fac-ulty (Tryzelaar 1993b, 11). Not only did his testimony ignore power differ-ences in the teacher-student relationship but it also obscured the hierarchy of gender in the academy. Although he was, in fact, not dating a "traditional" student (the woman was director of a special-program dormitory and was sit-ting in on this professor's class), from his privileged position as a white male (albeit junior faculty), the professor implied that, because the woman was older than most undergraduates, power differences were negated. The impli-cation here is that age is an equalizer. While this disclosure revealed just how gendered the discourse of autobiography is in this context, most people I spoke with didn't interpret this act as emblematic of larger gender inequities or discursive patterns; rather, they isolated or dismissed the disclosure as evi-dence of this person's foolishness or ignorance of parliamentary protocol. The relationship may, in fact, have been consensual, but the tendency to read this autobiographical script as *foolishness* ignores the potential power relations at play and the gendered dynamics of the pedagogical situation.

Following this particular disclosure, a white male member of the admin-istrative and professional staff of the general faculty [A&PS] reportedly said, "It's been my experience that students perceive faculty . . . to be in some posi-tion of power over them . . . what is perceived [by] a faculty member to be a straightforward approach . . . [might be] perceived [by students as] harass-ment" (Tryzelaar 1993b, 11). What this A&PS member realized (and the visit-ing assistant professor ignored) was the potential confusion of the consent/nonconsent binary. Carol Smart, in *Feminism and the Power of Law*, argues that the consent/nonconsent dyad does not account for the "complexities of a woman's position when she is being sexually propositioned or abused. . . . A woman may agree to a certain amount of intimacy, but not to sexual intercourse. . . . Having submitted, but failing to meet the legal criterion of nonconsent, women are deemed to have consented to their violation" (34). Additionally, women submit (in ways that may appear to some men as consent) because of fear of violence, of losing their job, or of failing a course. In other words, submission can be confused with consent. Although the inclusion of the consensual-relations clause within the context of the sexual-offense policy implies that such relations are imbued with power, the legal language of consent can disguise how much certain sexual behavior sanctions domination. To focus solely on whether or not a woman consented to a sexual relationship is to minimize the extent to which power defines consent (see Diamond and Quinby). The consensual relations clause became the flash point in discussions among the general faculty because it was most explicit about how power affects the most intimate and seemingly benign relations.

Those who opposed the consensual-relations clause claimed that the institution was replacing more private mechanisms such as self-regulation, good judgment, and a sense of values with public policy, and protested that the clause conflated the public and private realms. One problem with this perspective is that it denies institutional power inequalities and isolates individuals from their social contexts. Several older white men expressed their concept of privacy through a neoconservative rhetoric that implied that individuals must be protected from regulation. A white female professor said in a private interview, "I remember someone saying that this is going to infringe on my First Amendment rights. What First Amendment rights—to fuck students?" The privacy-rights argument was used to reify the notion of universal rights, an argument that functions as tacit autobiography in that it does not recognize the rights of certain groups are significantly restricted in this society.

A white male professor saw the consensual-relations clause as manifesting a puritan desire for punishment. He argued that, by regulating this behavior, the institution eroticized the act and consequently would produce a desire to break that law; in other words, by prohibiting consensual relations, the policy would generate more of them. According to a white male associate professor who supported the policy, one reason why so many men opposed the consensual-relations code was because they felt it "would create the occasion of harassment where it would never have existed previously." He continued:

> The men who were opposed to the clause have this purified idea about what the student-teacher relationship is. There is this attitude that

anything I do is just for educational purposes. There was also the sense that this policy opened up questions about their whole career and their whole understanding of what they were doing in the classroom. This, for instance, was very much the situation of one of our senior male faculty who was simply unable to accept that sexuality could in any way at all have entered into his interactions with students.

In another instance, a senior white male professor claimed that sexual harassment occurs only in the workplace, not in the academy. "The academic situation is different from the workplace," he said. "Professors do not put up pornographic pictures in their offices" (quoted in Tryzelaar, 1993a). By diverting attention from women's historical oppression and institutionalized sexism, this autobiographical script portrays professors as innocent, asexual beings. It perpetuates an image of the academy as a haven of "pastoral innocence, and of its highly cognitive and theoretical workers—seemingly 'disinterested' intellectuals" (Blair et al., 385).

What this statement ignores is the history of sexual harassment in the academy, not to mention the long history of consensual relations between students and professors at the college. In fact, one of the latent subtexts in discussions about the consensual-relations clause among the general faculty was the knowledge of faculty whose spouses or partners were at one point students at the college. A feminist administrator who avidly supported the inclusion of the consensual-relations clause expressed to me in a private interview that she had attempted to persuade those who objected to contextualize these relations historically. Here is her account:

> What was acceptable ten, fifteen, twenty years ago reads quite differently now, and that's a very hard thing to say to people who have dated students, who have married students . . . to say, look, the situation in which your courtship and marriage took place fifteen or twenty years ago was not charged in the same way with relations of power, hierarchy, and sexuality in the way it would be today. . . . We are not trying to tell you, you had a false experience; rather, that this is how we as a community should think about how we want to set our standards now. . . . We are not asking you to relive your life, but to evaluate where you want to go.

While a certain level of historical relativism is inescapable because relations are context specific, this reading of sexuality and history tends to gloss over the institutional power differences that may have defined some of these relationships. Nevertheless, highlighted here is the acute perception that the academy is undergoing significant changes with regard to understandings of sexuality and power. Clearly, consensual-relations codes have unsettled established codes of conduct in academe and elicited new autobiographical scripts and new forms of self-disclosure, which, despite narrative similarities, can be used to mobilize contrary political and pedagogical agendas.

Jane Gallop's recent book, *Feminist Accused of Sexual Harassment,* is a vivid example of the new politics of disclosure prompted by consensual-relations codes under the more general rubric of sexual-offense policies. In 1992, Gallop was accused of sexual harassment by two female graduate students at the University of Wisconsin. The university did not find Gallop guilty of discrimination, but it did find that she had violated the university's policy, labeling her behavior toward one of the two students as "consensual amorous relations." Gallop found herself in a contradictory position—a feminist accused of sexual harassment—and she regrets that antiharassment laws, largely a creation of the women's movement, are being used against feminists. Gallop thus nostalgically longs for a time when the intellectual and sexual were blurred, when learning and pleasure presumably were at the root of what it meant to be a feminist in the academy, when teaching was not separate from eros. Gallop's pedagogical stance is resonant with public positions articulated by a number of male faculty in the 1990s, who claimed that sexual relations with their female students were formative educational experiences for the women; these disclosures often were accompanied by autobiographical scripts of female students as hysterical and uncontrollable seductresses (see "New Rules About Sex on Campus," *Harpers* 1993, 33–42). For Gallop, there is an experiential link between feminist empowerment and consensual relations, which depends on a binary between power and sexuality that implies that feminist empowerment is not also predicated on feminist power. Although Gallop expresses that she no longer has affairs with her students, she looks back fondly on these liaisons, as she does on her own affairs with professors, as transformative pedagogical experiences.

I agree with Gallop that codes that presume that consensual relations are automatically discriminatory rewrite sexual-harassment policy as a crime of sexuality. However, I find it professionally unethical (though perhaps not illegal) for teachers to enable intellectual and sexual tensions to be articulated through sexual relations with their students, particularly when the student is in a structurally vulnerable position (e.g., the teacher has the power to evaluate, grade, and so on). First, it is precisely because feminists are in positions of authority that they should be held accountable for abuses of power when and if such abuses occur. Second, to claim that consensual relations between students and teachers are a signature of feminist community, sexual liberation, and liberating feminist pedagogy resecures essentialized notions of identity and community that hark back to the privileged discourse of early white feminism. In sum, the nostalgia for a feminism *outside* of power and for a pedagogical past when power differences between students and teachers were ignored dismisses the potentially coercive use of this power and divorces pedagogical practices from professional ethics. While we certainly need more debate about the ethics of consensual relations between faculty and students and a moral understanding that the community can support, we must not conflate this moral understanding with juridical processes. In the climate of the late 1990s, when attacks against sexual-harassment policies are finding support even in the courts, it is imperative that institutions of higher education recognize situations in which power is articulated on behalf of certain subject-positions and that antidiscrimination cases are grounded in a materialist analysis.

## *The Politics of Self-Disclosure*

It's not like you are respected for disclosure . . . you "kissed and told". . . it's like you're supposed to keep a dirty little secret and we haven't gotten past that. It's only after an incredibly long period that women can come forward and disclose. There are only a small minority of women at the top of the hierarchy in stable positions who can talk, who can afford the discourse of autobiography. The risk is even greater for those in less stable positions, for example, those who aren't tenured. (black female administrator)

For my generation and I think for the women older than I there seemed to be this unspoken assumption that women were somehow weaker or more easily victimized . . . it felt like if we talked about the crap we'd been through, we would be putting ourselves in the victim role. Maybe that was too much allowing the continuation of the public rhetoric around sexual harassment to take over . . . I felt like I wouldn't be able to control how people saw me after that. . . . Women are always seen as making things personal and incapable of making institutional decisions, or seeing things other than their own experiences. (white female faculty member)

These excerpts from private taped interviews with women at Oberlin College illustrate how gender, race, and class hierarchies shape public discourse in academia.[4] The first example emphasizes that the risks of disclosure are greater for women and others in structurally vulnerable positions. It also suggests that institutional procedures and protocol can reinforce certain silences; at Oberlin, for example, service workers and administrative staff, who are not also members of the faculty, do not participate in the larger public debates on the floor of the general faculty. A number of A & PS members stated that not bringing these various groups together to debate such issues in public forums reinforces the institutional and intellectual-class hierarchy. Another administrator of color concurred, saying that the process of revising the policy in the general faculty meetings "represented the epitome of the problems with faculty governance: as a system it reproduces some of the essential disabling hierarchies and elitism of the college. It [faculty governance] positions faculty at the top of the hierarchy, as the best, most informed, etc. . . . At Oberlin, decision making is done at the 'academic' level, and administrators and staff don't have real access to or voice within the governance system."[5] Although most of the people on the committee were, in fact, administrators and staff and the policy reportedly was presented to the A&PS Council before it was discussed on the floor of the general faculty, these expressions of exclusion highlight the prioritizing of faculty/student relations in public debates. (I should point out that the policy governs different groups in the college; however, the body that hears cases differs from group to group. Further, the two unions on campus have their own procedures for cases against another union member or administrator. Likewise, student co-ops have their own policy; a student in a co-op could bring charges under those procedures.)

The second quote focuses on the gendered presumptions governing social and institutional perceptions of autobiographical discourse—namely, its association with what is traditionally considered feminine. Many junior and senior women faculty with whom I spoke who had access to the meetings said they did not speak out because they feared they would be placed in the victim role or labeled as "deviant," "hysterical," or "evil man-hating feminists." These characterizations make the use of autobiography for women in public arenas in the academy even more risky and increase the likelihood of a biographical frame-up, the projection of an autobiographical script onto women. In other words, anything women say may get read as autobiographical.

Both the women quoted above highlight struggles over representation and how institutional practices represent and deploy power. A significant difference between their statements has to do with the subject-position and location of each. The first speaker addresses the issues of access and exclusion and how certain women's silences are structurally reinforced: "Our process is what shut me down. My silence has more to do with how the college is structured rather than the policy itself. The sexual-offense policy brought these aspects to the forefront." The second epigraph, on the other hand, demonstrates how women faculty, who have access, chose not to narrate the identities prescribed for them. Taken together, these excerpts illustrate how women with different positions in the academy are caught between social relations of power, representational practices, and autobiographical scripts.

Certain autobiographical scripts are projected onto those genders or races marked "other." Indeed, as these epigraphs suggest, dominant narratives of identity are mapped onto certain bodies and subject-positions. For instance, women (and people of color) need not expose their autobiography; the institution already projects its autobiographical scripts onto their visual selves. In the conclusion, I focus on the pedagogical scripts that the institution imposes on minority teachers; here, I want to concentrate on the projection of gendered and racialized autobiographical scripts onto women among the general faculty in policy debates, and examine women's internalization and negotiation of these scripts through particular discursive strategies, including silences. Although I consider silence a discourse of self-representation, I do not want to re-create a facile oppositional relationship between silence and self-disclosure. Silences can be a strategic form of resistance, but the inclusion of women's stories, disclosed in private interviews, to counter such silences also risks co-option. The risks of autobiography extend beyond the risks of speaking out in a dominant public space.

Countering institutional silences with women's disclosures does not necessarily challenge the expressionist notions of autobiography as a truth-telling, authenticating discourse; instead, it could very well reinforce uncritical uses of women's testimonies and gender essentialism. The temptation to read these disclosures as the "real" story is connected to the expressionist feminist approaches to autobiography discussed in previous chapters. Rather than reiterate my earlier critique of expressionism here, I will simply point out that expressionist uses of women's testimonies are implicated in the biographical frame-up and the politics of projecting an autobiographical script onto women. My intent is not to counter a presumably "false" masculine discourse with a "true" feminine one, but, rather, to use these disclosures to explore further the politics of self-representation in the academy and to examine how women's silences, the marginality of women of color, and the risks of autobiography are produced by institutional and bureaucratic individualism and reinforced by liberal feminist platforms. Both the epigraphs and my interviews provide an opportunity to consider the problematic of agency and to see how resistance in the academy is tied to the politics of self-representation.

The testimonies included in this chapter emerge from the collision of cultural narratives, which is why I urge readers to focus on the context of the disclosure and the relation between material conditions and the rhetorical occasion, and to concentrate on the institutional and personal consequences of certain identity narratives (inequality, exclusion, silence, and injury). Autobiographical acts of self-disclosure thus can be viewed as contact zones—as practices through which individuals negotiate conflicting identities and contradictory discourses. This view pushes us beyond merely identifying silences toward an understanding of the politics of self-disclosure and how, as an autobiographical act, self-disclosure reconfigures identity and agency by negotiating and sometimes appropriating institutionally sanctioned discourses. The two epigraphs do not give us the "real" story; rather, they reveal struggles over identity and representation itself.

Sexual-offense policies are designed to force those in power to confront the privilege of their autobiographical locations in ways never before demanded by the institution. For example, these policies ask faculty to examine how power is manifested in their actions toward students. As the faculty member quoted earlier pointed out, those with access to the public arenas of debate often suppress or abstract their personal experiences as a survival strategy; some women express a legitimate fear of dismissal or reprisals for speaking out—an example of the biographical frame-up.[6] A white administrator noted:

> Many women felt hurt, there was a sense of injury, about a lack of recognition that sexual harassment was something they had experienced, a kind of blindness about this . . . There was a group of people who were making the victims of sexual harassment to be those who might unjustly be accused of sexual harassment as opposed to those people who suffered from or at whom sexual harassment was targeted. There was this confusion about who were the real victims.

The narrative of victimization and injury conveyed in this excerpt also risks co-option. Invoking a claim of victim status offers us insight into power relations and the institutional invisibility of male power and its consequences. As the excerpt highlights, the claim itself is not neutral. People in positions of power often appropriate the discourse of victimization to secure their power. This is not to say that the discourse of victimization is futile as a strategy of resistance, but to point out that a claim of victimization does not insure legitimacy; it depends on who can speak and under what circumstances. Consider the following example.

As I mentioned earlier, at one meeting, after a senior white male faculty member argued that sexual harassment did not occur in the academy, a white female assistant professor complained that senior white men were controlling the discussion. "One of the things that strikes me [is] who's talking. How much harassment is involved [in] that?" she asked. "We don't seem to know much about sexual harassment. I have been at a department faculty meeting where [a member of the department] handed around a *Spy* magazine cover [with] Hillary Clinton in a red, white, and blue bustier" (Tryzelaar 1993a, 7).

The speaker risked a biographical frame-up by pointing out that gender harassment is embedded in the general faculty's communication rituals as well
as in its systematic distortion of harassment in the academy. Her autobiographical gesture could be interpreted as tactical resistance to the community's notion, defined by parliamentary rules, of what is speakable. One could
argue, for example, that she exposed the depoliticization of identity and erasure of power relations in the exchanges among the general faculty. By sharing
a personal observation, which implicated a senior colleague, she put herself in
a vulnerable position, taking a risk that this disclosure would be used against
her in the future. Although several junior women thanked her for speaking
out, a few senior women suggested she should not have spoken so candidly in
the meeting, claiming that such comments might further jeopardize her pre-
tenure position. When this faculty member made a claim of "realness," no
one listened to her or backed her up; her statement trailed off into silence and
was "reordered into the community's normative patterns of speakability"
(Smith and Watson 1996, 16).

I recall only one other time when a woman on the faculty, who was also
an administrator at the time, explicitly invoked the autobiographical in the
public meetings. Her statement was about the discrimination that women as
a group have endured, and here is how she recounted it.

> What was the point of taking this job if I couldn't speak out about the
> issues I really care about? While I've been told that Oberlin doesn't want
> its [administrators] to be too far out in front, I felt like this is a point at
> which I'm protected. I felt I could speak. I had a certain amount of in-
> stitutional position and power that I was willing to put on the line
> here . . . I felt what was important was to remind people of the experi-
> ences of a cohort of women that we had been touched by.

Several junior and senior women perceived this administrator as taking a
leadership role. Her persistent advocacy did "turn the tide at more than one
meeting," recalled a white female associate professor. However, her use of
autobiography in the excerpt quoted positioned autobiography within a liberal feminist discourse, which diminished its transgressive potential through
its strategic but nevertheless uncritical reliance on the hierarchy of institutional structures.

When I asked another senior white woman why she didn't invoke the
autobiographical at the meetings, she said she thought it would be both self-
defeating and agonizing. "Sexual harassment," she said, "is one of the most
painful experiences. All people want is to have it stop. By bringing it up in
public, you're bringing the specter of it up again." This woman voiced the fear

that autobiography will turn women into spectacles. "Weakness invites aggression," a senior white female administrator said. "There is this fear that we carry around, if I allow my vulnerability to be seen, rather than have my colleagues close ranks around me, which is really what you want, it is expressed as if you didn't know how to take care of yourself; that's the fear." Implicit here is the apprehension that those in positions of power will categorize anything women say as autobiographical and presumably private and that the statements of women who do speak autobiographically will be co-opted back into dominant discourse, such as the inverted victim-narrative.

Women have internalized the gendered scripts of institutional discourse, often with great pain. For example, a white associate professor said she feared that if she spoke about her own experiences of sexual harassment, she would probably get all flustered, her voice would tremble, and eventually she would break down. Another white female administrator characterized the process of working on the policy as painful. "It was personally frustrating . . . I was horrified at the level to which the discussion sank in the general faculty meetings and the level of bitterness. I would go home after those Tuesday faculty meetings and sob for an hour just to get it out of my system. For me, it was the first time I had been public in the general faculty about something, so it was really important for me to feel professional and in control and not to get shaken at all. I would just steel myself." "There's all this posturing, mostly male posturing," another white female administrator noted. "I feel like I'm walking into a boys' debating club, and it's as much about the rules and who makes the rules as it is about any kind of substance." The administrator recognized that the discourse was, in fact, gendered, but she also realized that "if it wasn't these rules then it would be something else." She continued, "The point here is that at least they are published someplace . . . if you get rid of the formal rules, then you are even more at the mercy of the informal rules. . . . To me, it's not a question of the rules themselves being unfair, but it's true most of us girls didn't grow up studying parliamentary procedure and the guys did, so we have a little remedial work to do in order to make [these rules] transparent."

Whether women need to challenge the institutional norms and disciplinary discourses or adapt to them is debatable, even among feminists. For example, the woman quoted above implies that all women need to do is learn to work better within the existing frameworks. Missing from this perspective, however, is the fact that the rules insure that larger social issues do not get explored. I contend that the frameworks themselves—the rules—need to be challenged and disrupted for fundamental change in the power structures to occur. The junior faculty women (most on temporary appointments) whom I interviewed were the most ambivalent about working with bureaucratic and disciplinary discourses of the institution. They criticized what they saw as the institutional co-option of feminist goals, and expressed concern over women's silences and how the institution defined antidiscrimination policies from a white male perspective. Although women may be exercising power in other contexts, such as on councils, in professional-conduct-review panels, and so on, women's silences on the floor of the general faculty, however strategic, reinforced traditional gender roles, such as polite deference to men in power. Silence can be a strategic form of self-representation, but it can also reinforce existing power relations; in various ways, it functions as a kind of tacit autobiography.

It was precisely because of the risk of a biographical frame-up, however, that some women opted to appropriate institutionally dominant discourses, such as statistical evidence and other realist strategies, to counter the privatization of sexual offenses in both explicit inversions of the victim narrative and tacit uses of autobiography by those in positions of power. In fact, several senior women achieved authority by talking about their experiences on mediating committees and in grievance proceedings within the college, pointing out which procedures seemed to work and which hindered the process. One senior woman, who was working on a sexual-offense policy for one of Oberlin's programs abroad, offered statistical evidence to counter claims made by opponents; by dealing with statistics, she felt she could stop the spiraling legalistic discussion. Statistical evidence enabled her to produce circumstances in which she could "speak out and sound like an expert." As she put it, "this strategy established her credibility."

The need to engage the debate in terms other than autobiography was echoed by a senior white professor, who emphatically stated during my interview with her that "testimony just ain't where it's at. It's not going to work in this public-political arena." She elaborated:

> [The] model of individual capability—well-being—full expressiveness . . . is not what concerns me; it is what policies are we getting through, how are we going to chip away at the administration. It's like old-style political questions. . . . I see the people I strategize with as allies, not as friends or personal support. I see it as political. But I really think my politics are of someone from an earlier generation [the 1960s]. My notion of what politics are and what it is for me to be a political activist comes out of principles and beliefs but not a sense of my own place and trying to widen that place or trying to make a place for myself, my group, my identity.

This professor is making a distinction between collective political action and identity politics (where one's politics are based on a sense of personal and social identity). As she suggests, identity politics has a significant influence on critical behavior in the academy. In recent years, there has been something of a stalemate between the emergent politics of identity (with its excessive particularization along the lines of race, ethnicity, sexuality, age, and gender) and an earlier feminist politics of collectivity (which, despite its imagined collectivity, was quite exclusionary). Debates over the virtues and vices of each position have preoccupied feminist politics for quite some time. The above excerpt illustrates that autobiography figures prominently in these debates and can, therefore, serve as a segue to a consideration of the larger theoretical questions about the role of autobiography in feminist politics prompted by these women's disclosures. More particularly, I will compare the politicized discourse of identity and conceptions of a collectivity in feminist theory, as each wrestles with or omits the politics of self-representation and problematics of experience. These distinctions have profound implications for how we understand the pedagogical dynamics of autobiography in the academy.

### "Testimony Just Ain't Where It's At"

More and more feminists are returning to earlier configurations of collectivity to counter the ineffective discourse of identity politics, which is often conflated with autobiography. Some feminists criticize identity politics on the grounds that it fractures alliances among people across differences, that it privileges identity and not politics, and that it gets readily co-opted back into the dominant institutional discourse of bourgeois liberalism. They see identity politics as an uncritical and nostalgic return to the early feminist principle that "the personal is political"; it is considered uncritical because it doesn't account for the exclusion and racism within early feminism (which prioritized the experiences of white middle-class women), and nostalgic because it is bound to regard women's voices and experiences as "truth." Some feminists argue that the return to women's experiences in feminist politics is a modernist reaction to postmodernism's deconstruction, disunification, and decentering of the subject and its denaturalization of identity. Wendy Brown, for example, claims, "Contrary to its insistence that it speaks in the name of the political, much feminist anti-postmodernism [positions that she and others associate with the work of Benhabib, Christian, Di Stefano, Hartstock, and Tompkins] betrays a preference for extrapolitical terms and practices: for Truth (unchanging, incontestable) over politics (flux, contest, instability) . . . for separable subjects armed with rights and identities over unwieldy and shifting pluralities" (37). Likewise, Linda Kauffman in "The Long Good-bye:

Against Personal Testimony, or an Infant Grifter Grows Up" argues that the pro-experience, anti-theory projects of feminists such as Tompkins and Christian conceive the purpose of feminism as the self-discovery of victimhood (267). Moreover, Kauffman questions the political efficacy of the desire for the integration of feeling/knowledge and emotional/abstract common to such work on the grounds that it "belie[s] a nostalgia for a clear, transparent language that never did exist" (268). As Brown puts it, "dispensing with the unified subject does not mean ceasing to be able to speak out our experiences as women, only that our words . . . cannot be anointed as 'authentic' or 'true' since the experience they announce is linguistically contained, socially constructed, discursively mediated, and never just individually 'had'" (40–41). While I don't deny that there is a residue of expressionism in some of these works, what Brown does not consider, and what Kauffman seems to dismiss altogether, is the potential transformative role of autobiography in feminist politics and pedagogy. Contrary to their efforts, Brown's and Kauffman's critiques actually offer strategies to imagine ways of recuperating autobiography's transformative potential.

Like Kauffman, I too find problematic feminist practices that are vulnerable to gender essentialism, idealize women's superior moral sense, discourage the investigation of complicating factors that weaken the stance of victimization (e.g., questions of complicity and collusion with institutions), and reinscribe in their expressionism uncritical notions of experience and authenticity. Kauffman does not, however, account for the ways her own critique participates in an essentializing process. She is critical of feminists who view autobiography as inherently or universally resistant, yet her essay creates the impression that autobiographical discourse, particularly personal narratives, is inherently or universally complicit. I find her analysis of the risks of autobiography and her call to challenge the boundaries of realism perceptive; but her outright rejection of autobiography in feminist politics is disheartening. Kauffman concludes her essay with this warning to feminists:

> Feminism is far more than the effort to "express" "women's personal experience," . . . By resisting the flattering temptation to talk solely to and about ourselves, we can concentrate on defying repressions that have already come to seem "normal.". . . The pace of contemporary events is like a speeding convertible; we can ill afford to be enchanted by the rearview mirror. Rather than mythologizing ourselves or the past, can't we total those disabled vehicles and—at long last—wave good-bye to all that?" (274–75).

But isn't it precisely *because* of the insatiable, relentless resilience of individualism that we need the rearview mirror to reveal how autobiography gets co-opted and to make visible the blind spots in our thinking?

Kauffman correctly contends that autobiography is not, by definition, a feminist mode. Nor, however, is it an inherently hegemonic discourse; it is simply used in ways that secure particular moral, social, and political projects. As Jana Sawicki wisely points out, "There are no inherently liberatory or repressive [narrative] practices, for any practice is co-optable and is capable of becoming a source of resistance" (quoted in Smith and Watson 1996, 17). Moreover, Kauffman glosses over some of the more nuanced aspects of the works she critiques. For example, while there is certainly residue of expressionism in Barbara Christian's essay "The Race for Theory," it seems to me that Christian is primarily concerned with how personal lives get appropriated and abstracted by theory. Kauffman argues that both Christian and Tompkins reify the binaries of theory/experience and male intellect/female intuition, yet she does not account totally for the extent to which autobiography is an arena of cultural struggle. How feminists negotiate these struggles and contradictions in the contact zones of the academy is the blind spot in each of these accounts—pro- and anti-autobiography.

Both Kauffman and Brown fail to acknowledge how certain autobiographical practices fracture notions of the unified self and the free-floating agent common to bourgeois individualism and liberalism.[7] This is not to romanticize these works, which may nevertheless be appropriated in criticism and pedagogy in ways that resecure uncritical notions of authenticity and truth. Thus, the transformative potential of autobiography need not involve a nostalgic return to modernist notions of the unified subject and authenticity. What is needed instead is an expanded sense of autobiography as a countergenre that negotiates asymmetrical power relations and participates in the transformation of the cultural production of identity, social relations, and historical memory. We must distinguish between counterautobiographical practices that expand generic boundaries and challenge uncritical notions of identity and authenticity and those that reify them. The challenge, as I see it, is not to move beyond identity, as in a developmental schema where identities are asserted and then abandoned in order presumably to move toward a politics of collectivity, but to release autobiography from the confines of liberalism, where it is mobilized in ways that reinforce individualism. Earlier, I quoted an Oberlin faculty member who characterized autobiography as representing "individual capability, well-being, and full expressiveness." Missing from this characterization is, in fact, the distinction between liberal notions of autobiography as an expression of individual identity and cultural materialist and resistance postmodernist notions of autobiography as the construction of social identities produced through historical relations, social practices, and systems of representation. But what can this reframing of auto-biography actually accomplish? Are these two stances mutually exclusive? Do autobiographical acts always risk being co-opted by institutionalized and bureaucratic narratives of identity?

The conflict between universal representation (politics of collectivity) and individualism (identity politics) is latent in liberalism. Feminist calls for a politics of collectivity often reinscribe the universal "we" that reiterates a de-politicized "I" (Brown, 56). In this sense, the push for politics of collectivity removed from the particularities of the autobiographical can slip into the dis-ciplinary power of liberalism and its neutralization of identity. Rather than seeing identity and politics as separate or as sequential—moving from one to the other—feminist politics should recognize that identities are not given but are constructed within and through politics. A critique of an essential identi-ty does not necessarily mean the rejection of any concept of identity whatso-ever (Mouffe, 381). Academic feminists and activists need to develop "an awareness of the *mediated* nature of all experience and of the ways that power differentials permeate these mediations" (Kruks, 7). Language and represen-tation are sites where power is contested and subjectivities constituted in so-cially specific ways.

One possible feminist response to the reactionary identity narratives (in-verted victim narrative) in debates over the sexual-offense policy at Oberlin College might have been to foreground the social practices and historical di-visions of labor in the academy that foster such identity narratives and enable sexual abuse. In principle, such a strategy would not necessitate the globaliza-tion or essentializing of women's positions but would allow for accounts from multiple standpoints. Those of us interested in building coalitions in the academy around this issue should consider how autobiographical perspec-tives and critical positions can be translated across a network of institutional, cultural, and personal connections and differences. Finally, we have to imag-ine how translations of experiences can be institutionally acted upon, not simply asserted. But how? And what difference will the articulation of differ-ences make?

## *What Difference Does Difference Make?*

In order to consider the progressive potential of autobiographical acts upon policy formation, we must first discover how the discourse of rights "frames" autobiography within particular institutional contexts. That is, we need to ask ourselves what the discourse of rights covers up and what will be the consequences of articulating the differences it hides. Perhaps an even more pressing question is: What impact will the deconstruction and denaturalization of the unified self and free-floating agent have on the discourse of rights? Rather than imagining how autobiography might have been used to disrupt the "rules of order" in the general faculty meetings at Oberlin College, I want to contemplate further the feminist translation of autobiography into identity-based rights, and consider the risks in repositioning autobiography within the confines of institutionally dominant narratives of identity as well as liberal feminism.

Catharine MacKinnon is perhaps the leading proponent of feminist jurisprudence, especially in the domain of sexual harassment and sexual assault. For MacKinnon, the object is to intervene and revise rights discourse so that it responds to, rather than masks, systematic gender subordination. She "seeks to make the law 'gender equal' . . . and 'gender sighted'" (Brown, 129). Her goals are to legalize "the capacity to recognize stratifying social power" (129), to expose gender inequalities obscured by abstract formulations of rights, and to remove the social obstacles that prevent women from claiming the rights they theoretically have. MacKinnon's work is frequently criticized as being vulnerable to gender essentialism. For instance, her inattention to the complexities of racial differences as they intersect with sexual offenses ignores how racial identities have figured in historical notions of sexual equality and how they have shaped legal practices.[8] A similar criticism could be made about sexual-offense policies in general. Gender is the formative subtext. The rhetoric of most sexual-offense policies does not reflect the full social web of identities or account for the very likely possibility that alleged victims will experience interpersonal and institutional sexism and racism through judicial procedures. The language of policy and the formation of grievance procedures do not sufficiently acknowledge or account for the ways race, gender, and sexual politics interact to promote a campus climate conducive to sexual and racial harassment and violence.

Many factors interact to foster an environment where sexual harassment and sexual assaults occur and to deter both white women and women of color from filing grievances.[9] Because men (mostly white men) control institutional resources and rewards and thus serve as the gatekeepers to future jobs and/or graduate school, women know that they may be revictimized by the system in other ways. In addition, the regulation of sexual offenses in the academy is often slow and cumbersome, and support systems are typically feminized (sex-segregated) and thus marginalized. Social stereotypes and myths about women also persist and help foster an opportunistic climate for sexual offenses. Assumptions about race make women of color even more vulnerable to sexual harassment and assault and to being revictimized during the grievance process. For example, women of color have been historically deprived of the respect that would enable men to see them as victims of sexual harassment or assault. Although sexual-offense policies are designed to assure individuals the right to a safe workplace, the traditional liberal focus on rights does not address the problems, risks, and institutional obstructions that hinder the ability of certain groups to claim such rights.[10] The discourse that characterized the debates at Oberlin College exemplifies this very problem. Omitted in the discussions on the floor of the general faculty were the ways in which gender, race, sexuality, and disability may be interlocking factors in sexual-harassment and sexual-assault cases. Additionally, because sexual-harassment and sexual-assault policies presume a compulsory heterosexuality, power relations within gay and lesbian communities were not brought into the public debate, although these discussions did occur in less public contexts, such as the Lesbian, Gay, and Bisexual Concerns Committee, and related concerns were integrated into the policy eventually. Oberlin's policy differs from that of other colleges because it acknowledges sexual orientation and how "outing" is enmeshed in a wider web of social inequities.[11] More particularly, making a person's sexual orientation known without his/her consent and with the intent to denigrate that person sexually can be considered an act of sexual harassment under the college policy. This definition of sexual harassment suggests that language can inflict injury, a position I endorse. However, in order for "outing" to be legally actionable as a form of harassment, concrete discriminatory effects must be shown. As I argued in the previous chapter in my discussion of the problematics of hate-speech codes, even those narrowly defined, we need to distinguish between the consequences and effects of speech acts and the idea that the speech act performs the injury itself (Butler 1997, 18). Although this language expresses the college's important commitment to creating an inclusive, tolerant, and civil campus climate, to code "outing" as a form of sexual harassment is to conflate speech with conduct, to presume that the speech act of "outing" performs the injury itself and that the disclosure of a "secret" functions according to the principles of extortion. I don't deny that "outing" can have serious consequences for individuals, but I suggest there is an inherent danger in conflating speech with conduct and the ethical with the legal realm. Indeed, one could argue that such codes reify the very sexual-identity categories that "outing" uses as the basis for a threat.

Presumably, one way to approach the problem of overlapping oppressions is to revise sexual-offense policies to extend their range of inclusion. Likewise, liberal feminists have attempted to address the problem of gender essentialism and universalistic legal perspectives by extending identity-based rights in relation to specifications of difference. Zillah Eisenstein, for example, in *The Coloring of Gender: Reimagining Democracy* proposes a notion of equality and rights that she identifies as radical liberalism and that rests on an understanding of both race and gender differences. Radical liberalism contrasts with both "old style" liberalism, which did not privilege lived differences or particularity, with what Eisenstein calls neoconservative revisionist liberalism, which focuses on universal rights and foregrounds the concept of liberty over equality (4). In order to reimagine democracy and reconstruct the discourse of rights, Eisenstein suggests that white women need "to be accountable to women of color" (199). I share Eisenstein's goal of being attentive to issues of race and the implication that sexual-offense policies must account for how race and gender oppressions interact in sexual offenses. But I am troubled by a feminist politics that simply adds on differences without sufficent attention to whiteness as a racial category. The title of Eisenstein's book—*The Coloring of Gender*—reflects this tendency to prioritize gender by superimposing race onto the white gendered body. Eisenstein does not acknowledge how the endorsement of the "racialized" experiences of women of color may, in fact, resecure the white/other binary that she seeks to unsettle.

Without disputing the importance of recognizing overlapping oppressions and the need for identity-based rights, especially in a backlash political climate, feminists should consider how rights discourse focuses our attention on an increase of protections that may reinscribe the very identity categories that have been used to oppress. Wendy Brown describes this phenomenon as the "paradox of rights discourse," and in *States of Injury,* she argues that political projects that focus on extending the range of rights mirror the configurations of identity and power they purport to oppose (3). Drawing on Foucault, she claims that "progressive efforts to pursue justice along lines of legal recognition of identity corroborate and abet rather than contest the 'political shape' of domination in our time" (28). Brown argues that identity-based rights are constrained by, and thus reinstall, the very terms and categories that have functioned as modalities of subordination or exclusion. While there are moments in history when rights have been the force of emancipation, such as the American civil-rights movement, identity-based rights function as regulatory practices and instruments of subordination when they disguise how hierarchical power relations stratify social positions and identities (120). According to Brown, social injury (sexual harassment, hate speech, etc.) becomes coded in rights discourse as something "which is 'unacceptable' and 'individually culpable' rather than that which symptomizes deep political distress in a culture; injury is thereby rendered intentional and individual, politics is reduced to punishment, and justice is equated with such punishment . . . and with protection" (27–28). The paradox of identity-based rights makes it even more difficult to imagine a transformative feminist politics of autobiography, precisely because it suggests that its transformative potential lies within our capacity to locate the opportunities and the perils for a counterhegemonic political project within institutional contexts defined by bourgeois individualism.

My analysis of the revision of the sexual-offense policy at Oberlin College shows how autobiographical practices get regulated and read in ways that constrict their political efficacy and how those in power re-create hierarchical power relations through tacit as well as explicit uses of autobiography. Moreover, this case study illustrates how institutional and bureaucratic discourses of liberalism actively produce and re-create culturally dominant narratives of identity. Even if sexual-offense policies are adopted by our institutions and grievance procedures are made more accessible, these policies and methods do not guarantee that institutional and disciplinary narratives of identity and power will change. There will be an ongoing need for intervention at levels other than the legalistic, for the reformation of demands for equality grounded in the complexity of sexual offenses and social identities, and for the creation of counterpublic spaces for contestation. As Wendy Brown insightfully puts it, "The question here is not *whether* denaturalizing political strategies subvert the subjugating force of naturalized identity formation, but *what kind* of politicization, produced out of and inserted into *what kind* of political context, might perform such subversion" (55, emphasis in original). Brown suggests that differences can make a difference only if articulated as political effects of power (not as privatized individual accounts of experience). Like Brown, I argue that the *risks* of autobiography are, in part, produced and reinforced by liberalism. The challenge of redefining sexual politics in the academy and constructing narratives that position historically marginalized people as agents, rather than simply as victims in need of protection, requires an analysis of the limitations of rights discourse. Indeed, if this case study teaches us anything, it is that the formation and revision of policy is only one stage of a much larger transformative pedagogical project.

We need to move beyond a narrow identity politics that addresses these struggles in terms of individual cases and rights and draws attention away from larger structural problems and historical domination. When we account for larger structural problems and historical domination, we must remember that identities and subject-positions are situationally constructed. Indeed, as Susan Stanford Friedman suggests, "A feminist analysis of identity as it is constituted at the crossroads of different systems of stratification requires acknowledging how privilege and oppression . . . shift in relation to different axes of power and powerlessness" (1995a, 7). For instance, the terms of membership in the arenas where policy is formulated must be made more democratic, the process of making policy must be accessible to all constituents, and the rules and forms of exchange must be questioned. If, as Brown suggests, political subjects always "run the risk of resubordination through the discourses naming and politicizing them" (62), we must ask what types of autobiographical practices would not resubordinate the historically marginalized? What types of autobiographical practices can both destabilize the formulation of identity as fixed and singular and sustain being overtaken by the resilience of individualism? How would a politics of diversity, which configures identity as relational, contestable, and multiple, transform the idiom of identity-based political practices in the academy? What kinds of political recognitions and disruptions can identity-based claims seek? In the following chapter, I consider the potential of autobiography to foster counterhegemonic spaces in a community that too often resorts to policy as its major paradigm of action.

# 6

IN AND OUT OF THE FLESH:
AUTOBIOGRAPHY, PUBLIC-ART ACTIVISM,
AND THE CRISIS OF WITNESSING

*I'm so terrified . . . A lot of my abuse was being watched while I was tak-*
*ing a bath by my grandfather. One of my perpetrators had me undress*
*and dance. I'm feeling like everyone is watching me again, that's why I*
*am so upset.* (Clothesline)

A white female incest survivor spoke those words when she was interviewed
for a documentary about the central Pennsylvania regional Clothesline
Project, which was assembled as part of Dickinson College's 1993 Public Affairs Symposium on Violence in American Society. The Clothesline Project is
a form of public-art activism[1] that takes as its subjects violence against women,
memories of abuse, and women's healing and recovery. It is a performance
piece in the form of an actual clothesline from which survivors or family and
friends of victims hang T-shirts that represent a particular woman's experience.
Since the project's inception in 1991 by the Cape Cod Women's Agenda, a
branch of the Women's International League for Peace and Freedom,[2] dozens
of clotheslines have been constructed on college campuses and at YWCAs,
rape crisis centers, libraries, and other public spaces across the country. The
first national Clothesline was enacted in Washington, D.C. in the spring of
1995. According to the National Clothesline Project literature, the purpose of
the project is fourfold: (i) to bear witness to survivors and victims of sexual
abuse and violence; (ii) to help with the healing process for those who have lost
a loved one or who are survivors; (iii) to educate, document, and raise social

119

awareness about the problem of violence against women; and (iv) to provide a nationwide network of support for women.[3]

The epigraph for this chapter was recorded for a documentary, not as part of the Clothesline Project itself. The forty-three-minute documentary *Clothesline,* produced by Rose and Malmsheimer, is based on interviews with women who contributed artwork to the regional Clothesline.[4] The video brings together the images that women created with survivors' testimonies about the significance of the images and their experience in creating the artwork. The survivor quoted above created a blue T-shirt (blue shirts represent survivors of incest or child sexual abuse), which she called "The Color of Silent Tears."[5] Before she explained to the interviewers what the images on her shirt represented, she told them she was terrified; the camera made her feel as if she were being positioned as a spectacle and thus violated all over again. As she put it, "I'm feeling like everyone is watching me again; that's why I'm so upset." The power of the camera's gaze and voyeuristic elements of the interview and documentary format are particularly problematic for this survivor because of the nature of her abuse. She explained that the images she had sewn onto her T-shirt, which she had cut from pieces of clothing she had worn as a child, represented physical beatings by her father, her mother's rejection, and the voyeuristic sexual abuse by her grandfather.

I begin this chapter with this incest survivor's testimony because it draws attention to the difficulty and danger of transforming private pain into public and political acts and foregrounds the methodological challenges of representing another person's trauma. It also complicates our understanding of the use of autobiography in subaltern counterpublic spaces—that is, in "discursive arenas where members of subordinate social groups invent and circulate counterdiscourses, which in turn permit them to formulate oppositional interpretations of their identities, interests, and needs" (Fraser 1990, 67). Although counterpublic spaces (such as the space created by the documentary and clothesline enactments) enable women to disseminate survivor discourse, these spaces are not unequivocally safe or without risk. Moreover, as the epigraph suggests, the critical desire to document survivors' experiences can produce contradictory effects. The contradiction lies in positioning survivors as both subjects and objects of meaning. Although the survivor quoted above is a subject of the documentary, the voyeuristic power of the camera suppresses her agency as a subject and repositions her as a spectacle—an object of desire—at the same time it provides an opportunity for her to break the silence by speaking out. While survivors report that speaking out is an important and often transformative step from being a passive victim to an active survivor (a common narrative in survivor discourse), we must realize that trauma and survival narratives can function in ways that both counter the invisibility of violence against women and reinscribe existing subject-object relations. This is not to imply that survivors are paralyzed by such contradictions, but rather that autobiographical acts and their documentation can serve contrary pedagogical and political agendas. Nevertheless, as Linda Martin Alcoff and Laura Gray argue, we must recognize the potential recuperation of such disclosures by the very structures and discourses that silenced such speech in the first place, and thus diminish the transgressive and interventionist potential of speaking out. This epigraph provides a critical lever for thinking about the dynamics of self-disclosure in counterpublic spaces and the dialogic nature of personal and political agency.[6] First, these contradictions and risks suggest that a subject's agency is fluid, not static, and that personal and political agency exists in relation to and emerges from particular historical struggles, institutional contexts, and power relations. As I argued in the previous chapter, we need to account for the structural regulations, power relations, and discourses that organize and constrain what can be disclosed and how an utterance will be heard. In other words, we must consider the dialogic relationship between the intratextual realm (formal properties of autobiographical representation) and the intertextual dimension (the social, political, and institutional contexts within which such representations circulate).

The structural regulations, power relations, and risks exposed by the survivor include the relationship between a researcher and her subject, the risks of retaliation and public humiliation, and the link between technology as an instrument of power and violence against women. The epigraph prompts us to consider how, as cultural critics and teachers, we negotiate these contractions, risks, and relations in our teaching, reading, and writing practices. The risks involved in representing survivors' stories include the critical risk that we may reinscribe fear, humiliation, and pain in our representations. The unease we experience in reading this quote and being implicated in this voyeuristic abuse can serve important critical ends; moments such as these force us to become more self-conscious about the risks of self-disclosure and to consider how survivors negotiate dominant cultural narratives in their translation of experience and how we as scholars and teachers then reframe their representations in our research and in our classrooms. If we fail to engage the project of transforming victims into public actors, we run the risk of re-creating the silences, fatalism, and cancellation long associated with victims of interrelational violence and sexual abuse.

The epigraph highlights the recuperative potential and dangers of self-disclosure. Moreover, it raises questions central to critical work on memory, trauma, and the use of autobiography in declared counterpublic spaces. These questions include: How can scholars, activists, and teachers (locations not exclusive of one another) engage representations of trauma in ways that do not revictimize those represented? How can they avoid the charge of voyeurism when doing this kind of documentation and witnessing? What role can counterautobiographic practices play in fighting violence against women? What are the risks? What do these risks tell us about women's struggles for personal and political agency? How can an investigation of competing cultural representations of violence against women enhance our critical understanding of women's resistance? Is a survivor's agency determined by her ability to expose and negotiate conflicting cultural representations?

I turn to the documentary and public enactments of the Clothesline Project to illustrate the risks inherent to the critic's recognition of a subject's agency and the potential replication of voyeurism. More particularly, I consider how cultural systems of representation—namely, tactics of self-disclosure, documentation, and cultural criticism—mobilize competing and often irreconcilable interests. A close comparative reading of the strategies of representation that shape the Clothesline Project and the documentary reveals the dialogic relationship between oppositional and dominant cultural practices and discourses and how survivors' agency is shaped by hierarchical relations, conflicting cultural representations, and social contexts. To claim that pain and violence are constructed by and within a matrix of cultural spaces, relations, and discourses is not to deny their corporeality but, rather, to shift attention to the conditions of their articulation and the relationship between the material and symbolic. As critical educators and cultural critics, we must not get caught in the collision of signs or become immobilized by the contradictions; rather, we must examine how successfully oppositional practices are in articulating and contesting dominant ideologies within particular contexts and how and whether such practices get recuperated into the dominant public spaces and modes of representation. Rather than look at counterpublic spaces as utopian and nonconflictual, we should view them as contact zones. In this chapter, I argue that if counterautobiographical practices are to function as forms of resistance, then activists, educators, and cultural critics need to recognize the heterogeneity of counterpublic spaces as they exist in relation to, not "outside" of, dominant culture. The dialogic conceptualization of dominant and resistant discourses and the contradictions of autobiography in counterpublic spaces have profound pedagogical and methodological implications, which are linked to the dangers of recuperation and the risks of self-disclosure.

## Tales of Excess and the Question of Agency

In order to understand how survivors of sexual violence transform private pain into public discourse and negotiate a sense of agency among contradictory discourses, we must recognize how dominant systems of representation construct victims and perpetrators. The dominant discourse of individualism and privatized self-help shapes the way we understand violence against women in the United States. Rather than link crime and violence against women to power inequities, the mass media and the state cast rapists and batterers as deviants and aberrations in an otherwise fair and normal world. Tales of excess shape the national discourse on violence against women. Media reporting, television docu-dramas, and mainstream films about domestic violence perpetrate tales of excess by demonizing abusers, objectifying and eroticizing survivors, and sensationalizing violence (see Kozol 1995). Mainstream entertainment genres tend to turn abusers into psychopaths and monsters and frame the problem of violence against women within the thriller genre. In *Sleeping with the Enemy*, for example, Laura's husband, Martin, obsessively stalks her until the final scene, when, crazed and out of control, he attacks her and she kills him (1995, 657). This film, like many others, conforms to cultural expectations of domesticity and traditional views of gender and the family. As Wendy Kozol insightfully points out, "*Sleeping with the Enemy* juxtaposes Martin, who threatens domesticity and the social order, with the 'normal' man, Ben, with whom Laura falls in love. . . . [and thereby foregrounds] heterosexual desire in this narrative of survival against the threat to domesticity" (657). Moreover, mainstream entertainment genres depict domestic violence as a problem of the private sphere and resistance as stories about individuals (664). As I pointed out in the previous chapter, similar patterns characterize how sexual harassment and violence against women are dealt with on college and university campuses; such acts often are privatized and construed as conflicts between individuals.

The discourse on violence against women is also complicated by institutionalized racism and racist ideologies, which have persisted in American culture since slavery. Media representations of violence against women, for example, reinforce racist stereotypes of black men as offensive, dangerous, and threatening, particularly in relation to white women (658). Although interracial sexual violence accounts for less than 10 percent of reported rapes, the myth of the black male rapist persists. Historically, racist ideologies have depended on the myth of black male deviance, yet another tale of excess, to legitimize white superiority, lynching, and other forms of racialized state violence (James, 28). Assumptions about race also make women of color more vulnerable to revictimization by the state. For instance, as Joy James points out, "The image of black women as promiscuous, which was manufactured by white males, deflected attention from racialized sexual violence inflicted by white men" (142). Black women share experiences of violence with all women, but their experiences are magnified by social myths and tales of sexual excess, particularly the myth of a "wild" African sexuality, and institutionalized racism. Because prosecution of sexual violence is administered by a racialized state, these social myths proliferate and deny black women respect and credibility as victims (144).[7]

The Clothesline Project may absorb many of the forms of dominant culture (tales of excess, T-shirts as a canvas of consumer culture, and tactics of self-disclosure), but it attempts to turn the "othering" gaze back on itself, to deprivatize the rhetoric of self-disclosure, and to deregulate the state's control of the female body by envisioning the systemic nature of abuse and the links between individual crises and social-institutional acts of dominance. The project can be seen, therefore, as a response to the individualization of cases of violence and the sensationalizing of women's trauma. While individual shirt-makers may draw on tales of excess, the project attempts to reframe these tales by placing them in a larger social and political context. In contrast to the documentary, the Clothesline Project directly challenges the construction of women as spectacles by refusing to provide corporeal entities within the T-shirts. One need only think of the marketing and advertising practices exemplified by the phenomenon of wet T-shirt contests, which categorize women according to their breast and waist measurements. The Clothesline Project negotiates the risks of self-disclosure and mediates dominant tales of excess through the public staging and display of the vanishing body; it at once employs and unsettles notions of the body as spectacle. But what is involved in the translation of private pain into public memory? And whose experiences are made visible? Moreover, do survivors re-create the voyeuristic impulse through tactics of self-disclosure? Do the documentary and enactments of the clothesline function in ways that reproduce or eliminate the risks of disclosure and the antipolitics of voyeurism?

### Translating Private Pain into Public Memory: The Dialogics of Survivor Discourse

The clothesline, as the most public of private spaces, where one's private life is under constant view, functions as a metaphor for the historical silence about, and displacement of, sexual violence against women. It is a place for women, as one contributor put it, "to air our dirty laundry." By exposing their stories

Figure 5. From the National Clothesline Project (1995), Washington, D.C. Photo by the author.

of abuse, recovery, and resistance as crafted on T-shirts, and hanging them from the line for the public to see, contributors turn a domestic ritual into a moment of protest (see figure 5.) The clothesline is also symbolic of the labor that launders the violence. For instance, in the legal sphere, the violence of women's stories of sexual abuse is often bleached, whitewashed, and sanitized by lawyers who subject these narratives to antagonistic scrutiny. Women often are revictimized by the state, which embodies masculinized hierarchies, "delimits the boundaries of personal/domestic violence . . . criminalizes 'deviant' and 'stigmatized' sexually . . . structures collective violence in the police force, prisons, and wars" (Mohanty et al., 21). Unlike the legal sphere and the documentary, the testimonies crafted on T-shirts as part of the Clothesline Project are anonymous. Because the identities of survivors are shielded, as a social and political performance the clothesline functions as a relatively safe space for women to tell their stories. For legal reasons, the Clothesline Project insists that the identities of perpetrators remain anonymous. The significance of survivors' anonymity, which is retained in actual enactments of the Clothesline but sacrificed in the documentary, becomes clear when the survivor quoted above reveals why she is hesitant to disclose her story. While survivors may be empowered by reporting sexual violence, as Alcoff and Gray point out, "the sense of empowerment generally does not outweigh the pain and humiliation of disclosure and its recollection of the frightening and agonizing assault and abuse" (269).

To the extent that the Clothesline Project and the documentary enable survivors to tell their story and to interconnect with the stories and experiences of others, the victimization and/or disintegration of the survivor metamorphoses into an act of self-translation. Each shirt represents a return to—a retelling—of the initial trauma. Each survivor bears witness to a past experience through a new social and psychological translation. As Felman and Laub point out, "The testimony is itself a form of action, a mode of not merely accounting for, but of going through a change" (163). Elaine Scarry's argument in *The Body in Pain* is useful for exploring the translation of private pain into public memory. Scarry argues that "even the elementary act of naming this most interior of events entails an immediate mental somersault *out of the body* into the external social circumstances that can be pictured as having caused the hurt" (16) (my emphasis). The Clothesline Project represents a breakdown of the distinctions between the symbolic and material by highlighting how survivors internalize dominant discourses and appropriate them in their own struggles for power and in the process of healing. Scarry suggests that corporeal experiences of pain and trauma and the discursive realm of representation are interdependent and in constant tension. This interdependence of the material and symbolic is painfully vivid, for instance, in survivors' representations of sexual abuse through the visual construction of an *out-of-body* experience. Images of disembodiment are commonly used to express bodily pain and loss. Many psychologists who specialize in working with victims of sexual abuse have pointed out that images of dissociation are common defense mechanisms to which abused women and children often resort. Numerous survivors of child abuse have described the experience of imagining themselves leaving their bodies, watching the abuse enacted on them from a distance (Herman).

Additionally, there are numerous examples of survivors who negotiate a sense of agency by marking the words of the abuser with the survivor's own intentions. For example, on a yellow shirt (which signifies women who have been battered or assaulted), one survivor inscribed the words "Bitch/Tramp." On a red shirt (which signifies a woman who has been raped), the following narrative appeared: "I hate you sleazy bitch, tramp. You're nothing, ugly fat whore. I know I raped you." One of the more visually striking shirts had an image of a woman whose face was badly beaten accompanied by the words: "Have you had your face done lately" (see figure 6). These three shirts demonstrate the dialogic nature of survivor discourse and how women negotiate dominant and resistant narratives. The embedding of hegemonic narratives

Figure 6. "Have You Had Your Face Done Lately?" Shirt hung on National Clothesline Project (1995), Washington, D.C. Photo by the author.

within resistance discourse, particularly hierarchies based on race, became more clear to me when I reviewed a segment of the documentary in which a white woman described a dark shadowy image on her shirt as the "tar baby" that lived on her back. This survivor described the "tar baby" as "shame, fear, the confusion, and the guilt, and just the weight of all this that I've been carrying around with me, mostly without having any idea what it was, for almost all of my life—forty years." She continued, "Sometimes she gets smaller when I'm feeling better and sometimes she gets bigger when I'm feeling worse." To use the image of the tar baby to depict the lingering pain and trauma that accompany sexual abuse is to use a racist image that not long ago permeated cartoons in the mainstream media: "a nigger baby that sticks to the body of whites."[8] Here, the image signifies the constant burden that this woman feels but seldom sees—an invisible yet felt burden of repressed emotions, which are signified as black. Rather than reproduce an individualist-oriented criticism that blames the woman for subsuming her pain in racist literary conventions, we critics and educators need to ask what in the dominant cultural narrative of race, violence against women, and trauma enables this representation. Moreover, we need to consider how survivors respond viscerally to certain signs and images. For instance, the image of the tar baby as an emblem of racial oppression may trigger traumatic memories for survivors of sexual abuse (Tal, 16–17).

Nevertheless, the visual connection between the white female survivor and the image of the tar baby—a connection the documentary creates— reproduces a historical pattern that positions the white female body as the norm. Racial difference gets configured as a ghostlike shadow, a looming and somewhat threatening presence. Paradoxically, the categories of blacks and women create a black/female axis that secures that whiteness will be coded as an invisibility, as nonraced, or as a lack of race. This coupling of blacks and women has resonance in abolitionist writing and echoes the economy of the visual that defines modernity and early feminism, when white middle-class women's exclusion from the public sphere was compared to the experience of black slaves (Wiegman, 45). This coupling is, of course, still with us today. The popularization of this coupling is internalized by this particular survivor through the therapeutic discourse of victimization. The positioning of the white body as the norm deflects attention away from the survivor's racial privilege through her racialization of the experience of sexual abuse. Complicating this situation is the fact that if we had seen this shirt on the Clothesline, we would not necessarily have known that the survivor was white. The documentary draws out, perhaps unintentionally, the continuing significance of the figures of invisibility and visibility for racial hierarchies in feminist politics and survivor discourse. The tar-baby sequence exposes the racial politics of trauma narratives, and it makes visible a discourse that is grounded in the construction, and often internalization, of the "other" as excess. The tar-baby example demonstrates the dialogic relationship between resistant and hegemonic discourses, and thereby points out that even in created counterpublic spaces, the strength in speaking out is implicated in dominant discourses. This is not to say that women's agency (or human agency more generally) is overdetermined; nor does it reduce the complexity of critical work on violence against women to a "damned if you do, damned if you don't" fate. But it does suggest that personal and political agency are predicated on historical and cultural frames of reference and power relations. In other words, agency is a discursively situated practice.

Yet another example of how resistant discourses rely on dominant narratives can be seen in the way the Clothesline Project and the documentary configure public and private spheres. Both the project and the documentary partake in the feminist practice of self-naming and are guided by the feminist principle "the personal is political," which emerged from women's consciousness-raising groups of the 1960s. Although these groups were inspired by the civil-rights movement in the United States, race and class differences among women presumably were downplayed compared with the focus on women's common oppression. One could argue that the clothesline metaphor reproduces a nostalgic narrative of women's labor and that, like the tar-baby image and early feminism, it effaces differences of race and class. The clothesline signifies communities of women—namely, working-class women in urban settings or apartment complexes who gather around clotheslines to discuss news of the day. But how many poor and working-class women have access to local and national Clothesline Projects? The Clothesline Project rests on class-based notions of domesticity that are, in many instances, at odds with the experiences it represents; that is, the experiences of women who lack access to public facilities or spaces where clotheslines are enacted are not represented. Class hierarchies also are signified on shirts where personal trauma narratives get caught up in "expert systems"—the world and language of professionals. A vivid example of this phenomenon are those shirts that depict the circle of recovery and those that are more concerned with personal self-help than with political and social movements. The emphasis on personal recovery and overcoming oppression at the interpersonal level—feminist therapy—represents the strategies most used by white middle-class women. As Hurtado suggests, "Ethnic and racial political movements in the United States fight vehemently against the use of therapeutic treatments which depoliticize and individualize their concerns by addressing social problems as if they emerged from the psychology of the oppressed" (850). Thus, we must ask, whose experiences does the Clothesline Project make visible? Whose experiences remain silenced?

Organizers of the national Clothesline Project express a commitment to challenge outward and internalized homophobia, racism, sexism, and other oppressions and to make explicit the connection between this violence and the violence women experience. The Clothesline Project attempts to create a sense of solidarity among women. Race, national identity, and sexuality are marked on individual shirts through language, geographical markers and maps, national logos, and photographs. But despite its grassroots efforts to be inclusive, the Clothesline Project may inadvertently create less empathy for white poor and working-class women and women of color than for white middle-class women. These absences point to the limits of symbolic representation and its potential contribution to the reproduction of historical silences. To explore further the problematics of representations of trauma and the risks of self-disclosure, I will now focus on the dynamics of autobiography in contrasting media of representation, particularly the documentary and actual enactments, and on how they determine and mediate survivors' stories.

## Autobiography and "Technologies of Truth"[9]

The use of personal testimonies in the documentary operates under the influence of feminist documentary-film practices that brought "renewed credibility . . . to the importance of people owning and being able to determine the terms of how they are visually represented" (Horrigan, 170). In the documentary, the T-shirts are recognizable as autobiographical; they are situated in a biographical and thus more individualized narrative that reincorporates ideologies of individualism—namely, the subject overcoming adversity—through the body of the survivor. The two interviewers, who sit beside the survivor as she explains what each image or word on her shirt signifies, do not challenge, judge, or question the survivor's rendition of her experience. Rather, they listen to each woman's story. The positioning of survivors as experts is significant because it challenges the idea that women's accounts of sexual abuse are evidence of madness or theatrics (Bronfen, 265). Underlying both the activist project and the film production is the assumption that the act of self-disclosure, of telling one's story, is beneficial to survivors. The premise of this process, called "the talking cure," is that through telling her story a survivor can render the self well or whole. While healing can come through the re-marking of the symptoms, the problem, as I pointed out earlier, is that this process of making the "private" public involves a number of risks, not the least of which is that in the documentary the identity of the survivor is now known (Phelan, 160). The documentary does not preserve the confidentiality of the survivor but, rather, erases the "tracelessness" of the material body inaugurated in the activist project by marking the body permanently visible (Phelan, 148–49). The documentary also reproduces an uncritical notion of authenticity because the survivors' expertise is seemingly unmediated by the narrative of the documentary itself.

The Clothesline Project negotiates the risks of self-disclosure (fear of humiliation, retaliation, etc.) more successfully than does the documentary. In actual Clothesline enactments, the risks of self-disclosure are part of the performance. The Clothesline Project offers the viewer a tactile, embodied experience that reorganizes the voyeuristic tradition: the survivor's body is not on stage. The documentary, on the other hand, engages a form of self-representation and documentation that appears to give the viewer access to the survivor and thus the "real" meaning of the shirt, whereas the Clothesline Project itself presumes a historical referent but does not supply it. The project implicates autobiography through the disappearance of the body. In contrast, the documentary presents autobiography as truth through the presence of the body. The visualization and corporeal presence of the survivor in the documentary also invoke notions of authenticity that the Clothesline Project challenges. Public enactments of the Clothesline Project challenge simplistic notions of authenticity and agency by drawing attention to the risks of self-disclosure and the necessity of anonymity. The anonymity and invisibility of survivors amplify the commonality of abuse and foster a sense of community. As I suggested earlier, however, the sense of community created by the project must not go unchallenged. As witnesses of the Clothesline Project, we become aware of the risks in creating survivors as both subjects and objects of meaning, and we are compelled to negotiate our way through these contradictions. In contrast, as viewers of the documentary, it is difficult to work through these contradictions when placed in the uncomfortable role of voyeur.

When I first viewed the documentary, I was struck by the power of these women's testimonies and their courage to speak out, to find a narrative where historically there has been none. The more I viewed the film, however, the more uncomfortable I became with the medium itself and its status as an "imprint of the 'real'" (Renov, 4). The derivation of the noun *documentary* is linked to the concept of historicity; its semantic clusters either have to do with teaching and with evidence or with proof. The 1989 edition of the revised *Oxford English Dictionary* defines *documentary* as "factual, realistic, applied especially to film or literary work, etc., based on real events or circumstances, and intended primarily for instruction or record purposes" (quoted in Rosen, 65–66). The film's apparent styleless mode—documentary realism—is, of course, a style in and of itself. Its seemingly unmediated rendition of experience inscribes a rhetoric of fact or what might be called a rhetoric of the real. As Trinh T. Minh-ha points out, when the real becomes the only referent in documentary then the "result is the elaboration of a whole aesthetics of objectivity and the development of comprehensive technologies of truth" (94). Minh-ha convincingly argues that such a preoccupation is in actuality a relentless pursuit of naturalism, wherein the "emphasis is again laid on the power of film to capture reality 'out there' for us 'in here'" (95). The filmmaker as a mediator and the medium itself are assumed to be value-free and transparent (96).

The narratives told by survivors for the *Clothesline* documentary attain a privileged status for their factuality; they are presented as analogs of reality—as documents. In this way, the documentary brings personal testimony closer to its use in the judicial context; the historical event that the testimony describes is foregrounded over the process and risks of disclosure. Unlike the judicial context, however, the survivors' testimony is not scrutinized by the interviewers. The two interviewers in the documentary offer only supportive words and affirmative gestures as survivors tell their stories. Survivors do not have to convince the interviewers of the truth of their stories; all they are asked to do is explain their representation (i.e., what various aspects of their T-shirt signify) and let the details and narrative serve as evidence. The film unsettles the victim-expert split by positioning survivors as the sole producers of meaning. The documentary eliminates the role of the expert mediator, which has the effect of denying the recuperation of the survivor's story into an expert narrative. In this sense, the documentary "creates a space where survivors are authorized to be both witnesses and experts" (Alcoff and Gray, 282). However, except for the transgressive segment, when the survivor addresses the voyeuristic gaze of the camera and thus implicates the audience in the construction of her as other, the film does not explore fully the co-creative relations among interviewer, survivor, and audience. While critics and researchers also may be survivors, in the context of documentation, they/we are in a very different social position. Therefore, those of us concerned with documenting survivors' stories must turn the "othering" gaze on ourselves.

The documentary constructs a set of relationships for the viewer, interviewers, and the victim that depends on the explanatory force of personal psychology and the therapeutic discourse of victimization. The relation between the interviewers and each survivor resembles the constructed relations between therapist and client—that is, the survivors' speech is coded as the expression of inner feelings. The construction of the body as spectacle and narrative of voyeurism is repeated through the staging of a kind of penitent/confessor relationship between survivor and viewer. These T-shirts are not simply confessions, for neither the witness nor the shirt-maker completely controls the exchange. As Felman points out, "Because trauma cannot be simply remembered, it cannot simply be 'confessed': it must be testified to, in a struggle shared between a speaker and listener to recover something the speaking subject is not—and cannot be—in possession of. . . . feminine auto-biography *cannot be* a confession. It can only be a testimony: to survival. And like other testimonials to survival, its struggle is to testify at once to life and to death—the dying—the survival has entailed" (16).

The documentary makes visible and audible the experiences of women; this is an important tactic in fighting violence against women and a step in the process of healing and recovery. With the exception of the woman who draws attention to the camera's gaze, however, the documentary does not draw attention, as does the play of absence and presence in actual enactments of the clothesline, to "historical processes that, through discourse, position subjects and produce their experiences" (Joan Scott, 779). The documentary does not critically engage the volatile relationship between a survivor's story and the social and material conditions that make survivors' stories vulnerable to recuperation. This is not to suggest that filmmakers should stop making documentaries about violence against women and women's resistance; there are many fine documentaries about the crisis of witnessing and violence against women.[10] But perhaps the *Clothesline* documentary would have been more effective had it engaged explicitly in the risks of self-disclosure and visibility. While recuperation is not inevitable or total, when representing survivors' stories, researchers need to maximize the transgressive potential of these disclosures. Obviously, I am not denying the value of speaking out. The assertion of agency in making survivors' stories public is significant; survivors' stories have far too long been coded as culturally unspeakable. As Smith and Watson suggest, "In citing new, formerly unspeakable stories [e.g., stories of child sexual abuse, incest, battering, etc.] narrators become cultural witnesses insisting on memory as agency in its power to intervene in imposed systems of meaning" (1996, 15). Moreover, speaking out builds communal identification. Nevertheless, we must not ignore the risks of self-disclosure and the possibility that such disclosures will be recuperated back into dominant cultural narratives and systems that silenced them in the first place. Self-disclosure is not an unequivocally empowering discourse. I am not advocating that we stop bringing sexual violence into public discourse. On the contrary, as Alcoff and Gray wisely put it, what we need to do is "to create new discursive forms and spaces . . . not to confess, but to witness . . . sexual violence in ways that cannot be contained, recuperated, or ignored" (287–88). The risks of self-disclosure are contingent upon many factors, including the structural regulations of discourse that organize what can be disclosed and how an utterance will be heard. I suggest that we look at both the production and the reception of survivor discourse to see how meanings are altered by particular contexts. In order to explore further the potential of survivor discourse to counter the invisibility of violence against women and how spatial configurations and material conditions mediate and constrain survivors' testimonies, I turn to an enactment of the Clothesline Project on the Oberlin College campus.

## Oberlin College's Clothesline Project and the Crisis of Witnessing

During the spring of 1994, the Sexual Assault Support Team (SAST) organized the staging of the Clothesline Project on the Oberlin College campus during sexual-awareness month. Students in charge of organizing and advertising the project did not follow the guidelines suggested by the national project. Instead of limiting the clothing to color-coded T-shirts that depicted violence against women, members of SAST invited survivors, both male and female, to use any piece of clothing as a canvas for their story, including men's boxer shorts, women's aprons and dresses, and children's clothing. Students argued for an inclusive clothesline, claiming that by excluding men's shirts they would deny healing opportunities for men. This decision was also informed by the mission of SAST, which recognizes and supports both men and women who have been sexually assaulted and/or abused. It might be argued that the clothesline on campus redefined the notion of public by challenging the association of the private as a female realm. In other ways, however, the decision to include the stories of male and female survivors reconceived the mission of the project.

Under the hot sun of an early April afternoon, two college women from SAST unwrapped a long cord of clothesline, stretching it catty-corner from one side of the porch of the student union to the other. Another SAST member worked on the poster that was going to be hung in front of the porch to advertise the project, while others were inside setting up the counseling room or unpacking clothes (many were picked up at a local thrift shop) for survivors and friends and family of survivors/victims to create pieces for the exhibit. The student union, Wilder Hall, is an enormous sandstone building with large arched windows and a wide cement porch; unlike an urban tenement, a farmhouse, or a suburban apartment complex, it is an unusual place to find a clothesline.

By noon, about an hour into the project, two shirts had been hung on the clothesline: my own, which I had done for a friend who had been sexually assaulted as a young girl, and another done by a student, who depicted the sexual abuse of a small child. The communal nature of testimony and the sense of empowerment that comes from telling another's story became clear to me while making my shirt. I remembered my horror when a close friend from graduate school told me about her experience of sexual abuse; she would keep her bedroom windows locked, afraid that her neighbor, the man who repeatedly molested her, would come and get her during the night. She said that the act of telling her story to me was very important to her, that it somehow helped the healing process. Making a shirt for her also taught me the significance of witnessing and the paradox of her absence and the story's presence. Breaking the silence is a common metaphor in survivor discourse. Each piece of clothing testifies to the continual struggle of victims to be heard. In fact, this type of reciprocity and communal witnessing is essential to the project. The public is cast into a relationship of "intimate citizenship" (Plummer's coinage, 17) as the Clothesline Project attempts to reform the public sphere and to create communities of remembrance and resistance.

The other contributor who had hung a shirt on the line inscribed these words on a white, long-sleeved blouse with a blue ribbon woven around the collar: "I have 2 friends who were raped when they could fit into a shirt this size. One by her babysitter and the other by her father." On the back of the shirt, she wrote, "They still have to deal with this everyday of their lives. I guess I am the lucky one who only has to live in fear (everyday of my life) that this could happen to me." Each shirt, apron, or dress enables the viewers to be more aware of the history of their own physical, emotional, and political involvement. For example, as I watched the woman hang her shirt, duck under the line, and walk away, I thought about how every arrival and departure would incorporate yet another kind of silence, a protective silence, into the narrative of my witnessing. I thought about how the Clothesline Project breaks the silence only to reassert it once again. The presence and subsequent disappearance of survivors also are essential to the project's effect. The inevitable disappearance of material bodies from the space and the anonymity of survivors (shirts are often hung by organizers of the project) highlight the vulnerability of survivors and account for the dangers faced in disclosure.

The Clothesline Project enacts a tension between the vanishing body and the actual historical event. There is, one might say, a "politics of disguise and anonymity that takes place in public view" (James Scott, 19). Paradoxically, each staging defines the female body through its disappearance. Because it is a temporary event that does not leave behind any visual trace, other than the shirts themselves and photographic representations, spectators and participants are prompted to consider "the generative possibilities of disappearance" (Phelan, 27). The Clothesline Project both assumes a body (each piece of clothing takes a contoured materiality—a torso, arms, or neck, etc.) and figures the body as an absence—an absence that points to the body's fragility and, at the same time, suggests that a trace of the body is present through its absence. Absence becomes the body's echo. Each piece of clothing hung on the line is both a representation and a production of loss; what each T-shirt references is essentially irrecoverable. The event enacts something that makes its materiality (namely, the body of survivors) vanish or, at least, disguises it through anonymity. As I suggested earlier, the disappearance constitutes the particular historicity of the event. Making a shirt for my friend enabled me to experience this doubleness—the play of absence and presence—that not only offers a critique of violence against women and historical silences about women's suffering (one aspect of the crisis of witnessing) but also points to the critic's inability, by virtue of her mere presence, to escape the shadows of absence. We witness what has happened to others through our own body. We embody the absence.

By two o'clock, approximately a dozen women either contributed to or witnessed the project, and one male faculty member and one male student were present. Unlike the women participants, the men maintained their distance from the clothesline. Later, in fact, the one male faculty member who attended while I was present told me he felt like he was invading the space. This man's sensitivity to his position contrasts with an experience I had earlier that day. In the center of Wilder Bowl (a square of lawn bounded by the student union, library, old gymnasium, and administration building), there was a startling spectacle. Among the students lying on the grass, reading, playing Frisbee, talking, and listening to music were two conspicuous young men. One of them was naked and lying flat on his back on a portable metal table; the other, half-clothed, was bent over him. Apparently, the man standing was giving the other a massage. The noise from Wilder Bowl and the presence of an exposed white male body did not diffuse the silence surrounding the clothesline; on the contrary, it deepened it by highlighting the community's apparent indifference. Was the pain of victims of sexual abuse really all that invisible? Several women at the project commented on how "free" these men must have felt exposing themselves this way. This spectacle at Wilder Bowl vividly reminded us that the spaces women can safely occupy are limited, and it demonstrated how counterpublic spaces exist in dialogue with dominant public spaces and how the boundaries between "resistance" and "dominance" are fluid, not fixed. As I suggested earlier, this dialogic quality of resistant and dominant discourse also is vividly apparent in survivors' narratives.

Consider the following narrative produced by a shirt-maker for the Oberlin clothesline. On the front and back of a large white T-shirt, one survivor wrote:

I was raped by a man I met in a dance club in Rome. He followed me home and held me down on the floor of a bathroom, under a sink. I still dream about the drainpipe over my face. All I could see, and not being able to breathe. I told the chaperon of my tour group. He said it was my fault. People in the group stopped speaking to me. I went home and didn't tell anyone for a year. I still believed it was my fault. IT WASN'T. This is not easy. I haven't told very many people because when I do I always feel like I'm making it up. It was on a train. It wasn't my fault they were drunk. I wasn't drunk. They weren't my friends. I wanted them to like me. They held me down. It was on a train. I'm not making this up. This happened on the same tour. I didn't tell anyone because I didn't think they'd believe me.

The survivor is depicted in dialogue with herself; the two constructed voices in this text include her own experiential memory and the internalized voices of others, which are characterized by scrutiny and doubt. Because the people she spoke to did not believe her, the process of telling her story left her open to further victimization and alienation. The disbelief of the survivor's story is, of course, a common and deeply embedded "master narrative" in our culture, one that is perhaps most prevalent in the courts, where victims' stories are often discredited and/or pathologized as "evidence of women's or children's hysterical or mendacious tendencies, or even as testimony to women's essential nature as helpless victims in need of patriarchal protection" (Alcoff and Gray, 268). This shirt exposes the "master narrative" and highlights the risks women face in making their stories public.

This rape story represents a modernization of classic rape stories in the nineteenth and early twentieth centuries, when narratives of rape (articulated by dominant groups) incorporated a model of female sexuality that positioned women who were raped as temptresses, seductresses, or impure "bad girls" who "asked for it." These narratives were accompanied by nineteenth-century notions of female sexuality as a response to male sexuality. That is, men were viewed as active and driven by sexual need and women as passive. Thus, "good girls" submitted to men and "bad girls" were raped. While these narratives remain with us today, the antirape movement has challenged them by creating new narratives. As Ken Plummer points out, the narratives that emerged after 1970 became those "of power and gender rather than sex and desire" (67). Three strategies are involved in creating these new narratives. These include: "the debunking of myths [including the presumption that women invite rape and that men act on uncontrollable sexual impulses], the creation of a history, and the writing of a political plot" (Plummer, 67). The revision of the classic rape story on the Oberlin clothesline reveals that "though bodies in culture are always inscribed by exterior signifiers, it matters whether the woman does the translation into [a] semiotic category or has it done to her" (Bronfen, 154).

## The Pedagogical Implications of Critical Witnessing

In contrast to the documentary, enactments of the Clothesline Project demonstrate how the autobiographical subject can be constructed as a displacement of corporeal identity. This particular narrative of displacement suggests that oppressed subjects are "always 'somewhere else': doubly marginalized, displaced always *other* than where he or she is, or is able to speak from" (Hall, 44). As one watches bodies move in and out of the space carved out by the clothesline, one loses track of the autobiographical subject. It is precisely within this double movement toward and away from the material body—in and out of the flesh—that the survivor's agency lies. The project uses the trope of absence—namely, the absence of the bodies of victims and survivors—to highlight the crisis of violence that occurs on women's bodies. This double movement, the fact that the autobiographical subject cannot be fixed and that the survivor can simultaneously reveal and conceal her identity, is an integral part of the project. The film locates the subject's agency in the telling, in the remaking of the narrative of abuse, whereas the project locates agency in the movement between the material and the symbolic. One might argue that the film complicates this movement by visually fusing the material and the symbolic: now the shirts are attached to, though not worn by, survivors. The project more explicitly engages the ways women's bodies are inscribed in a struggle that is both material and representational.

The clothesline does not simply take what was previously unspoken or unseen and move it into the public realm, but, rather, it ends the silence and invisibility, only to reassert them again. This absence becomes vividly apparent when looking at rows and rows of white shirts that depict women who have been murdered: "Belinda strangled to death 6-6-93"; "Teresa stabbed in front of 10 year old son: died several weeks later"; "Margie shot by husband 4-1-93"; "Emily Hernandez 9 months old, beaten, broken-bones, raped, dead" (see figure 7). When we look at the white shirts, we confront the literal absence of life. Thus as critics, we must contemplate what is missing and the impossibility of claiming the object of vision (Bhabha 1987, 5). Although the identities of the shirt-makers elude us, each shirt "leaves a resistant trace, a strain of the subject, a sign of resistance" (6).

The space created by the Clothesline Project reorganizes the voyeuristic tradition of seeing art and implicates the material body of the viewer and critic in profoundly new ways. First, the project frustrates the voyeuristic de-

Figure 7. Rows of white shirts hung on the National Clothesline Project (1995), Washington, D.C. Photo by the author.

sire to fix and contain the other as object by forcing viewers to contemplate the crisis of witnessing (7). Second, it overwhelms the viewer by the physical space it consumes; like the AIDS Names Quilt, Clothesline Projects are usually sprawled on lawns or spread between buildings or across fields. Third, it assumes a material witness and invites a tactile response; as one walks through and around the clotheslines, shirts flap in the wind, brushing against one's skin. If we are to carry out our function as critical witnesses, we must become part of the creation. But can the critical gesture become part of the creation, and if so, how? Therapeutic models of trauma and the process of healing call for an empathetic listener. As medical practitioner and theorist Dori Laub puts it, "The absence of an empathic listener, or more radically, the absence of an *addressable other,* an other who can hear the anguish of one's memories and thus affirm and recognize their realness, annihilates the story" (quoted in Felman and Laub, 68). For many survivors, this is the first time they are being public about what they have endured; their trauma has not previously been witnessed. Critical witnessing involves more than empathy and more than an affirmative therapeutic stance. It involves recognizing the ideologies that regulate the social body and the prevailing histories and accepted truths, as well as the risks involved in positioning survivors as both subjects and objects of meaning. The pedagogical and critical challenge for educators, critics, and activists who strive to contest the antipolitics of voyeurism is to recognize the potential resistant function of testimony as well as the risks of self-disclosure. We cannot position ourselves above or outside of these contradictions and risks; instead, we must negotiate these conflicting pedagogical demands.

If one were to take a pedagogical cue from my readings of actual enactments of the Clothesline Project and the documentary *Clothesline*, one would argue that as witnesses we are not blank slates onto which memory, trauma, or resistance is innocently inscribed. In other words, our presence also is interwoven with and constitutive of systems of representation. Witnesses cannot transcend dominant strategies of representation, but, rather, they too must negotiate a sense of personal and political agency among contradictory discourses and technologies. Whether we are actual witnesses to human trauma or secondary witnesses to its artistic representation, bearing witness is a socially mediated and complicated act that helps define the social imagination and the publicness of remembering.

The juxtaposition of the Clothesline Project and the documentary highlights the problematics of representing the experiences of survivors of sexual abuse and draws attention to our contradictory subject positions as researchers mediating representations of an other. Because the Clothesline Project more consciously exposes the paradoxes of autobiography and the risks of disclosure in counterpublic spaces, it challenges pedagogical and critical paradigms that exoticize the other as spectacle and that uncritically position survivors as autonomous free-floating agents. Although the project is predicated on the material presence of witnesses, part of its social and political aesthetic is what slips away—the movement between absence and presence, the space between visibility and invisibility. The clothesline subverts the visibility of the other (marked by the body) and puts forth an aesthetic of impermanence, based on the metonymic figures of missing, absence, and disappearance.[11] I use the term *metonymy* to refer to a figure or trope that is not a mere substitution of the part for the whole (the traditional view) but which, as a substitute, "produces no relief, its place is assigned in the structure by the mark of an emptiness" (Jacques Derrida in Bhabha 1987, 8). Some readers might argue that my formulation of an aesthetic of impermanence erases or abstracts the subject's agency. But I contend that this formulation allows viewers/participants to witness the temporal and historically shifting nature of their own and the subject's agency. Moreover, the concept of impermanence foregrounds the importance of historical memory, which "moves beyond the boundaries of the singular corporeal body" (Simon, 1), and the ethical responsibility of critics, researchers, and teachers to respond to testimonies of human trauma in a way that captures the "ambiguities and paradoxes of an always incomplete testimony which initiates fissures or breaks in what can be 'said'" (7). The Clothesline Project urges educators and critics to become more adept at witnessing the paradoxes of autobiography and the contradictions within which we are caught and to recognize that "resistance inheres in the very gaps, fissures, and silences of hegemonic narratives" (Mohanty et al., 38). In other words, these contradictions can become a point of pedagogical inquiry in our classrooms, in activism, and in cultural criticism. Tony Bennett puts it this way: "If a brief for criticism [and, I would add, pedagogy] is called for . . . it is one that will enable critical practices to operate variably and in multiple ways on the sites of such contradictions rather than—in constructing a totalizing contradiction of its own—outside and independently of them" (138).

Contemporary criticism and pedagogy should not partake in the historical conspiracy of silence by dismissing representations of human suffering as narcissistic and self-pitying "victim art," a claim dance critic Arlene Croce made about Bill T. Jones's "Still/Here," a modern dance epic about people living with terminal illnesses.[12] As Joyce Carol Oates so eloquently put it, "Only a sensibility unwilling to attribute full humanity to persons who have suffered injury, illness or injustice could have invested such a crude and reductive label" (1). As cultural critics, researchers, and educators, we must distinguish between forms of voyeurism and critical witnessing, and recognize both the transgressive and recuperative uses of self-disclosure, because these distinctions are what make resistance possible. Likewise, feminists must challenge the facile equivalence of self-disclosure and opposition. We must realize that the project of representing the experiences of others is not purely hermeneutical but is an interventionist practice with risks. As my analysis of the Clothesline Project and documentary suggests, critics, researchers, and teachers must take a more dialectical position that acknowledges the embodiment of contesting discourses (such as political and therapeutic discourses) and the tensions between activist politics and processes of signification. How these tensions shape representations of violence and trauma and whether they provide new alternatives for a transformative praxis are questions that remain to be explored by contemporary critics, activists, and educators. The challenge is to configure autobiography as transformative cultural practices in ways that sustain its political efficacy and guard against its recuperation. In my conclusion, I contemplate further the pedagogical obstacles and the risks of disclosure as manifested in the cultural contact zones of professional conferences.

# Conclusion

TRAVELING FRAMES: AUTHORITY,
AUTHENTICITY, AND THE PEDAGOGY
OF LOCATION

> *It is imperative that we take individual and institutional responsibility*
> *for critically examining the practices of our own institutions, and for*
> *initiating and maintaining an open dialogue that will ultimately nur-*
> *ture the possibilities for growth and change within our institutions.*
> *(Gilmore et al., 91)*

On the second evening of the 1997 Pedagogy of the Oppressed Conference, hundreds of academics, students, artists, and community activists gathered in a large lecture hall at the University of Nebraska in Omaha for a "mass dialogue." Standing in front of the large lecture hall, the facilitator, a leading spokesperson for critical democratic pedagogy, asked participants to form small groups to discuss both global and local concerns regarding the pedagogy of the oppressed.[1] These concerns would presumably function as generative themes and serve to focus the mass dialogue. When the larger group reassembled, several participants immediately interrogated the facilitator's framing method, claiming that as mutually defining spheres, the global and local could not be functionally separate. Immediately following this discussion, a number of participants individually testified to experiences of alienation and invisibility at the conference. For instance, several undergraduate students said they felt they had been positioned categorically as pedagogical "objects of analysis" at some of the sessions; a woman of color objected to the lack of diversity among participants and organizations represented at the conference. The facilitator, a white male, acknowledged the problem and then suggested to the woman of color (a professor) that she join next year's conference committee on diversity to help address the problem of minority representation. He responded to the undergraduates by asking them to come to the front of the lecture hall so they could address the entire group about their concerns. Instead of guiding the audience to think about the larger implications of these personal testimonies (which would have been one of many possible strategies to focus the dialogue), the facilitator enabled, no doubt unintentionally, a pedagogical process by which marginalized individuals were put on display as spectacles or further tokenized.

The facilitator's invitation to the undergraduate students to come to the front of the lecture hall so their concerns could be made visible is a well-intentioned pedagogical impulse because it is seemingly empowering and sympathetic. But what the facilitator did not experience from the other side of the podium was the positioning of students as pedagogical spectacles. This moment at the mass dialogue, like the scene in the *Clothesline* documentary discussed in the previous chapter where the survivor expresses reluctance to disclose her story in front of the camera, foregrounds the pedagogical contradiction produced by the critical desire to represent the experiences of those classified as other. Visibility may seem to challenge historical silences and absences, but as a pedagogical strategy it too often reinforces the subject-object dichotomy and differences in social power rather than dislodging them.

The woman of color who was asked to serve on a committee to address the presumed lack of diversity at the conference further exemplifies the contradictory effects of the pedagogy and politics of visibility. Clearly there was a need for better representation of historically nondominant groups in positions of authority. But the suggestion that this woman serve on next year's committee does not address the problematics of the current situation; instead, it repositions her as a cultural other and as an educator of difference— a classic example of institutional tokenization. Likewise, this example resonates with the institutional pedagogical pattern wherein the "racialized personal other is called on to authenticate the academic enterprise" (Hum, 3). One could argue that the undergraduate students and the woman of color who spoke out at the mass dialogue were implicated in a larger pedagogical narrative, in which notions of authenticity were tied to oppositional politics and institutionally driven autobiographical scripts propelled by the underrepresentation of women and minorities. These two gestures of presumed inclusion in effect conflated identity with visibility and shifted the responsibility for social change back onto the marginalized subject. On the institutional level, pedagogical gestures of inclusion can function in ways that betray the groups they claim to help, reducing the transformational potential of inclusion by containing it within dominant paradigms and superstructures. As Sue Hum perceptively points out, "A change in cultural content and symbols cannot account adequately for any critical revision of a grand narrative" (3). Thus, the very institutional hierarchies and pedagogical postures that the conference sought to challenge were reproduced.

It is precisely the contradictions between the theory and practice of critical pedagogy that were ignored at the mass dialogue. The larger betrayal narrative here, of course, is that the critical methods (visibility politics, tokenization, etc.) betrayed the critical aims (inclusion, equity, etc). My critique of the mass dialogue is not directed toward individuals (which is why I decided not to use proper names) but toward institutional postures and their pedagogical consequences. I suspect that the facilitator felt unfairly attacked by some conference participants; in an academic climate fraught with hostilities from both the left and right, he got caught, and was essentialized as an antagonist, in an even larger betrayal narrative. These incidents reveal the difficulty of enacting liberatory pedagogy in Western institutional contexts, and offer a place for critical teachers to think through the problematics of visibility politics and of making structural inequalities visible without reproducing hierarchical subject-object relations. Indeed, the dialogue prompted me to think about the scripts of my own "professionalism" and pedagogical interactions. My purpose is not to judge the behavior of particular individuals but to urge critical educators to unmask our own systemic and pedagogical complicity (both individually and collectively) in re-creating the spectacle of the pedagogical other. As I argued in the previous chapter, we must recognize the contradictions of liberatory pedagogy and use this knowledge self-critically; instead of being immobilized by such contradictions, we should use them as starting points for building coalitions and for carving out new counterpublic spaces from which to speak and act. Of course, "living with contradictions," as Elspeth Probyn wisely points out, "does not necessarily enable one to speak of them, and in fact for concrete reasons, it may be dangerous to do so" (1990, 182). Nevertheless, those of us who can should.

The mass dialogue demonstrates the potential of autobiography to expose and destabilize existing power relations and, conversely, to fracture groups working for social change. Moreover, the mass dialogue exemplifies how even declared counterhegemonic spaces are not immune to identity politics and struggles over self-representation. This example further suggests the transferability and usefulness of an analysis of the pedagogical dynamics of autobiography in contexts beyond the classrooms and campus of a small liberal arts college. Like the pedagogical scenarios discussed in earlier chapters (writing classrooms, faculty meetings, student protests, etc.), the mass dialogue can be seen as a pedagogical contact zone wherein knowledge, identities, and social relations were produced and struggled over and where conventions of communication and notions of authenticity and authority collided (Giroux 1994a, 155). Moreover, the mass dialogue demonstrates the usefulness of the concept of the contact zone for understanding pedagogical sites outside the classroom, as teachers, students, and activists "meet, clash, and grapple" with one another (Pratt 1991, 34).

The Pedagogy of the Oppressed Conference *did* create spaces for new collaborations, activist learning, and strategies of resistance. It featured panels and workshops on the translation of Freirian pedagogy in American educational contexts and the challenge of establishing productive collaborations between community activists and academics. Most panels examined these issues as they played out in particular institutional sites and pedagogical locations, including elementary, secondary, and post-secondary classrooms, correctional facilities, community centers, and public health, arts, and literacy projects. Despite its progressive and revitalizing effects, however, the conference functioned in contradictory ways. As a culturally encoded text, the conference provides an opportunity to reflect further on how power, authority, and resistance align variously through autobiographical practices. More specifically, it illustrates the extent to which the interventionist potential of critical pedagogy depends upon an understanding of the dynamics and problematics of autobiography in counterpublic spaces. Most importantly, it highlights the need for greater self-social reflexivity on the part of critical educators about our practices and how they are contained within (and thus appropriated by) institutions (Roman 1997, 271). In other words, as McLaren suggested in his keynote address at the 1996 Pedagogy of the Oppressed Conference, "Critical pedagogy is ultimately a dream, but one that is dreamt in the wakefulness of praxis. . . . an individual cannot say he or she has achieved critical pedagogy if he or she stops struggling to attain it" (1996, 9). It is in the spirit of critical self-reflexivity that I use professional conferences as concluding pedagogical sites of inquiry and as a way to review and reframe some of the pedagogical issues discussed in earlier chapters. These issues include: the relationship between authenticity and oppositional politics, the problematics of pedagogical tourism and visibility politics, the complex interactions between present and historical representations of marginalized groups, and the tensions between the pedagogical narratives about the other (articulated by those in positions of power) and those that emerge from those written or spoken about.

## Pedagogical Narratives of Betrayal and Redemption

There are several pedagogical responses to the tensions described above. One response is the pedagogical narrative of identification, wherein the white Western subject comes to know his/her own estranged racialized self and frames his/her disclosure as an act of identification with those traditionally marked as other. An exchange at a recent composition and rhetoric conference highlighted this narrative for me. At a panel on academic representation and contrasting disciplinary discourses, one panelist, who grew up in Malaysia, stood before a room of mostly white professors and graduate students and said how difficult it was for her to speak in this context and how it had taken her ten years to write her paper, a critique of pedagogies of inclusion and the canonization of a grand narrative of liberal pluralism in composition studies. She interspersed her critique of the profession with personal narrative. She described herself as a "border crosser," a hyphenated identity whose intellectual practice and pedagogy were the product of many cultural and linguistic intersections. And she called for a pedagogy that created "spaces for the interrogation of 'betweenness.'" Implicit in her narrative was a call to distinguish between the liberal humanist discourse of travel and mobility and the forced movements of historically disenfranchised groups. At the end of her session, a few white men established their authority by claiming their own status as border crossers and hyphenated identities by referring to their ethnic and class backgrounds.

While it is certainly true that class and visibly unmarked (though often audible) cultural differences condition one's access to and experience in the academy, the act of making the invisible visible is not the same as being visibly marked as a racial other. I'm not suggesting that one social location is more authentic than the other but that the impulse to make the invisible visible can function in certain contexts to resecure racial privilege. Thus, while the attempt may have been to fracture the solidification of identity categories and challenge gender and race essentialism, attention was nevertheless drawn back to the visibly marked white male body. The polemics of such "identifying moves," as I suggested in chapter 4 in my discussion of the institutional responses to the activism of students of color and the defacement of the Memorial Arch on the Oberlin College campus, is that they often manifest themselves, or are interpreted, as forms of white defensiveness. Empathy and identification are important aspects of our humanity. However, empathetic stances need to be interrogated; while empathy may work on an individual level, it can be seriously inadequate as a strategy for change at the institutional level. Here, reflexivity about one's social location gave way to an assertion of difference unaware of its own complicity in reinscribing existing power relations. Although the white males' disclosures do complicate white identity (as fractured, multiple, shifting, and hyphenated by language, class differences, histories of migration, immigration, etc.), they do not account for the particular history of race politics in this country, which encodes how certain bodies are perceived as racially marked while others are not. Moreover, these acts of identification ignore how self-disclosure gets coded differently in various contexts, depending upon who does the disclosing. Pedagogical narratives of identification need to be historically contextualized and examined for their shortsightedness because they may very well (as they did at this conference session) obstruct the building of coalitions based on a shared purpose and a social analysis of material conditions and differences. I label identification narratives as redemption narratives because they function as repurchasing acts: whiteness is taken back and resecured at the center of each narrative. Identification narratives share a reliance on Western modernist discourses of self-other, which reinscribe the center-periphery formation through cultural and economic practices of othering.

Self-other and subject-object binaries remain integral to formations of resistance as well, often in ways that reduce their transformative potential. For instance, these binaries structure the discourses of identity that emerged in the 1980s and early 1990s in feminist criticism of postmodernism. The self-other binary often is manifested in such critiques as a kind of "nostalgia for the full subject as the basis of praxis" (Grewal, 244). The pedagogical aim articulated was that those traditionally marginalized needed to become full subjects and that deconstruction denied them that. Many of these arguments were written in response to increasing visibility of postmodern theory, which some feminists and leftist critics saw as a threat and a betrayal of the marginalized person's subjectivity and agency (232). As I discussed in chapter 1, multiplicity and the fracturing of subjectivity became equivalent in such critiques to the loss of agency (244).

The trope of betrayal also has been used in divisive ways within marginalized communities, especially by those who see identities and locations enunciated at the intersections of gender, race, and sexuality as a kind of betrayal. For example, as Leslie Bow points out, in discussions of Asian-American women's writing,

> racial and gender identifications are often experienced as oppositions. . . .
> As tensions between American and ethnic home cultures are played out
> over issues of gender (particularly in regard to feminism and sexuality),
> cultural nationalism and feminism appear as mutually exclusive. In this
> context, discussions of the "strategic assertion of identity" as a means of
> dealing with multiple categories of identity across lines of race, class,

gender, and sexuality can fail to acknowledge the contentious framework in which Asian American women and other women of color are
forced to negotiate identity. If feminism is positioned as a betrayal of
ethnic culture, the question of alliance becomes not one of strategy, but
of loyalty (31).

While Bow is critical of these imposed disloyalties, she is also careful to point
out that, in the current climate, it seems that "more attention is devoted to fur-
thering the concept that we can 'shuttle between identities' than how we go
about it or what it means to make that attempt. The theoretical emphasis needs
to focus on the consequences of such shifting, "how the subject negotiates between often contradictory positions" and how social locations are enunciated
and animated in practice, with degrees of mobility (31). Likewise, as I argued in
my discussion of the use of tropes of travel, hybridity, and border crossing in
feminist-writing pedagogy in chapter 2, we need to consider whose identities
are shifting and who is moving into which cultural and pedagogical contact
zones. We must ask who travels and from where to where. To guard against
pedagogical tourism and the presumption of whiteness as the normative location from which everyone moves, we must acknowledge unstable zones of contact where struggles for autobiographical voice are staged and where identification narratives and cultural tourism collide with the identity narratives and
enforced movements of the other, as in diasporic border crossings.

## Performing Identities: Autobiography Scripts Pedagogy

Recent scholarship on multiple subjectivities, crossing the boundaries of
identity (impersonation, passing, cross-racial and cross-gender writing, etc.),
and living in the borderlands challenges fixed notions of identity and agency
and of the conflation of authenticity with the perceivable racial, ethnic, and
gendered self. Tropes of traveling, hybridity, and crossing (which feminists of
color and postcolonial theorists such as Alacrón, Anzaldúa, Bhabha, Grewal,
Kaplan, Mohanty, and Spivak have engaged for some time) are beginning to
take hold in pedagogy studies, particularly critical pedagogy and composition pedagogy—for example, in discussions of code-switching, signifying,
and intercultural literacy.[2] Pedagogy: The Question of Impersonation, edited by
Jane Gallop, is just one example. Indira Karamcheti's "Caliban in the Classroom," an essay in the collection, is particularly relevant to my discussion
here. In chapter 5, I discussed how faculty in positions of power projected
autobiographical scripts onto women faculty in debates over the sexual-
offense policy. In her essay, Karamcheti problematizes visibility politics and
highlights how the biographical frame-up (the projection of an autobiographical script onto another) works in classroom pedagogy.

She argues that most minority teachers, "encased in the personal and visible facts of [their] visible selves," are "walking exemplars of ethnicity and of race" (138). She points out that the minority teacher "does not necessarily have the choice of deliberately engaging the machinery of the personal in order to problematize authority. Authority has already been problematized by the fact of visible difference" (138). For instance, authority is often awarded or denied minority teachers on the basis of their visible selves. According to Karamcheti, the pedagogical roles available to the visibly marked other are limited; they include the role of Caliban as the native informant—a pedagogical position often imposed on people of color that essentializes difference and positions the cultural other as representative—and the role of the revolutionary—that is, the racialized body encoded into a narrative of resistance (142). Karamcheti continues:

> According to the narrative, resistance is discovered in every margin and periphery: show me an other, a subaltern, a marginalized figure; I'll show you resistance. The narrative of resistance has a ready-made role for Caliban: the authentic, organic intellectual (read revolutionary) seeking to overthrow Prospero's rule, the postcolonial guerrilla fighter waging battle in the belly of the beast. The politicization of the role is clear, and brings Caliban closer, if not close enough, to the sources of power, Prospero's books.
>
> But Caliban's resistance is no real threat. The postcolonial playing the role of the academic revolutionary is safely contained within the recognizable role of resistance. . . . The unspoken subtext here is certainly an anti-intellectualism, more certainly a distrust of the native or subaltern intellectual, most certainly a sense that the "authentic" postcolonial is the grass-roots peasant, living oppression, not the indigenous or cosmopolite intellectual, theorizing postcoloniality. (143)

Another role available to minority teachers, she claims, is that of the hybrid postcolonial intellectual, the figure of Ariel in Aimé Césaire's *A Tempest,* a revisioning of the play from the colonized point of view, not in Shakespeare's *Tempest.* Ariel is a mulatto in Césaire's play, whom Karamcheti describes as a "native intellectual having an identity crisis (as Césaire's Prospero derisively mocks him) . . . [Ariel is] "deeply implicated in the very structures that enslave him, [and seeks] to mediate and achieve synthesis between exploiter and exploited" (143). Prospero himself—or, rather, Caliban impersonating Prospero—is the last of the potential dramatic roles for the minority teacher, a role, as Karamcheti suggests, that denies visual evidence of difference and instead "insists on the authenticity of guild membership" (143).

These pedagogical roles and institutional postures, though schematic and oversimplified, nevertheless offer a way for critical educators to begin to think through the problematic of visibility and the projection of autobiographical scripts onto students and teachers. Given the inevitability of the personal in the classroom and the ways that material bodies are coded by cultural stereotypes, Karamcheti calls for a Brechtian performance of difference, wherein the actor (read teacher) alienates the viewer (read student) from the spectacle and unsettles rather than fulfills audience (student) expectations (145). To explore further the pedagogical possibilities of using autobiography to counter the projection of authority or an essentialist autobiographical script onto the cultural other and to work through the contradictions in constructing the other as both a subject and object of critique, I turn to two additional pedagogical sites at the Pedagogy of the Oppressed Conference.

In his improvisational workshop, on the afternoon following the evening of Mass dialogue, Augusto Boal encouraged participants to collaborate on a representation of the conference by creating a tableau. Boal, the founder of many centers of the Theater of the Oppressed around the world, focuses on theater as a form of social criticism. While tableaux usually are motionless and silent, the conference tableau was a living, breathing sculpture. Boal began the workshop by describing the process as one in which some individuals would function as sculptors and others as "sculptees," or representations of each sculptor's vision of the conference. He offered participants the following guidelines: Sculptors were not to speak to the sculpted but only to model the image or sound they wanted by molding the sculptee's body or modeling it themselves; sculptors were not to create forms that might harm another person; and individuals who were chosen to participate could decline. The audience was part of the sculpture as performance. People moved in and out of roles; at any given moment in the improvisation, they could be switched from spectator roles to participant roles, either as sculptors or sculptees. In this sense, the improvisation disrupted the spectator/participant boundaries. Not everyone experienced the fluidity of these roles; some stood on chairs and cheered, while others, like me, watched in awe from the sidelines. One might say that as onlookers we assumed a voyeuristic stance; however, our "looking" functioned as a spectacle for the sculptors and sculpted. Thus, our gestures and postures were part of the performative and pedagogical narrative. Spectators were not merely witnesses but participants—spect-actors—in a social and pedagogical drama (Cohen-Cruz, 113). Nevertheless, the improvisation fractured the us/them, subject/object binaries lingering in our memory of the mass dialogue. In contrast to the mass dialogue, Boal's workshop enacted Freirean pedagogy and provided a model of critical self-reflexivity, cooperation, and participatory learning—all staples of Freirean pedagogy.

The tableau was built one body-image-text at a time. Two bodies were positioned in chairs, their hands and facial expressions crafted to simulate conversation; another person was manipulated into the classic thinker position, sitting hunched forward, hand on chin, elbow on knee; another was positioned on the edge of a chair, her hand raised above her head; another was placed upright, his arm extended and fingers curled as if holding a piece of chalk and writing on a blackboard; another wandered aimlessly, a look of despair on his face. A diverse group formed a circle, hands held at their sides, heads tilted toward the sky. Two women stood side by side, bent over at the waist and repeating a series of motions as if on an assembly line; first, they grasped the air in front of them and cupped their hands as if catching something, and then they pulled back and let the invisible object fall to the ground. Sounds animated the ever-changing image. Sounds like a steam press. Like a cash register. Like wind. Like rain. Then a layering of sounds. Rhythmic, syllabic, nonreferential vocalizations. Sssshhhhhhuuuuuh waffle prlprlprlring prlprlprlring thromthrumthromthrum gwawthrom gwawthrum zzzzzzzzz zip zip. Sssshhhhhhuuuuuh waffle prlprlprlring prlprlprlring thromthrumthromthrum gwawthrom gwawthrum zzzzzzzzz zip zip. Cacophony. Visions and experiences coming together. Themes emerging, disappearing, then reappearing. Sounds surfacing and descending. Falling apart. Points at which the ability to make sense of the sound or image vanished. Dissonance. Gradually, the surface anarchy resolved into some kind of unified vision. The image and sound of the conference metamorphosed before us.

One of the last body-image-texts to become part of the living sculpture was that of the facilitator of the mass dialogue, who was guided by a participant/sculptor to lie on the floor in front of the buzzing, chugging conference machine. After the sculptor molded the facilitator's body into the form of a cross, another participant was guided to stand over him, his foot suspended a few inches from the facilitator's chest as if ready to release a forceful, crushing blow. At that point, the improvisation seemed to take on a referential function, not to mention the violence of representation scripted onto it. What this pivotal scene revealed for me was how social agency, identity, and power are mediated through and inscribed on the flesh of the symbolic as well as the material body. The improvisation exposed how authority is mobilized through the biographical frame-up, the projection of an autobiographical script onto another: now the facilitator was "framed."

This image of the facilitator of the mass dialogue, as martyr could be seen as an act of empathy or identification and thus part of a larger redemption narrative. It also could be viewed as representing or perhaps even enforcing critical reflexivity. Or one could look at this body-image-text as a recontextualization of the facilitator's authority and, therefore, as an illustration of the consequences of confusing the authority of one's position with the authority of one's knowledge. Finally, this image could be seen as representing implicit violence, which itself is not an unproblematic response to authority. One could argue that at this moment the improvisation slipped into the discourse of identity politics, but I found the self-conscious imaging of the facilitator as spectacle (which he graciously and humbly enabled) a gesture that foregrounded the complex politics of self-representation and the interdependent relation between the body and ideology that typifies Boalian theater. It was precisely the body-image-text of the facilitator—the biographical frame-up—that revealed that the material body cannot in the end free itself from ideological discourses, cultural narratives, and historical memories. As Philip Auslander puts it, "The Boalian body . . . cannot exist outside ideology . . . but can only try on different ideological positionings as they are inscribed on the body" (131). This is not to say that bodies are determined by ideologies but that social agency emerges from the negotiation and resignification of embodied discourses and practices.

Likewise, Reanae McNeal's play, *Don't Speak My Mother's Name in Vain,* which focused on sexual violence against African-American women from enslavement to the present, drew attention to the historical and ideological discourses inscribed onto the material body, particularly the black female body, and how as members of the audience we are implicated in the production and reception of the cultural other and the violence of representation. McNeal is a storyteller and performance artist.[3] Her play, consisting of eight character sketches animated with dance, blues, and spiritual songs, is informed by the deep belief, as McNeal notes in her mission statement, that "the tongue of the wise brings healing" (Proverbs 12:18). All eight sketches are about the power of memory and the embodiment of historical trauma, as well as the role of multiple and contradictory discourses in shaping the historical struggles, pain, and healing of African-American women (spiritual, legal, Afrocentric, etc.). The sketches focus on the violence of slavery, white women's complicity in the violence against black women in the South during the Reconstruction era, white supremacy, sexism within the Marcus Garvey movement, incest, and heterosexism within the black community, among other issues. While all the sketches are vivid and compelling, the last two are particularly relevant to my discussion because they highlight the projection of autobiographical scripts onto those marked as cultural others.

In the seventh sketch, a woman addicted to crack cocaine turned the othering gaze on the audience, in this case comprised mostly of white women, and urged us to see her as both a subject and an object of critique and to witness the struggles in these contradictions. This powerful piece worked both *with* and *against* the re-creation of the spectacle of the cultural other. McNeal accomplished this by having the crack addict speak directly to the audience and by implicating us as characters in her narrative. For instance, as the woman listed the common stereotypes people have about poor black women, she assured members of the audience that just because she gesticulated as she spoke, she was not going to explode into violence. She told the audience how she couldn't break the cycle and asked us how it felt to have a statistic talk back. This character sketch not only exposed the projection of certain auto-biographical scripts onto poor black women, but it also highlighted the self-other binary and how it facilitates unequal relations. Like Boal's workshop, this sketch is an example of the Brechtian performance of difference that Karamcheti advocates, a performance that calls attention not only to the speaker but to how the speaker is heard.

The eighth and final sketch took an unexpected autobiographical turn. Here McNeal reframed the self-other binary by conveying to the audience how she has internalized and negotiated certain autobiographical scripts and the historical legacy of violence against African-American women. She talked directly to the audience about her experiences of rape and sexual assault at college and then declared, "You thought that this was a play, but it is me breaking the cycles of generations, and I am a survivor." One could argue that the trope of survival at the end of the play consolidates the multiple subjec-tivities depicted in earlier sketches. In contrast to this reading, I would sug-gest that the effect of this autobiographical disclosure does not so much rein-force uncritical notions of a unified and fixed subjectivity as it opens up the possibility of reading the autobiographical subject as part of a "multiple-voiced subjectivity," itself contingent upon historically changing material and discursive contexts (Alarcón quoted in Grewal, 235). One might argue, then, that the autobiographical gesture in the final sketch provided a frame for participants to experience the performance of identity and the theatrical-ity of autobiographical subject in the process of becoming. In sum, McNeal's performance and Boal's workshop exemplify the potential of autobiography to expose and work through the risks of constructing the other as a pedagogi-cal spectacle.

## Pedagogy and the Politics of Location

My analysis of the dynamics of autobiography at particular conference sites reveals how struggles over cultural representation are not isolated in college classrooms. We must not, however, conflate pedagogical locales. Indeed, the process of moving from one pedagogical contact zone to another throws into relief the extent to which methods of enframing are contingent upon and situated within particular contexts. Rather than conclude this study with a litany of universal claims or pedagogical prescriptions, I want to call for additional site-specific pedagogical studies, which focus on the "different levels at which the articulation of theory and practice may proceed" (Probyn 1990, 177). Elspeth Probyn defines these different registers as the locale, the local, and the location. The locale refers to a place or setting for an event (discursive or nondiscursive); location refers to the methods used to locate sites of research and "delineates what we may hold as knowledgeable" (178); and local refers to the temporal and the articulation of a specific time. Location is not simply a metaphor for place or identity; it also includes the processes and methods by which research sites are selected, enframed, and studied. According to Probyn, local, locale, and location are dynamic; they do not exist in a pure state. In order to account for these dynamics as they shape our analysis of particular pedagogical sites, teachers-researchers should first recognize that local knowledge and locales are not natural or autonomous but that they exist in dialogue with larger cultural narratives and locations. While meanings are shaped by local sites and social arrangements, just as people at the mass dialogue called for the reinterpretation of the global and local, we have to ask how those inside and outside (or those who cross through, etc.) demarcate the local, which is both a rhetorical and a material site. Probyn's configuration of the levels at which articulation of theory and practice may proceed prompts a reexamination of the concept of the "politics of location." The term (coined by Adrienne Rich in her seminal essay "Notes Toward a Politics of Location"), as Kaplan points out, marks the "eruption of 'difference' in both activist and academic discourses" (1994, 140) and the "North American feminist articulation of difference . . . [and process] of interrogating and deconstructing the position, identity, and privilege of whiteness" (139). However, as the examples of the identification narratives at the composition conference illustrated, "reference to location is not transformative in and of itself. . . . Specifying location . . . is a standard gesture in the West, part of the production of value and knowledge that creates canons, races, genders, and a host of other marked categories" (149). The difference between a politics of location that repositions whiteness at the center and one that explores the convergences among local, locale, and location is that material bodies, contexts, and historicized struggles are foregrounded in the latter.

The implication of this reframing for autobiography studies, autoethnography, and pedagogical scholarship in particular is that autobiographical acts cannot "be read off the surface" (Probyn, 181). They must *not* be seen in isolation from the locale (place), the local (time), and the pedagogy and politics of location (methods of enframing). Questions about the transferability and replicability of my study become important in this regard. A staple of ethnographic methodology and qualitative research is that knowledge becomes generalizable through the accumulation of related inquiry and that the only things transferable are the methods themselves, though even they change as they are animated in new contexts. Like Lillian Mulero's *Untitled Mirrors,* discussed in the preface, the meaning of which would shift if the work was installed in a dressing room at Victoria's Secret, surrounded by the halls of Ellis Island, or hung among the mirrors in the Palace of Versailles, pedagogy emerges from particular projects, cultural discourses, and historical sites. What travels is not the transmission of pedagogical truths but critical aims and goals. What travels is the desire to develop dialogic pedagogical spaces, to understand how human agency is shaped by particular material, social, discursive, and historical contexts. What travels is the need to explore the links between cultural crises of representation and material and formal structural inequities. What travels is the need to document the hidden transcripts and the costs of silencing and exclusion, to track the consequences, pedagogical contradictions, and transformative potential of institutional policies, to create and critique counterpublic spaces where silences are interrupted and anger and passion can be transformed into action. What travels is the understanding that pedagogy is "a shifting set of theoretical and political interventions into the relationship between knowledge and authority" (Giroux 1994a, 155).

*Framing Identities* investigates the convergences among the locale, location, and the local through the practices of critical reflexivity, autoethnography, and the cultural and material analysis of the rhetorical configurations of autobiography and their consequences. This study of autobiographical acts (oral, written, performative, and visual) shows the links between the politics of pedagogy and the politics of self-representation. Additionally, it demonstrates how autobiographical acts play out in vexed and contradictory ways and how they become sites of cultural struggle in American institutions of higher education. I hope that *Framing Identities* will provide a model for teachers-researchers across the disciplines to study the performance of autobiography at the intersections of the material and discursive realms at their own institutions, to explore its contradictory uses and consequences (progressive and reactionary), and to enable them to imagine ways of using this knowledge to carve out new pedagogical spaces from which they and their students emerge as social, political, and intellectual subjects. Integrating our self-reflections with cultural, rhetorical, and material analysis, and encouraging our students to do the same, not only will go a long way toward justifying attention to the personal in the classroom but it also will help us move beyond a naive and reductive identity politics. I suggest that we turn the pedagogical looking glass upon ourselves and that we use the knowledge gained from critical reflexivity to rewrite the stories we tell about ourselves, our students, and our institutions.

Figure 8. From the *Untitled Mirrors* series (1990), by Lillian Mulero. Used by permission of the artist.

*Introduction*

1. There are numerous studies of the history of Oberlin College, its religious traditions, its role as an abolitionist center, and its renowned students, such as Lucy Stone (Fletcher, Lasser, Merrill, Solomon). A fascinating feature of reading these studies is seeing how various historians and local writers engage Oberlin's image of itself. (See Bigglestone, Blodgett, and Hosford for analyses of these constructions.) Although Oberlin was one of the first colleges to admit women, as Geoffrey Blodgett, a history professor at the college points out, the admission of women was not so much an indication of the school's enlightened approach to sexual equality but a way to produce as many Christian teachers and missionaries as possible—a more recent example of the gaps between the college's goals and practices has to do with support for lesbian, gay, and bisexual students on campus. Although Oberlin was the site of the first student lesbian, gay, and bisexual organization (1971), William Norris, a sociology professor at the college, argues that, despite extensive attitudinal support for these individuals at Oberlin, there was also widespread victimization. Norris argues that this paradox draws on institutional characteristics, culture, and priorities—namely, a liberal ethos that focuses on equal rights and a heterosexual orthodoxy. While it is interesting to analyze the stories that Oberlin tells about itself, this is not the focus of my current study. I provide those aspects of Oberlin's history that are essential to understanding my experience and study of particular events and the pedagogy and politics of identity on campus from 1991 through 1996.

2. According to a report by the statistician at Oberlin College, of the 2830

students enrolled in the fall of 1995, 220 were African-American; 6, Native American; 270, Asian-American; 113, Latino; 2072, white; and 149, "foreign." The 1995 Oberlin student body was comprised of students from seventeen foreign countries and forty-eight states. The cost of one year of education and room and board at Oberlin is approximately $28,000. A survey of the student self-reported family income for the 1994 incoming class estimated that 5 percent of the students were from families with incomes of $14,999 or less; 15 percent were from families with incomes between $15,000 and $29,999; 27 percent were from families with incomes between $30,000 and $59,999; 36 percent were from families with incomes between $60,000 and $149,000; and approximately 9 percent were from families with incomes of $150,000 or more (Office of Institutional Research, Oberlin College). For more current figures, see the website of the Oberlin College Office of Institutional Research (http://peacock.adm.oberlin.edu/ir.html). The average SAT scores of Oberlin students is V601 and M629. The statistics for 1995 show that 51 percent of those admitted were in the top 10 percent of their graduating class and 76 percent in the top 20 percent. Oberlin competes for students with colleges such as Amherst, Carleton, Grinnell, Haverford, Middlebury, Pomona, Swarthmore, Vassar, Wesleyan, and Williams and with universities such as Brown, Chicago, Duke, Pennsylvania, Stanford, and Yale.

3. In "Multiculturalism vs. Hegemony: Ethnic Studies, Asian Americans, and U.S. Racial Politics," E. San Juan Jr. questions the use of social-identity categories as oppositional strategies, arguing that they do not challenge the logic of liberal individualism and consumerism. Also see Jon Cruz's "From Farce to Tragedy: Reflections on the Reification of Race at the Century's End," in which he urges us to view multiculturalism as part of a "social logic of late capitalism." He argues that multiculturalism "mediates capitalism and modern social identities" (21).

4. See, for example, Villanueva, hooks (1994), James and Farmer, Zandy, Roof and Wiegman, Malinowitz, Kirsch (1993), and M. Rose.

5. For examples of this trend in feminist criticism, see Anzaldúa, Bannerji, Bauer, Bulkin, Grewal, Griffiths, hooks, Kaplan, Kuhn, Martin, N. Miller, M. B. Pratt, Smith and Watson, Tompkins; in critical and feminist pedagogy, see Ellsworth, Gallop, Grumet, Humm, Thompson and Wilcox, Weiler; in sociology of education, see Fine, Mohanty, Stanley; in anthropology, see Behar, Okely; and in literacy and composition studies, see L. Bloom, Brodkey, Chiseri-Strater, Gilyard, Hesford, Kirsch, Lu, Malinowitz, R. Miller (1996), Ritchie, Royster, Schlib, Soliday, N. Sommers, Worsham, and Villanueva, among others.

6. See, for example, the attack on Tompkins's "Pedagogy of the Distressed" in *College English* (53, no. 4 and 5 [1991] and 54, no. 4 [1992]) and the debate between Daphne Patai (Feb. 23, 1994) and Ruth Behar (June 29, 1994) in the *Chronicle of Higher Education*. Also see "Four Views of the Personal in Scholarship," *PMLA* (Oct. 1996): 1063–79.

7. Cultural-production theory is itself influenced by a variety of intellectual traditions, including the Frankfurt School of Marxist critical theory, Italian

Marxist Antonio Gramsci, the cultural theory of Raymond Williams, and the educational theory and practice of Paulo Freire. (See Weiler, 1–25.)

8. Hélène Cixous, Jacques Derrida, and Luce Irigaray are among those she labels ludic postmodernists.

9. Donna Haraway, Joan Scott, Gayatri Spivak, and Ebert herself are among those she labels resistance postmodernists.

10. For further discussions of the intersections of gender, race, and the "practice of theory," see Awkward, Collins, hooks (1989), McDowell, Rebolledo, B. Smith, V. Smith, and West.

## 1. Memory Work

This chapter was inspired by Annette Kuhn's compelling autobiography, *Family Secrets: Acts of Memory and Imagination,* and by Marianne Hirsch's *Family Frames: Photography, Narrative, and Postmemory,* which affirmed my belief in the transformative power of autobiography as a form of cultural criticism.

1. See Jeeves for a discussion of the history of labor and mining in South Africa.

2. See L. Bloom for a discussion of middle-class values in relation to the field of composition.

3. Similarly, Elizabeth Bruss maintains in *Autobiographical Acts: The Changing Situation of a Literary Genre* that an act is autobiographical if: (a) the author is both the creator and subject matter; (b) claims are made for the truth-value of what the autobiography reports—that is, the autobiography makes claims to historical veracity; and (c) the autobiographer believes what she or he claims (10–11). These three criteria constitute the "autobiographical contract," or as Philippe Le-Jeune argues in his influential work *On Autobiography,* the "autobiographical pact." The focus on the mimetic relationship between the author and narrator privileges a legalistic rhetoric of pacts and contracts, which ignores how legal rhetoric is shaped by particular ideologies of the self. I return to this notion of legal narrative of the self in chapter 5.

4. For instance, in the fourteenth century, the confession was used to police the language of mysticism (as defined by women mystics) and the contradictions between this language and the language of patriarchal ecclesiastical authority. Gilmore argues that the confession has functioned as a discourse that policed the authority of women mystics and maintained their marginality (see 56–61).

5. The publication of Estelle C. Jelinek's *Women's Autobiography: Essays in Criticism* in 1980 marked a change in attitude toward autobiography: writing by women previously regarded as nonexistent or unworthy was now accorded serious attention. In fact, the 1980s signaled a period of increased critical attention to the history of the genre and its configuration of gender and racial differences, as seen in publications such as: *Autobiography: Essays Theoretical and Critical,* edited by James Olney (1980); Domna Stanton's collection, *The Female Autograph* (1984);

Paul John Eakin's *Fictions in Autobiography: Studies in the Art of Self-Invention* (1985); Sidonie Smith's *A Poetics of Women's Autobiography* (1987); *Life/Lines: Theorizing Women's Autobiography,* edited by Bella Brodzki and Celeste Schenck (1988); *The Private Self,* edited by Shari Benstock (1988); Felicity Nussbaum's *The Autobiographical Subject: Gender and Ideology in Eighteenth-Century England* (1989); and Françoise Lionnet's *Autobiographical Voices: Race, Gender, and Self-Portraiture* (1989), among others. In addition to those studies already mentioned, several other significant works have contributed to the transformation of autobiography studies. These include: Felski; Gilmore; N. Miller (1988), (1991); Smith and Watson (1992), (1997); Stanley; Ashley, Gilmore, and Peters; and Thompson and Tyagi.

6. Soon thereafter, in *Sade Fourier Loyola* (1971), Barthes talks of the "return of the author" as if, in fact, the death of the author has occurred. As Burke points out, "A little like Dionysus, or Christ, the author must be dead before he can return" (30). In fact, the author "reappear[s] as a desire of the reader's, a spectre spirited back into existence by the critic himself" (30). This complicates the disappearance of the author in interesting ways. Here, the reader is seen as constructing the author. While there is a certain allure in this theoretical position, what is not central is recognition of how the reader's and writer's contexts come into contact and shape moments of production and reception.

7. For instance, in the 1960s and 1970s, in response to an increasingly diverse student population, the removal of admissions barriers, and an increase in financial aid for those previously denied access to a college education, the focus in composition pedagogy shifted from the written product and its correctness to the process of writing. Many in the field considered the shift progressive because one of its primary goals was to enable writers from diverse backgrounds to claim authority through the written word. But the process movement, shaped by modernist notions of the self, did not sufficiently account for the ways that cultural identities and differences complicate the writing process. Since the 1980s, there has been a growing interest in composition studies in the politics of writing and the cultural locations of writers.

8. In a 1990 report, the National Institute against Prejudice and Violence stated that 65–70 percent of U.S. minority students reported some form of harassment (Lawrence et al., 1). According to Ehrlich (1994), over the past seven years an average of one million such incidents have occurred on campuses per academic year. For more background and statistics on racial hate crimes on American campuses, see Aguirre (1990); Delgado (1991), Laramee (1991), and the U.S. Commission on Civil Rights (1990).

9. See Bizzell, Lu (1994), R. Miller (1994), Selfe and Selfe, Jr., and Van Slyck, for discussions of the pedagogical and curricular implications of the concept of the contact zone.

10. The pedagogical challenge I continually confront is finding ways to get students to move beyond mere descriptions of their experience to cultural analy-

sis. I have designed a number of assignments that invite students to experiment with autobiography as a form of cultural criticism and to facilitate the integration of theory and experience in their academic writing. For example, one essay option invites students to consider how familial and cultural stories have shaped or influenced the construction of their identity. If family members do not tend to tell stories or if family storytelling was so unimportant or insignificant an event, students can focus their papers on the significance of these facts. In other words, students could examine what might account for the lack of prominence of storytelling. I offer the following questions to help students generate ideas for their essay. Who tells the stories in your family? When are they told and where? Are there favorite stories that you or members of your family tell and retell? Are stories usually about the family or are they about the wider world? What values or moral lessons do the stories convey? Are some of the stories intended to be inspirational? Are some intended to induce guilt? Do family stories tend to be serious or humorous or do they fall in between? Who are the heroes of these stories? Who are the villains? What constitutes success, and what constitutes evidence of failure for the characters in these stories (e.g., material wealth, religious fervor, determination, education, a good marriage, etc.)? Whose interests do the stories represent? Does someone or some group of people within the family tend to control the storytelling mechanism? What is (or has been) your own role in your family's storytelling? Do you tell stories? Appear in stories? Or simply listen to stories? Do you or other members of the audience for a story sometimes disagree with the narrator about the accuracy of stories whose events you have also experienced? Have you experienced any changes in your views of, or attitudes toward, family stories? For instance, have you come to appreciate certain stories more in retrospect, or have you become suspicious of the intent behind stories you once enjoyed and accepted at face value? (I thank Len Podis for his refinement of this assignment.)

I also designed a writing assignment that invites students to investigate how the family is inscribed within visual systems of representation. The goal of this assignment is to help students understand the importance of cultural work and its effects. Photographs are useful in this regard as pedagogical texts in that they facilitate inquiry into the socially mediated nature of identity construction. For example, photographs of social functions are often tied to ideology of the modern family. Prior to this writing assignment, students would have read several essays that consider the role of visual culture in the family, the shifting contexts in which family photographs are seen, and how family photographs have the effect of naturalizing cultural practices and ideologies. For example, Marianne Hirsch's *Family Frames,* Kuhn's *Family Secrets,* and Jo Spence's *Family Snaps* all bring together the personal with the familial, the cultural, economic, and historical through an analysis of family photographs.

This essay option invites students to use family photographs as a basis for telling stories and to work with family photographs in ways similar to Kuhn,

Hirsch, and Spence—that is, to move among description, autobiography, and cultural and historical analyses and to become aware of the complexity of their own subjectivities and histories. Following are some of the questions I offer to help students generate ideas for their critical essays: Are the photographs you have chosen to work with part of an unofficial history of your family? In what ways is the family album or particular snapshots a way to represent the family and their everyday lives? Does the photograph represent an idealized image of your family, yourself, or particular family members? What does the family album or particular snapshots tell you about power relationships within the family? Does a particular series of photographs represent power struggles between men and women or between adults and children? Try to remember key events—emotional, social, or economic—that link up to the years you are dealing with in the photographs. How did these events shape the family's image of itself? In what ways do these photographs prompt you to reconsider your "self-history"? What is missing from the photograph? What pictures might have been taken but never were? What events or people were not recorded? What might have been impossible to represent? What scenarios are seen as possible subject matter for the family album? In other words, what remains invisible within family archives? What do these photographs tell you about the ways in which particular people (e.g., genders) are positioned in the world? What social and cultural values and ideas shape the family's visual representation of itself? Do Kuhn, Hirsch, or Spence provide a critical vocabulary and interpretive strategies to help you generate your own interpretation of your family's representation of itself? (Some of these questions are drawn from Kuhn's *Family Secrets* and Spence's *Cultural Sniping*.)

## 2. Autobiography and Feminist Writing Pedagogy

1. Also see S. Clark's discussion of the provisional nature of Flynn's earlier argument.

2. Centrist approaches to diversity are becoming more prevalent in composition through the inclusion of multicultural readers; these are published by large corporations that profit enormously through the production and marketing of difference. Although a few multicultural readers do historically and socially contextualize autobiographical acts, many perpetuate the myth of America as a cultural melting pot simply by stressing greater visibility of historically underrepresented groups, but they lack a critique of the unequal power relations of those who are looked at and those who look.

3. For a cultural and rhetorical analysis of the dynamics of 'zines, see McLaughlin, especially chapter 3, "Criticism in the 'Zines: Vernacular Theory and Popular Culture."

4. In "Essentialism and Experience," hooks reminds us of the ways essentialism is expressed from locations of privilege. Others remind us how essentialism is often used as a contingent strategy of empowerment and resistance. Joy

Ritchie, for example, in "Confronting the Essential Problem" highlights the ways students in a feminist-literature course shifted from naive essentialist positions to strategic essentialist positions as the semester progressed.

5. Feminists in fields other than composition have challenged liberal models of autobiography and essentializing tendencies in their pursuit of antiracist and antisexist pedagogies. See, for example, the work of Bannerji et al. and of Tokarczyk and Fay. Their work also offers an expanded conception of autobiographical practices as a form of cultural politics. For an insightful critique of the dominant metaphors and essentializing tendencies in creative-writing pedagogy, see Bishop 1988.

6. I want to thank Hans Ostrom for this insight.

### 3. Writing Identities

1. For additional critiques of expressionism, see Berlin, "Rhetoric and Ideology"; Bernstein; Catano; Clifford; Flannery; Hill; Jarratt; LeFevre; and Neel.

2. For extensive critiques of appropriations of expressionism in feminist composition, see Bernstein; Dingwaney and Needham; Jarratt; and Ritchie, "Confronting the Essential Problem."

3. See Spivak and Rooney; Higginbotham; hooks 1991.

4. For more on the dialogics of black literary traditions, see Henderson.

### 4. "Ye Are Witnesses"

1. For critiques of Western feminism, see Alarcón, Barrett, Brooks-Higginbotham, Davis, Ebert, Hennessy, hooks 1981, Lorde, and Spivak.

2. There are three phases of Oberlin's involvement in Asia. The first was the missionary phase. The second was the establishment of the Oberlin Shansi Memorial Association (OSMA, a nonprofit organization with headquarters on the Oberlin College campus), which oversaw the secularization of educational work, the development of middle schools in Asia, and the establishment of an agricultural department and a research center in China. The third is a mutual education exchange; currently, the association offers fellowships to any member of the Oberlin graduating class to teach English in universities in India, Indonesia, Japan, or the People's Republic of China for two years (Carlson). According to the OSMA website, "Shansi was founded in 1907 to provide support and guidance for consolidation of pre-1990 educational efforts begun by Oberlin College graduates in Taigu, Shanxi Province, China as early as 1881. . . . In addition to the educational exchange between Oberlin graduates and Asia, the Shansi Association sponsors many events on campus. It also sponsors an Asian Outreach program for the local schools, and provides books and materials to Asian institutions" (www.oberlin.edu/~shansi).

3. For a more detailed discussion of the complexities surrounding a histor-

ical appraisal of the Boxer Rebellion, see *Chinese Studies and History* (20) (spring/summer 1987).

4. First Amendment absolutists support unconditional protection of speech in all circumstances. See Smolla on the differences between absolute absolutism and qualified absolutism, especially pages 23–27.

5. I want to thank Adrienne Jones and Clayton Koppes for kindly giving me written copies of their speeches for my research.

6. For example, in *R.A.V. v. St. Paul,* the Minnesota State Supreme Court construed the burning cross found in front of a black family's house as "fighting words." This decision was later overthrown by the court, which argued that the burning cross constituted a "viewpoint" and thus was protected by the First Amendment. This decision is in marked contrast with the U.S. president's "don't ask, don't tell" policy on homosexuality in the military, where the simple declaration of homosexuality is understood to be a homosexual act—that is, speech is equated with conduct. In *R.A.V. v. St. Paul,* the court was willing to separate the burning cross as a sign of racial violence, not to mention the physical threat of injury by fire, from conduct, but in the case of sexual representation, the court felt compelled to collapse these distinctions (Butler, 21–22).

7. A now-classic example of the use of autobiography as a medium of social protest is the Combahee River Collective's autobiographical manifesto opposing racism of white middle-class feminism. As Sidonie Smith points out, autobiographical manifestos issue a call to action and foreground group identification over individuality (160–61).

8. Many recent multicultural readers reinforce these premises. For a more detailed discussion of institutionalized multiculturalism and the politics of multicultural education, see Giroux and McLaren, McCarthy, and Thompson and Tyagi.

9. For an analysis of race-management pedagogies and practices in the academy, see Mohanty, "On Race and Voice." For critiques of the rhetoric of equality and community in composition pedagogy, see Chordas, J. Harris, and Shirk.

10. I want to thank this student, whose name must remain anonymous, for giving me permission to use his paper and for his comments on an earlier draft of this chapter.

## 5. The Risks of Autobiography

1. A 1987 study conducted by two Oberlin students revealed that out of 331 Oberlin students polled, "49.4 percent of both female and male students had unwanted sexual experiences, with 28.9 percent engaging in unwanted coitus, oral and/or anal sex" (Redick and Harris, 6).

2. Oberlin's parliamentary procedures are based upon General Henry Roberts's *Rules of Order* (1876). Roberts, an Army engineer, originally devised the rules for organizations and men's clubs.

3. Similar patterns characterize the discourse against homosexuals in the military. For example, homosexuals are constructed as perverse; it is presumed that their presence will foster an atmosphere of harassment. The "don't ask, don't tell" policy on homosexuality in the military is, of course, a critique of homosexual "masculinity"; heterosexuality is the norm against which homosexuality is measured. For extended critiques of the constructed masculinity of the law, see Eisenstein, Frug, Grbich, and Wicke.

4. My discussion of women's contributions and silences is based upon selected conversations I had with junior and senior faculty, administrators, and professional staff a year after the policy passed. All the women I spoke with supported the policy, yet many did not participate in the discussions within the general faculty meetings, or if they did, they did not invoke autobiographical experiences. Moreover, because so many women faculty are overcommitted, many did not have time to attend all the meetings, which took place for several months. Because there are so few women of color on the faculty at Oberlin and because at least two professors of color were on leave during the year, their concerns were not heard in public forums. There are, of course, risks in speaking out about one's workplace. A woman of color on the staff told me over the phone that she felt the risks in speaking out were too great; she even hesitated to speak with me, fearing that if someone found out, she might lose her job. I wanted to understand why some women were silent at the meetings and what private assumptions and institutional barriers shaped their silences. During the interviews, I asked faculty and A&PS members who attended the meetings a number of questions, including: What is your perception of the general faculty meetings at which the sexual-offense policy was discussed? Why do you think so few women spoke at these meetings? How do you perceive or account for women's silences? Do you believe the primary purpose of these meetings was to pass the policy and/or to educate the community or something else? Do you believe the policy will contribute to progressive change?

5. Moreover, the recommended grievance procedures are based on an academic year, when the college is in session. Although the policy is supposed to cover all employee groups, if an incident occurs in the summer between, say, a staff worker and an administrator, victims may have to wait until the fall to resolve it.

6. Confidentiality—or, rather, the lack thereof—also hinders women's ability to speak out. As an administrator of color put it, "One would think that at such a small college we can do better at protection, at confidentiality. At any given time, there are at least ten people engaged on the hearing panel. . . . The promise of confidentiality is a wish . . . you can't have any litigation without it being public at some point." In order to take action or remedy the problem, one's anonymity and confidentiality are at risk.

7. See, for example, Caren Kaplan's 1992 essay on resistance literature and outlaw genres and my own discussion of strategic essentialism in chapter 3. For discussions of how marginalized groups substitute communal identities for the

bourgeois individual of traditional autobiography, see Anzaldúa, Henderson, Kaplan, Lionnet, D. Sommer, and Torres.

8. For further discussions of race and essentialism in feminist legal theory, see A. Harris.

9. I do not mean to deny the experiences of men who are victims of sexual harassment and assault; for example, gay bashing is on the rise on American campuses. Studies show, however, that women are more frequent victims of sexual harassment and violence.

10. For a discussion of the history of race and sexual violence in this country and on our nation's campuses and the factors related to African-American women, rape, and disclosure patterns, see Davis, Mitchell, Wriggins, and Wyatt. For discussions of sexual coercion and violence in gay male and lesbian relationships, see Duncan, Garnets et al., Hickson et al., Jenness and Broad, Lobel, Lowers, and Waterman et al. For discussions of patterns of sexual abuse involving victims with disabilities, see Grothaus, Merkin and Smith, and Sobsey and Doe. I thank Heather West, a former student at Oberlin College, for sharing her research on these intersections.

11. The clause that references sexual orientation occurs under the definition of sexual harassment. The particular section of the definition to which I refer reads as follows: "Behavior which is inappropriate to the academic or employment setting—for example, unwelcome or irrelevant comments, gestures, or touching—which may reasonably be perceived as a sexual overture or sexual denigration. This includes making known to other people a person's sexual orientation without his/her consent and with the intent to denigrate that person sexually" (from Oberlin College's Policy on Sexual Offenses, adopted by the general faculty on April 28, 1993, reprinted in the fall 1995 Information Guide from the Equity Claims office).

## 6. In and Out of the Flesh

1. Public-art activism, which emerged from political activism and the aesthetics of conceptual art in the late 1960s and early 1970s, often draws on the experiences of people from outside the art world and encourages community collaboration and public participation. Public-art activism is a prominent component of AIDS activism. For more information on public-arts activism as a movement, see Felshin, Gott, Kahn and Neumaier, and J. Miller.

2. The Women's International League for Peace and Freedom (WILPF) was established in 1915, nine months after World War I began. Women from nations at war united to demand peace. Throughout its eighty-three-year history, the WILPF has worked to promote peace, social justice, and gender and racial equality and to stop all forms of violence against women.

3. The National Network for the Clothesline Project and publisher of the national newsletter is located at P.O. Box 727, East Dennis, Massachusetts 02641. When the project was started in 1991, there was one clothesline with thirty-one

NOTES TO CHAPTER 6 — 169

shirts on it; a year later, forty-two Clothesline Projects were enacted with a total of fifteen hundred shirts; in February 1995, there were two hundred fifty clotheslines and thirty-five thousand shirts. These numbers reflect only a fraction of the women abused in the United States annually. According to the National Victim Center, in 1992 683,000 women were sexually assaulted in the United States. Every day 1,871 sexual assaults occur in this country. A reported rape occurs every six minutes, with only one in ten rapes actually reported. The National Resource Center on Domestic Violence estimates that every fifteen seconds a woman is battered in the United States. More than four million U.S. women are physically assaulted by a partner each year. According to the National Coalition of Rape Crisis Centers, one in four girls will have been sexually assaulted by the age of eighteen; 90 percent of children are raped by someone they know; 11 percent of all perpetrators are the victim's father or stepfather; and 29 percent of all rape victims are under age eleven. According to the National Gay and Lesbian Task Force, 40 percent of all lesbians are threatened with physical violence; one out of every five lesbians has been punched, hit, kicked, or beaten in her lifetime. The National Coalition against Domestic Violence estimates that every eleven days a woman is murdered by her husband or boyfriend in the United States, and sixteen hundred women were murdered by their partners in 1992 (National Network Clothesline Project literature).

4. I want to thank the producers of the film for inviting me to serve as commentator at the documentary's first screening at the 1994 Oral History Association Conference in New Mexico. My critique, based on the first cut of the film shown at the conference, has benefited from conversations with the producers as well as participants at the conference, particularly Kim Rogers. A third cut of the copyrighted film is now available through South Mountain Productions, 93 Old Town Rd., Gardners, Pennsylvania 17324. I would also like to thank Ethel Jensen for providing me background information and visual representations of the 1993 clothesline enacted at Dickinson College.

5. Organizers of the national project offer the following color codes to contributors as guidelines: White shirts indicate women who were murdered; yellow or beige shirts represent women who have been battered or assaulted; red, pink, or orange shirts represent women who have been raped or sexually assaulted; blue or green shirts represent women survivors of incest or child sexual abuse; and purple or lavender shirts represent women who have been abused simply because they are lesbian. These shirts are hung on the clothesline by the shirt-makers themselves or the organizers of local projects.

6. I distinguish between personal and political agency to highlight the fact that personal agency does not always lead to political agency. This is not to say that personal agency is inherently apolitical, for it too is shaped by political ideologies and struggles, but to suggest that the personal empowerment often associated with therapeutic models does not necessarily lead to political commitment or activism.

7. These patterns of representation are not limited to violence against women. They occur throughout social politics and the national discourse on crime, poverty, teenage pregnancy, and equal opportunity. For instance, the current backlash against affirmative action and the 1997 welfare-reform bill are examples of how the state and the media collaborate in constructing tales of excess, which position the disenfranchised as inferior and inadequate. The disenfranchised are cast as predators who deplete national resources and deprive the rest of the citizenry. The popularity of these retrenchment tales is based largely on their ability to invoke the myth of the American dream, the ideology of individualism, and the racist and sexist survival-of-the-fittest paradigm. The retraction of support services for the needy is linked to the spectacle of immigrants rushing national borders, a scenario that challenges "our" American Dream. The racial politics operative here are unmistakable. Mainstream media, like the state, serve up the racialized body (read black and poor) as commodities and reproduce the voyeurist gaze by constructing the other as a spectacle.

8. The tar-baby image appropriates an African folktale. The basic elements of the tale are that a trickster approaches a figure made of tar, rubber, or some other sticky substance. The trickster speaks to the figure and becomes angry when it fails to return his greeting. The trickster then strikes the figure and holds it until it can be apprehended. Versions of this folktale have been reported from the Guinea coast area, the Congo, and Angola, and are repeated throughout Africa. See, for example, "Anansi and the Gum Doll" and "Brer Rabbit" (*Standard Dictionary of Folklore, Mythology, and Legend*).

9. This subtitle is taken from Trinh T. Minh-ha's "The Totalizing Quest of Meaning," in *Theorizing Documentary,* edited by Michael Renov, p. 94.

10. These include *Fear That Binds Us, Rape Stories, Conspiracy of Silence,* and *First Person Plural.* I should point out that some these films raise problems of their own. *Conspiracy of Silence,* for example, does not define sufficiently the social obstacles and structural apparatus that define women's abuse as well as their healing. Most documentaries about sexual violence against women, at least those I have seen, position survivors as both subjects and objects of meaning. Some, however, such as *Rape Stories* and *First Person Plural* mediate these contradictions better than others.

11. My formulation of an aesthetics of impermanence is deeply influenced by the theoretical works of Shoshana Felman and Dori Laub on crises of witnessing in literature, psychoanalysis, and history and by the work of artists in concentration camps and ghettos. While we must not conflate cultural crises and victims, art created in the midst of a crisis, particularly a crisis of violence that is socially institutionalized and sanctioned by either direct participation or complicity, shares an aesthetic of impermanence and social action. Mary S. Costanza argues in *The Living Witness: Art in the Concentration Camps and Ghettos* that artists incarcerated in Nazi concentration camps, many of whom were moving toward an aesthetic of abstraction, resorted to the familiar art language of visual

realism in order to communicate the horrors they witnessed and endured. And we, she continues, "are the uncomfortable witnesses of these elegies in form and shape. . . . Looking at this art is not comfortable; it is meant to arouse the conscience and inflame some decent human outrage and indignation" (87).

12. Croce assumed that Jones had "crossed the line between theater and reality" by construing victimhood as an art spectacle. I say "assumed" because Croce never even saw the performance. She refused to see "Still/Here" because she thought it would force her into an "intolerably voyeuristic" position. Ironically, Croce's refusal to attend the performance turned the projected narcissism back onto herself: she became the subject of her review. Croce cast the critic as a victim, claiming that art about human trauma wounds the conscience of the critic. Her decision not to view "Still/Here" may have offered her a sense of protection and immunity, but her absence reinforced the historical silences and fatalism long associated with people with AIDS and other life-threatening illnesses. Implicit in the Croce-Jones controversy is a much larger debate about which communities get to position their stories as part of the cultural-aesthetic mastertext.

## Conclusion

1. In order to keep my analysis focused on institutional postures and their pedagogical consequences, to avoid the re-creation of individuals as pedagogical spectacles, and to limit the possibility of a biographical frame-up, I have decided *not* to identity individuals at the mass dialogue by name.

2. For critical uses of these tropes in critical pedagogy, see Giroux (1992) and Giroux and McLaren. For applications of these concepts in discussions about multicultural pedagogy in composition and literacy studies, see Severino, Guerra, and Butler, and Soliday; also see Bahri, Brodkey, Gilyard, Royster, Lu, M. Rose, and Smitherman. For investigations of these tropes as they play out in antiracist and antisexist pedagogy, see Bannerji, et al. and hooks (1994).

3. Reanae McNeal can be contacted through Imani Revelations, 2824 W. Locust Street, Suite B3121, Davenport, Iowa 52804.

# BIBLIOGRAPHY

Ackelsberg, Martha A. 1996. "Identity, Politics, Political Identities: Thoughts Toward a Multicultural Politics." *Frontiers* 16 (1): 87–100.

Aguirre, A., Jr., and J. Turner. 1995. *American Ethnicity: The Dynamics and Consequences of Discrimination.* New York: McGraw-Hill.

Alarcón, Norma. 1990. "The Theoretical Subject(s) of *This Bridge Called My Back* and Anglo-American Feminism." In *Making Face, Making Soul/Haciendo Caras: Creative and Critical Perspectives by Women of Color,* ed. Gloria Anzaldúa, 356–69. San Francisco: Aunt Lute Foundation Books.

Alcoff, Linda, and Laura Gray. 1993. "Survivor Discourse: Transgression or Recuperation." *Signs* 18 (2): 260–90.

Aloise, Connie, and Laura Lane. 1993. "Theorizing the Female Student for a Feminist Pedagogy." College, Composition, and Communication Conference. San Diego, Cal. April 1–3. Unpublished manuscript.

Altman, Meryl. 1990. "How Not to Do Things with Metaphors We Live By." *College English* 52 (5): 495–506.

Anzaldúa, Gloria, ed. 1990. *Making Face, Making Soul/Haciendo Caras: Creative and Critical Perspectives by Women of Color.* San Francisco: Aunt Lute Foundation Books.

———. 1987. *Borderlands/La Frontera: The New Mestiza.* San Francisco: Spinsters/Aunt Lute.

Ardener, Shirley, ed. 1975. *Perceiving Women.* London: Malaby Press.

Aronowitz, Stanley. 1994. *Dead Artists, Live Theories, and Other Cultural Problems.* New York: Routledge.

———. 1993. "Paulo Freire's Radical Democratic Humanism." In *Paulo Freire: A*

*Critical Encounter.* Ed. Peter McLaren and Peter Leonard. 8–24. London and New York: Routledge.

————, and Henry Giroux. 1985. *Education under Siege.* South Hadley, Mass.: Bergin and Garvey.

Arthur, John, and Amy Shapiro, eds. 1995. *Campus Wars: Multiculturalism and the Politics of Difference.* Boulder, Colo.: Westview Press.

Ashley, Kathleen, Leigh Gilmore, and Gerald Peters, eds. 1994. *Autobiography and Postmodernism.* Amherst: University of Massachusetts Press.

Auslander, Philip. 1994. "Boal, Blau, Brecht: The Body," in *Playing Boal: Theatre, Therapy, Activism.* Eds. Mady Schutzman and Jan Cohen-Cruz. 124–33. New York: Routledge.

Awkward, Michael. 1995. *Negotiating Difference: Race, Gender and the Politics of Positionality.* Chicago: The University of Chicago Press.

Bahri, Deepika. 1997. "Marginally Off-Center: Postcolonialism in the Teaching Machine." *College English* 59 (3): 277–98.

Bakhtin, Mikhail. 1986. *Marxism and the Philosophy of Language.* Trans. Ladislav Matejka and I. R. Titunik. Cambridge, Mass.: Harvard University Press.

————. 1981. *The Dialogic Imagination: Four Essays by M. M. Bakhtin,* trans. Michael Holquist and Caryl Emerson, ed. Michael Holquist. Austin: University of Texas Press.

Bannerji, Himani. 1995. *Thinking Through: Essays on Feminism, Marxism, and Anti-Racism.* Toronto: Women's Press.

Bannerji, Himani, Linda Carty, Kari Dehli, Susan Heald, and Kate McKenna. 1992. *UnSettling Relations: The University as a Site of Feminist Struggles.* Boston: South End Press.

Barrett, Michele. 1989. "Some Different Meanings of the Concept of 'Difference': Feminist Theory and the Concept of Ideology." In *The Difference Within,* ed. Elizabeth Meese and Alice Parker, 37–47. Philadelphia: John Benjamins Publishing Co.

Barthes, Roland. 1981. *Camera Lucida: Reflections on Photography,* trans. Richard Howard. New York: Hill and Wang.

————. 1977. "The Death of the Author." In *Image-Music-Text,* trans. and ed. Stephen Heath, 42–48, London: Fontana.

Bartky, Sandra Lee. 1988. "Foucault, Femininity, and Patriarchal Power." In *Feminism and Foucault: Reflections on Resistance,* ed. Irene Diamond and Lee Quinby, 61–86. Boston: Northeastern University Press.

Bauer, Dale. 1995. "Personal Criticism and the Academic Personality." *Who Can Speak: Authority and Critical Identity,* ed. Judith Roof and Robyn Wiegman, 56–69. Urbana and Chicago: University of Illinois Press.

Behar, Ruth. 1991. "The Body of the Woman, the Story in the Woman: A Book Review and Personal Essay." In *The Female Body: Figures, Styles, Speculations,* ed. Laurence Goldstein, 267–311. Ann Arbor: University of Michigan Press.

Belenky, Mary Field, Blythe McVicker Clinchy, Nancy Rule Goldberger, and Jill

Mattuck Tarule. 1986. *Women's Ways of Knowing: The Development of Self, Voice, and Mind.* New York: Basic Books.

Bennett, Tony. 1987. "The Prison-House of Criticism." *New Formations* 2: 127–44.

Benstock, Shari, ed. 1988. *The Private Self: Theory and Practice of Women's Autobiographical Writings.* Chapel Hill: University of North Carolina Press.

Bergland, Betty. 1994. "Postmodernism and the Autobiographical Subject: Reconstructing the Other." In *Autobiography and Postmodernism,* ed. Kathleen Ashley, Leigh Gilmore, and Gerald Peters, 130–66. Amherst: University of Massachusetts Press.

Berlin, James. 1988. "Rhetoric and Ideology in the Writing Class." *College English* 50 (5): 477–94.

Bernstein, Susan David. 1992. "Confessing Feminist Theory: What's 'I' Got to Do with It?" *Hypatia* 7 (2): 120–47.

Berthoff, Ann E. 1987. "The Teacher as Researcher." In *Reclaiming the Classroom: Teacher Research as an Agency for Change,* ed. Dixie Goswami and Peter Stillman, 28–38. Upper Montclair, N.J.: Boynton/Cook.

Bhabha, Homi. 1992. "A Good Judge of Character: Men, Metaphors, and the Common Culture." In *Race-ing Justice, En-gendering Power: Essays on Anita Hill, Clarence Thomas, and the Construction of Social Reality,* ed. Toni Morrison, 232–50. New York: Pantheon Books.

———. 1987. "Interrogating Identity." *Identity: The Real Me. ICA Documents* 6.

———. 1983. "The Other Questions—Homi K. Bhabha Reconsiders the Stereotype and Colonial Discourse." *Screen* 24 (6): 18–36.

Bigglestone, William E. 1981a. "Irrespective of Color." *Oberlin Alumni Magazine* 77 (spring): 35–36.

———. 1981b. *They Stopped in Oberlin: Black Residents and Visitors of the Nineteenth Century.* Scottsdale, Ariz: Innovation Group.

Bishop, Wendy. 1988. "Teaching Undergraduate Creative Writing: Myths, Mentors, and Metaphors." *Journal of Teaching Writing* 7: 83–102.

Bizzell, Patricia. 1997. "The 4th of July and the 22nd of December: The Function of Cultural Archives in Persuasion as Shown by Frederick Douglass and William Apess." *CCC* 48 (1) 44–60.

———. 1994. "'Contact Zones' and English Studies." *College English* 56 (2): 163–69.

Blair, Carole, Julie R. Brown, and Leslie A. Baxter. 1994. "Disciplining the Feminine." *Quarterly Journal of Speech* 80: 383–409.

Blodgett, Geoffrey. 1985. *Oberlin Architecture, College, and Town: A Guide to Its Social History.* Oberlin, Ohio: Oberlin College.

———. 1972. "Myth and Reality in Oberlin History." *Oberlin Alumni Magazine* 68 (May–June): 4–10.

Bloom, Allan. 1987. *The Closing of the American Mind: How Higher Education Has Failed Democracy and Impoverished the Souls of Today's Students.* New York: Simon and Schuster.

Bloom, Harold. 1994. *The Western Canon: The Books and Schools of the Ages.* New York: Harcourt Brace.

Bloom, Lynn. 1997. "American Autobiography and the Politics of Genre." In *Genre and Writing: Issues, Arguments, Alternatives,* ed. Wendy Bishop and Hans Ostrom. 151–59. Portsmouth, N.H.: Boynton/Cook.

———. 1996. "Freshman Composition as a Middle-Class Enterprise." *College English* 58 (6): 654–75.

Blue, Frederick J. 1989. "Oberlin's James Monroe: Forgotten Abolitionist." *Civil War History* 35 (4): 285–301.

Bordo, Susan R. 1989a. "The Body and the Reproduction of Femininity: A Feminist Appropriation of Foucault." In *Gender/Body/Knowledge/Feminist Reconstructions of Being and Knowing,* ed. Alison M. Jaggar and Susan R. Bordo, 13–33. New Brunswick, N.J.: Rutgers University Press.

———. 1989b. "Feminism, Postmodernism, and Gender-Scepticism." In *Feminism/Postmodernism,* ed. Linda J. Nichoson, 113–56. New York: Routledge.

Botstein, Leon, John Boswell, Joan Blythe, and William Kerrigan. 1993. "New Rules about Sex on Campus: Should Professors Be Denied Admission to Students' Beds?" *Harpers* 287 (1720): 33–42.

Bow, Leslie. 1995. "For Every Gesture of Loyalty, There Doesn't Have to Be Betrayal: Asian American Criticism and the Politics of Locality." In *Who Can Speak?: Authority and Critical Identity,* ed. Judith Roof and Robyn Wiegman, 30–35. Urbana: University of Illinois Press.

Brady, Laura. 1997. "The Reproduction of Othering." In *Feminism and Composition: In Other Words,* ed. Susan Jarratt and Lynn Worsham, 21–44. New York: Modern Language Association.

Braidotti, Rosi, Ewa Charkiewicz, Sabine Hausler, and Saskia Wieringa. 1994. *Women, the Environment and Sustainable Development: Towards a Theoretical Synthesis.* London: Zed Books with INSTRAW.

Brandt, Deborah. 1994. "Remembering Writing, Remembering Reading." *CCC* 45 (4): 459–79.

Bridwell-Bowles, Lillian. 1992. "Discourse and Diversity: Experimental Writing within the Academy." *College Composition and Communication* 43: 349–68.

Brodkey, Linda. 1987. "Writing Critical Ethnographic Narratives." *Anthropology and Education Quarterly* 18 (2): 67–76.

———, and Michelle Fine. 1992. "Presence of Mind in the Absence of Body." In *Disruptive Voices: The Possibilities of Feminist Research,* ed. Michelle Fine, 77–96. Ann Arbor: The University of Michigan Press.

Brodzki, Bella, and Celeste Schenck, ed. 1988. *LifeLines: Theorizing Women's Autobiography.* Ithaca, N.Y.: Cornell University Press.

Bronfen, Elisabeth. 1992. *Over Her Dead Body: Death, Femininity and the Aesthetic.* New York: Routledge.

Brown, Wendy. 1995. *States of Injury: Power and Freedom in Late Modernity.* Princeton: Princeton University Press.

Bruss, Elizabeth W. 1976. *Autobiographical Acts: The Changing Situation of a Literary Genre.* Baltimore: Johns Hopkins University Press.

Bulkin, Elly, Minnie Bruce Pratt, and Barbara Smith. 1988. *Yours in Struggle: Three Feminist Perspectives on Anti-Semitism and Racism.* Ithaca, N.Y.: Firebrand Books.

Burgin, Victor. 1982. *Thinking Photography.* London: MacMillan.

Burke, Seán. 1992. *The Death and Return of the Author: Criticism and Subjectivity in Barthes, Foucault, and Derrida.* Edinburgh: Edinburgh University Press.

Butler, Judith P. 1997. *Excitable Speech: A Politics of the Performative.* New York: Routledge.

———. 1993. *Bodies That Matter: On the Discursive Limits of "Sex."* New York: Routledge.

———. 1990. *Gender Trouble: Feminism and the Subversion of Identity.* New York: Routledge.

Cabusao, Jeffrey. 1996. "Asian American Studies Now!!!" *As I AM,* APA conference issue (spring) 19–21.

———. 1995. "Myths, Dreams, and Realities: Redefining Education As a Means of Resistance through Filipino American Experiences." Opening Doors Research Institute, Ohio State University. Unpublished paper.

Carlson, Ellsworth C. 1982. *Oberlin in Asia: The First Hundred Years 1882–1982.* Oberlin, Ohio: Oberlin Shansi Memorial Association.

Carr, Robert. 1994. "Crossing the First World/Third World Divides: Testimonial, Transnational Feminisms and the Postmodern Condition." In *Scattered Hegemonies,* ed. Inderpal Grewal and Caren Kaplan. Minneapolis: University of Minnesota Press.

Catano, James V. 1990. "The Rhetoric of Masculinity: Origins, Institutions, and the Myths of the Self-Made Man." *College English* 52 (4): 421–36.

Caywood, Cynthia L., and Gillian R. Overing. 1987. *Teaching Writing: Pedagogy, Gender, and Equity.* Albany: State University of New York Press.

Chambers, Iain. 1994. *Migrancy, Culture, Identity.* New York: Routledge.

Chien, Irene. 1995. "Autobiography and Feminist Discourse in Grrrl 'Zines." Unpublished manuscript.

Chiseri-Strater, Elizabeth. "Turning in upon Ourselves: Positionality, Subjectivity, and Reflexivity in Case Study and Ethnographic Research," ed. Peter Mortensen and Gesa E. Kirsch, 115–33. Urbana, Ill.: National Council of Teachers of English.

Chodorow, Nancy. 1978. *The Reproduction of Mothering: Psychoanalysis and the Sociology of Gender.* Berkeley: University of California Press.

Chordas, Nina. 1992. "Classrooms, Pedagogies, and the Rhetoric of Equality." *College Composition and Communication* 43 (2): 214–24.

Christian, Barbara. 1990. "The Race for Theory." In *Making Face, Making Soul/Haciendo Caras: Creative and Critical Perspectives by Women of Color,* ed. Gloria Anzaldúa, 335–45. San Francisco: Aunt Lute Foundation Books.

Cixous, Hélène. 1991. *"Coming to Writing" and Other Essays,* trans. Sarah Cornell et al., ed. Deborah Jenson. Cambridge, Mass.: Harvard University Press.

Clark, Gregory. 1990. *Dialogue, Dialectic, and Conversation: A Social Perspective on the Function of Writing.* Carbondale: Southern Illinois University Press.

Clark, Suzanne. 1997. "Argument and Composition." In *Feminism and Composition: In Other Words,* ed. Susan Jarratt and Lynn Worsham, 94–99. New York: Modern Language Association.

Clifford, John. 1991. "The Subject in Discourse." In *Contending with Words: Composition and Rhetoric in a Postmodern Age,* ed. Patricia Harkin and John Schilb, 38–51. New York: Modern Language Association.

*Clothesline.* 1994 (video). Produced by Susan Rose and Lonna Malsheimer. Gardners, Pa.: South Mountain Productions.

Cohen-Cruz, Jan. 1994. "Mainstream or Margin? US Activist Performance and Theatre of the Oppressed." In *Playing Boal: Theatre, Therapy, Activism,* eds. Mady Schutzman and Jan Cohen-Cruz, 110–23. New York: Routledge.

Collins, Jim. 1989. *Uncommon Cultures: Popular Culture and Post-Modernism.* New York: Routledge.

Collins, Patricia Hill. 1991. *Black Feminist Thought: Knowledge, Consciousness, and the Politics of Empowerment.* New York: Routledge.

Combahee River Collective, The. 1982. "A Black Feminist Statement." In *All Women Are White, All Blacks Are Men, But Some of Us Are Brave: Black Women's Studies,* ed. Gloria T. Hull, Patricia Bell Scott, and Barbara Smith, 13–22. Old Westbury, N.Y.: Feminist Press.

Cornell, Drucilla. 1991. *Beyond Accommodation: Ethical Feminism, Deconstruction, and the Law.* New York: Routledge.

Costanza, Mary S. 1982. *The Living Witness: Art in the Concentration Camps and Ghettos.* New York: Free Press.

Crenshaw, Kimberle. 1992. "Whose Story Is It, Anyway? Feminist and Antiracist Appropriations of Anita Hill." In *Race-ing Justice, En-gendering Power: Essays on Anita Hill, Clarence Thomas, and the Construction of Social Reality,* ed. Toni Morrison, 402–40. New York: Pantheon Books.

Croce, Arlene. 1994. "Discussing the Undiscussable." *The New Yorker* 70 (43): 54–60.

Crosby, Christina. 1992. "Dealing with Differences." In *Feminists Theorize the Political,* ed. Judith Butler and Joan W. Scott, 130–43. New York: Routledge.

Cruz, Jon. 1996. "From Farce to Tragedy: Reflections on the Reification of Race at the Century's End." In *Mapping Multiculturalism,* ed. Avery Gordon and Christopher Newfield, 19–39. Minneapolis: University of Minnesota Press.

Culley, Margo, ed. 1992. *American Women's Autobiography: Fea(s)ts of Memory.* Madison: University of Wisconsin Press.

Davis, Angela. 1983. *Women, Race, and Class.* New York: Vintage Books.

Delgado, R. 1991. "Campus Antiracism Rules: Constitutional Narratives in Collision." *Northwestern University Law Review* 85: 343–87.

De Man, Paul. 1979. "Autobiography As De-facement." *MLN* 94: 919–30.

DeMott, Benjamin. 1992. *The Imperial Middle: Why Americans Can't Think Straight about Class.* New Haven, Conn.: Yale University Press.

Denzin, Norman K. 1995. "The Experiential Text and the Limits of Visual Understanding." *Educational Theory* 45 (1): 7–18.

Diamond, Irene, and Lee Quinby. 1988. "American Feminism and the Language of Control." In *Feminism and Foucault: Reflections on Resistance,* ed. Irene Diamond and Lee Quinby, 193–206. Boston: Northeastern University Press.

Dingwaney, Anuradha, and Lawrence Needham. 1992. "Feminist Theory and Practice in the Writing Classroom: A Critique and a Prospectus." In *Constructing Rhetorical Education: From the Classroom to the Community,* ed. Marie Secor and Davida Charney, 6–25. Carbondale: Southern Illinois University Press.

Duncan, David F. 1990. "Prevalence of Sexual Assault Victimization among Heterosexual and Gay/Lesbian University Students." *Psychological Reports* 66 (1): 65–66.

Duster, Troy. 1991. "Understanding Self-Segregation on the Campus." *The Chronicle of Higher Education* (September 25): B1–B2.

Eakin, Paul John, ed. 1991. *American Autobiography: Retrospect and Prospect.* Madison: University of Wisconsin Press.

———. 1985. *Fictions in Autobiography: Studies in the Art of Self-Invention.* Princeton, N.J.: Princeton University Press.

Ebert, Teresa T. 1993. "Ludic Feminism, the Body, Performance, and Labor: Bringing *Materialism* Back into Feminist Cultural Studies." *Cultural Critique* (winter): 5–50.

———. 1991. "The 'Difference' of Postmodern Feminism." *College English* 53 (8): 886–904.

———. 1988. "The Romance of Patriarchy: Ideology, Subjectivity, and Postmodern Feminist Cultural Theory." *Cultural Critique* (fall): 19–37.

Ehrlich, H. 1994. "Reporting Ethnoviolence: Newspaper Treatment of Race and Ethnic Conflict." *Z Magazine* (June): 53–60.

Eisenstein, Zillah R. 1994. *The Color of Gender: Reimaging Democracy.* Berkeley and Los Angeles: University of California Press.

Ellsworth, Elizabeth. 1992. "Teaching to Support Unassimilated Difference." *Radical Teacher* 42: 4–9.

———. 1989. "Why Doesn't This Feel Empowering? Working through the Repressive Myths of Critical Pedagogy." *Harvard Educational Review* 59 (3): 297–324.

Faigley, Lester. 1992. *Fragments of Rationality: Postmodernity and the Subject of Composition.* Pittsburgh, Pa.: University of Pittsburgh Press.

Fairchild, James. 1984. *Oberlin: The Colony and the College. 1833–1883.* New York: Garland Publications.

Farris, Christine. 1996. *Subject to Change: New Composition Instructor's Theory and Practice.* Cresskill, N.Y.: Hampton Press.

Feldman, Allen. 1991. *Formations of Violence: The Narrative of the Body and Political Terror in Northern Ireland.* Chicago: University of Chicago Press.

Felman, Shoshana. 1993. *What Does a Woman Want? Reading and Sexual Difference.* Baltimore: Johns Hopkins University Press.

———, and Dori Laub. 1992. *Testimony: Crises of Witnessing in Literature, Psychoanalysis, and History.* New York: Routledge.

Felshin, Nina, ed. 1995. *But Is It Art?: The Spirit of Art as Activism.* Seattle: Bay Press.

Felski, Rita. 1989. *Beyond Feminist Aesthetics: Feminist Literature and Social Change.* Cambridge, Mass.: Harvard University Press.

Ferguson, Kathy E. 1993. *The Man Question: Visions of Subjectivity in Feminist Theory.* Berkeley: University of California Press.

Fine, Michelle. 1992. *Disruptive Voices: The Possibilities of Feminist Research.* Ann Arbor: University of Michigan Press.

Finke, Laurie. 1993. "Knowledge As Bait: Feminism, Voice, and the Pedagogical Unconscious." *College English* 55 (1): 7–27.

Fisher, Berenice. 1994. "Feminist Acts: Women, Pedagogy, and Theatre of the Oppressed." In *Playing Boal: Theatre, Therapy, Activism,* eds. Mady Schutzman and Jan Cohen-Cruz. New York: Routledge.

Flannery, Kathryn T. 1991. "Composing and the Question of Agency." *College English* 53 (6): 701–13.

Fletcher, Robert Samuel. 1943. *A History of Oberlin College: From Its Foundation through the Civil War.* Oberlin, Ohio: Oberlin College.

Flynn, Elizabeth. 1995. "Review: Feminist Theories/Feminist Composition." *College English* 57 (2) 201–12.

———. 1988. "Composing As a Woman." *College Composition and Communication* 39 (4): 423–35.

Foucault, Michel. 1983. *This Is Not a Pipe,* trans. and ed. James Harkness. Berkeley: University of California Press.

Fox-Genovese, Elizabeth. 1988. "My Statue, My Self: Autobiographical Writings of Afro-American Women." In *The Private Self: Theory and Practice of Women's Autobiographical Writing,* ed. Shari Benstock, 63–89. Chapel Hill and London: University of North Carolina Press.

Frankenberg, Ruth. 1996. "When We Are Capable of Stopping, We Begin to See: Being White, Seeing Whiteness." In *Names We Call Home,* ed. Becky Thompson and Sangeetz Tyagi, 3–18. New York: Routledge.

———. 1993. *White Women, Race Matters: The Social Construction of Whiteness.* Minneapolis: University of Minnesota Press.

Fraser, Nancy. 1992. "The Uses and Abuses of French Discourse Theories for Feminist Politics." In *Revaluing French Feminism,* ed. Nancy Fraser and Sandra Lee Bartky, 177–94. Bloomington: Indiana University Press.

———. 1990. "Rethinking the Public Sphere: A Contribution to the Critique of Actually Existing Democracy." *Social Text* 25/26: 56–80.

Freedman, Diane P. 1992. *An Alchemy of Genres: Cross-Genre Writing by American Feminist Poet-Critics.* Charlottesville: University Press of Virginia.

Freire, Paulo. 1985. *The Politics of Education.* South Hadley, Mass.: Bergin and Garvey.

———. 1970. *Pedagogy of the Oppressed,* trans. Myra Bergman Ramos. New York: Continuum.

Frey, Olivia. 1987. "Equity and Peace in the New Writing Class." In *Teaching Writing:*

*Pedagogy, Gender, and Equity,* ed. Cynthia L. Caywood and Gillian R. Overing, 93–106. Albany: State University of New York.

Friedman, Susan Stanford. 1995a. "Beyond White and Other: Relationality and Narratives of Race and Feminist Discourse." *Signs* 21 (1): 1–49.

———. 1995b. "Making History: Reflections on Feminism, Narrative, and Desire." In *Feminism Beside Itself,* ed. Diane Elam and Robyn Wiegman, 11–53. New York: Routledge.

Frug, Mary Joe. 1992. *Postmodern Legal Feminism.* New York: Routledge.

Fusco, Coco. 1995. *English Is Broken Here: Notes on Cultural Fusion in the Americas.* New York: The New Press.

Fuss, Diana. 1989. *Essentially Speaking: Feminism, Nature, and Difference.* New York: Routledge.

Gallop, Jane. 1997. *Feminist Accused of Sexual Harassment.* Durham, N.C. and London: Duke University Press.

———, ed. 1995. *Pedagogy: The Question of Impersonation.* Bloomington: Indiana University Press.

Garnets, Linda, Gregory M. Herek, and Barrie Levy. 1990. "Violence and Victimization of Lesbians and Gay Men." *Journal of Interpersonal Violence* 5 (3): 366–83.

Gates, Henry Louis, Jr. 1986. "Editor's Introduction: Writing 'Race' and the Difference It Makes." In *'Race,' Writing and Difference,* ed. Henry Louis Gates Jr., 1–20. Chicago: University of Chicago Press.

Gilligan, Carol. 1982. *In a Different Voice: Psychological Theory and Women's Development.* Cambridge, Mass.: Harvard University Press.

Gilmore, Leigh. 1994. *Autobiographics: A Feminist Theory of Women's Self-Representation.* Ithaca, N.Y., Cornell University Press.

Gilmore, Perry, David M. Smith, and Apacuar Larry Kairaiuak. 1997. "Resisting Diversity: An Alaskan Case of Institutional Struggle. In *Off White: Readings on Race, Power, and Society,* 90–99. New York: Routledge.

Gilyard, Keith. 1991. *Voices of the Self: A Study of Language Competence.* Detroit: Wayne State University Press.

Giroux, Henry A. 1994a. *Disturbing Pleasures: Learning Popular Culture.* New York: Routledge.

———. 1994b. "Insurgent Multiculturalism and the Promise of Pedagogy." In *Multiculturalism: A Critical Reader,* ed. David Theo Goldberg, 325–43. Boston: Blackwell Publishers.

———. 1992. *Border Crossings: Cultural Workers and the Politics of Education.* New York: Routledge.

———, and Peter McLaren. 1994. *Between Borders: Pedagogy and the Politics of Cultural Studies.* New York: Routledge.

Gitlin, Andrew, and Audrey Thompson. 1995. "Creating Spaces for Reconstructing Knowledge in Feminist Pedagogy." *Educational Theory* 45 (2): 125–50.

Gitlin, Todd. 1995. "Identity Politics: An Examination and a Critique." In *Higher*

*Education under Fire: Politics, Economics, and Crisis of the Humanities,* ed. Michael
  Berube and Cary Nelson, 308–25. New York: Routledge.

Glasser, Ira. 1994. "Introduction." In *Speaking of Race, Speaking of Sex: Hate Speech, Civil
  Rights, and Civil Liberties,* ed. Henry Louis Gates Jr. et al., 1–16. New York: New York
  University Press.

Gordon, Avery F., and Christopher Newfield, ed. 1996. *Mapping Multiculturalism.*
  Minneapolis: University of Minnesota Press.

Gott, Ted, ed. 1994. *Don't Leave Me This Way: Art in the Age of AIDS.* New York: Thames
  and Hudson.

Graff, Gerald. 1992. *Beyond the Culture Wars: How Teaching the Conflicts Can Revitalize
  American Education.* New York: Norton.

Grbich, Judith E. 1991. "The Body in Legal Theory." In *At the Boundaries of Law:
  Feminism and Legal Theory,* ed. Martha Albertson Fineman and Nancy Sweet
  Thomadsen, 61–76. New York: Routledge.

Grealy, Lucy. 1994. *Autobiography of a Face.* Boston: Houghton Mifflin Company.

Grewal, Inderpal. 1994. "Autobiographic Subjects and Diasporic Locations: *Meatless Days*
  and *Borderlands.*" In *Scattered Hegemonies: Postmodernity and Transnational Feminist
  Practices,* eds. Inderpal Grewal and Caren Kaplan, 231–54. Minneapolis: University of
  Minnesota Press.

———, and Caren Kaplan. 1994. *Scattered Hegemonies: Postmodernity and Transnational
  Feminist Practices.* Minneapolis: University of Minnesota Press.

Griffiths, Morwenna. 1995. *Feminisms and the Self: The Web of Identity.* New York:
  Routledge.

Grosz, Elizabeth A. 1994. *Volatile Bodies: Toward a Corporeal Feminism.* Bloomington:
  Indiana University Press.

Grothaus, Rebecca S. 1985. "Abuse of Women with Disabilities." In *With the Power of
  Each Breath,* ed. Susan E. Browne, Debra Connors, and Nanci Stern, 125–28.
  Pittsburgh, Pa.: Cleis Press.

Grover, Jan Zita. 1992. "Public Art on AIDS: On the Road with Art against AIDS." In
  *A Leap in the Dark: AIDS, Art, and Contemporary Cultures,* ed. Allan Klusacek and
  Ken Morrison, 58–69. Montreal: V'ehicule Press.

Grumet, Madeleine R. 1988. *Bitter Milk: Women and Teaching.* Amherst: University of
  Massachusetts Press.

Grundy, Shirley. 1987. *Curriculum: Product or Praxis.* New York: The Falmer Press.

Gunn, Janet Varner. 1982. *Autobiography: Towards a Poetics of Experience.* Philadelphia:
  University of Pennsylvania Press.

Gusdorf, George. 1980. "Conditions and Limits of Autobiography." (1956) Trans. James
  Olney. Rpt. *Autobiography: Essays Theoretical and Critical.* Ed. James Olney, 28–48.
  Princeton: Princeton University Press.

Hairston, Maxine. 1992. "Diversity, Ideology, and Teaching Writing." *College
  Composition and Communication* 43 (2): 179–93.

Hall, Stuart. 1987. "Minimal Selves." In *Identity: The Real Me,* ICA Documents 6: 44–46.

Haraway, Donna. 1991. *Simians, Cyborgs, and Women: The Reinvention of Nature.* New York: Routledge.

———. 1988. "Situated Knowledges: The Science Question in Feminism and the Privilege of Partial Perspective." *Feminist Studies* 14 (3): 575–99.

Harding, Sandra. 1993. "Eurocentric Scientific Illiteracy—A Challenge for the World Community." In *The "Racial" Economy of Science: Toward a Democratic Future,* ed. Sandra Harding, 1–29. Bloomington: Indiana University Press.

Harris, Angela. 1993. "Race and Essentialism in Feminist Legal Theory." In *Feminist Legal Theory Foundations,* ed. D. Kelly Weisberg, 348–58. Philadelphia: Temple University Press.

Harris, Joe. 1989. "The Idea of Community in the Study of Writing." *College Composition and Communication* 40 (1): 11–22.

Hayano, David M. 1979. "Auto-Ethnography: Paradigms, Problems, and Prospects." *Human Organization* 38 (1): 99–104.

Henderson, Mae Gwendolyn. 1990. "Speaking in Tongues: Dialogics, Dialectics, and the Black Woman Writer's Literary Tradition." In *Reading Black, Reading Feminist: A Critical Anthology,* ed. Henry Louis Gates Jr., 116–42. New York: Meridian Books.

Hennessy, Rosemary. 1993. *Materialist Feminism and the Politics of Discourse.* New York: Routledge.

Henning, Barbara. 1991. "The World Was Stone Cold: Basic Writing in an Urban University." *College English* 53 (1): 674–85.

Herman, Judith Lewis. 1992. *Trauma and Recovery.* New York: Basic Books.

Hesford, Wendy. 1997a. "Autobiography and Feminist Writing Pedagogy." In *Genres: Mapping the Territories of Discourse,* ed. Wendy Bishop and Hans Ostrom, 160–72. Portsmouth, N.H.: Boynton/Cook.

———. 1997b. "'Ye Are WITNESSES': Pedagogy and the Politics of Identity." In *Feminism and Composition: In Other Words,* ed. Susan Jarratt and Lynn Worsham, 132–52. New York: Modern Language Association.

———. 1997c. "Writing Identities: The 'Essence' of Difference in Multicultural Classrooms." In *Writing in Multicultural Settings,* ed. Carol Severino, Juan Guerra, and Johnnella Butler, 133–49. New York: Modern Language Association.

———. 1992. *Women Reading the Self, Word, World.* Ph.D. diss. New York University.

Hevia, James. 1992. "Leaving a Brand on China: Missionary Discourse in the Wake of the Boxer Movement." *Modern China* 18 (3): 304–32.

Hicks, D. Emily. 1991. *Border Writing: The Multidimensional Text.* Minneapolis: University of Minnesota Press.

Hickson, Ford C.I., Peter M. Davis, Andrew J. Hunt, Peter Weatherburn, Thomas J. McManus, and Anthony P. M. Coxon. 1994. "Gay Men as Victims of Nonconsensual Sex." *Archives of Sexual Behavior* 23 (3): 281–94.

Higginbotham, Evelyn Brooks. 1992. "African-American Women's History and the Metalanguage of Race." *Signs* 17 (2): 251–74.

Hill, Carolyn Ericksen. 1990. *Writing from the Margins: Power and Pedagogy for Teachers of Composition.* New York: Oxford University Press.

Hirsch, E. D., Jr. 1987. *Cultural Literacy: What Every American Needs to Know.* Boston: Houghton-Mifflin.

Hirsch, Marianne. 1997. *Family Frames: Photography, Narrative, and Postmemory.* Cambridge: Harvard University Press.

Holbrook, Sue Ellen. 1991. "Women's Work: The Feminizing of Composition." *Rhetoric Review* 9 (2): 201–29.

Holquist, Michael. 1990. *Dialogism: Bakhtin and His World.* New York: Routledge.

hooks, bell. 1994. *Teaching to Transgress: Education as the Practice of Freedom.* New York: Routledge.

————. 1992. *Black Looks: Race and Representation.* Boston: South End Press.

————. 1991. "Essentialism and Experience." *American Literary History* 3 (1): 172–83.

————. 1990. *Yearning: Race, Gender, and Cultural Politics.* Boston: South End Press.

————. 1989a. "feminist politicization: a comment." In *Talking Back: Thinking Feminist, Thinking Black,* 105–11. Boston: South End Press.

————. 1989b. *Talking Back: Thinking Feminist, Thinking Black.* Boston: South End Press.

————. 1984. *Feminist Theory from Margin to Center.* Boston: South End Press.

————. 1981. *Ain't I a Woman: Black Women and Feminism.* Boston: South End Press.

Horrigan, Bill. 1993. "Notes on AIDS and Its Combatants: An Appreciation." *Theorizing Documentary,* ed. Michael Renov, 164–74. New York: Routledge.

Hosford, Frances J. 1934. "Oberlin No-Myths." *Oberlin Alumni Magazine* 30 (March): 232–35.

————. 1933. "Oberlin Myths." *Oberlin Alumni Magazine* 29 (July): 232–35.

————. 1930. "The Oberlin Idea." *Oberlin Alumni Magazine* 26 (July): 296–98.

Hum, Sue. 1997. " 'Yes, We Eat Dog Back Home': Contrasting Disciplinary Discourse and Praxis on Diversity." Rhetoric and Composition Conference, Pennsylvania State University. Unpublished manuscript.

Humm, Maggie. 1989. "Subjects in English: Autobiography, Women, and Education." In *Teaching Women: Feminism and English Studies,* eds. Ann Thompson and Helen Wilcox, 39–49. Manchester and New York: Manchester University Press.

Hurtado, Aída. 1989. "Relating to Privilege: Seduction and Rejection in the Subordination of White Women and Women of Color." *Signs* 14 (41): 833–55.

Jacobson, Carl. 1995. "The 'Oberlin Band' in Shanxi, 1881–1900." Unpublished paper.

James, Joy. 1996. *Resisting State Violence: Radicalism, Gender, and Race in U.S. Culture.* Minneapolis: University of Minnesota Press.

————, and Ruth Farmer. 1993. *Spirit, Space and Survival: African American Women in (White) Academe.* New York and London: Routledge.

Jameson, Fredric. 1979. "Reification and Utopia in Mass Culture." *Social Text* 1: 130–48.

JanMohamed, Abdul R. 1994. "Some Implications of Paulo Freire's Border Pedagogy." In *Between Borders: Pedagogy and the Politics of Cultural Studies,* ed. Henry Giroux and Peter McLaren, 242–52. New York: Routledge.

Jarratt, Susan. 1991. "Feminism and Composition: The Case for Conflict." In *Contending with Words: Composition and Rhetoric in a Postmodern Age,* ed. Patricia Harkin and John Schilb, 105–23. New York: Modern Language Association.

Jay, Paul. 1994. "Posing: Autobiography and the Subject of Photography." In *Autobiography and Postmodernism,* ed. Kathleen Ashley, Leigh Gilmore, and Gerald Peters, 191–211. Amherst: University of Massachusetts Press.

Jeeves, Alan H. 1985. *Migrant Labour in South Africa's Mining Economy: The Struggle for the Gold Mines' Labour Supply 1890–1920.* Montreal: McGill-Queen's University Press.

Jenness, Valerie, and Kendal Broad. 1994. "Antiviolence Activism and the (In)visibility of Gender in the Gay/Lesbian and Women's Movements. *Gender and Society* 8 (3): 402–23.

Jikui, Li. 1987. "How to View the Boxers' Religious Superstitions." *Chinese Studies and History* 29 (3, 4): 98–112.

Kahn, Douglas, and Diane Neumaier, eds. 1985. *Cultures in Contention.* Seattle: Real Comet Press.

Kakalia, Narges. 1996. "DESI: Reflections on Starting Out." *DESI: Discourse Expressing South Asian Issues* 1: 4–5.

Kaplan, Caren. 1994. "The Politics of Location as Transnational Feminist Critical Practice." In *Scattered Hegemonies: Postmodernity and Transnational Feminist Practices,* ed. Inderpal Grewal and Caren Kaplan, 137–52. Minneapolis: University of Minnesota Press.

———. 1992. "Resisting Autobiography: Outlaw Genres and Transnational Feminist Subjects." In *De/Colonizing the Subject: The Politics of Gender in Women's Autobiography,* ed. Sidonie Smith and Julia Watson, 115–38. Minneapolis: University of Minnesota Press.

———. 1987. "Deterritorializations: The Rewriting of Home and Exile in Western Feminist Discourse." *Cultural Critique* 6: 187–98.

Karamcheti, Indira. 1995. "Caliban in the Classroom." In *Pedagogy: The Question of Impersonation,* ed. Jane Gallop, 138–54. Bloomington: Indiana University Press.

Kauffman, Linda. 1993. "The Long Goodbye: Against Personal Testimony, or an Infant Grifter Grows Up." *American Feminist Thought at Century's End,* ed. Linda Kauffman, 258–77. Oxford: Blackwell.

Kelsh, Deb. 1993. "The Feminization of Composition: Practitioners and Student Writers." College Composition and Communication Conference. San Diego, Cal. April 1–3. Unpublished manuscript.

Kendall, Elaine. 1975. *"Peculiar Institutions": An Informal History of the Seven Sister Colleges.* New York: G. P. Putnam's Sons.

Kirsch, Gesa. 1993. *Women Writing the Academy: Audience, Authority, and Transformation.* Carbondale: Southern Illinois University Press.

———, and Joy Ritchie. 1995. "Beyond the Personal: Theorizing a Politics of Location in Composition Research." *College Composition and Communication.* 46 (1): 7–29.

Knoblauch, C. H. 1988. "Rhetorical Constructions: Dialogue and Commitment." *College English* 50 (2): 125–40.

Kozol, Wendy. Forthcoming. "Can Feminist Pedagogy Find a Safe Space: White

Defensiveness and the Politics of Silence." *Concerns,* special issue, ed. Wendy Hesford and Lisa Jadwin.

———. 1995. "Fracturing Domesticity: Media, Nationalism, and the Question of Feminist Influence." *Signs* 20 (3): 646–67.

Kraemer, Don. 1991. "Abstracting the Bodies of/in Academic Discourse." *Rhetoric Review* 10 (1): 52–69.

Kruks, Sonia. 1995. "Identity Politics and Dialectical Reason: Beyond an Epistemology of Provenance." *Hypatia* 10 (2): 1–22.

Kuhn, Annette. 1995. *Family Secrets: Acts of Memory and Imagination.* London: Verso.

La Belle, Jenijoy. 1988. *Herself Beheld: The Literature of the Looking Glass.* Ithaca, N.Y.: Cornell University Press.

Lakritz, Andrew. 1995. "Identification and Difference: Structures of Privilege in Cultural Criticism." In *Who Can Speak?: Authority and Critical Identity,* ed. Judith Roof and Robyn Wiegman, 3–24. Urbana: University of Illinois Press.

Landau, Terry. 1989. *About Faces: The Evolution of the Human Face.* New York: Anchor Books.

Laramee, W. 1991. "Racism, Group Defamation and Freedom of Speech on Campuses." *NASPA Journal* 29: 55–62.

Lasser, Carol, ed. 1987. *Educating Men and Women Together: Coeducation in a Changing World.* Urbana: University of Illinois Press.

Lawrence, Charles III. 1993. "If He Hollers Let Him Go: Regulating Racist Speech on Campus." In *Words That Wound: Critical Race Theory, Assaultive Speech, and the First Amendment,* ed. Mari Matsuda, Charles Lawrence III, Richard Delgado, and Kimberle Williams Crenshaw, 53–88. Boulder, Colo.: Westview Press.

LeFevre, Karen Burke. 1987. *Invention as a Social Act.* Carbondale: Southern Illinois University Press.

LeJeune, Philippe. 1989. *On Autobiography,* ed. Paul John Eakin, trans. Katherine Leary. Minneapolis: University of Minnesota Press.

Leonard, Delavan L. 1898. *The Story of Oberlin: The Institution, the Community, the Idea, the Movement.* Chicago: Pilgrim Press.

Lionnet, François. 1989. *Autobiographical Voices: Race, Gender, Self-Portraiture.* Ithaca, N.Y.: Cornell University Press.

Lobel, Kerry, ed. 1986. *Naming the Violence: Speaking Out about Lesbian Battering.* Seattle: Seal Press.

Lorde, Audre. 1984. *Sister Outsider.* Trumansburg, N.Y.: The Crossing Press.

Lowers, Jane. 1995. "Rape: When the Assailant Is One of Our Own." *Deneuve* (September/October): 36–38.

Lu, Min-Zhan, and Bruce Horner. 1998. "The Problematic of Experience: Redefining Critical Work in Ethnography and Pedagogy." *College English* 60 (3): 257–77.

Lu, Min-Zhan. 1994. "Representing and Negotiating Differences in the Contact Zone." Paper presented at Oberlin College, Oberlin, Ohio.

———. 1992. "Conflict and Struggle: The Enemies or Preconditions of Basic Writing?" *College English* 54 (8): 887–913.

————. 1987. "From Silence to Words: Writing as Struggle." *College English* 49 (4): 437–48.

Lubiano, Wahneema. 1992. "Black Ladies, Welfare Queens, and State Minstrels: Ideological War by Narrative Means." In *Race-ing Justice, En-gendering Power: Essays on Anita Hill, Clarence Thomas, and the Construction of Social Reality,* ed. Toni Morrison, 323–63. New York: Pantheon Books.

Luke, Carmen, and Jennifer Gore, eds. 1992. *Feminists and Critical Pedagogy.* New York: Routledge.

Mailloux, Steven. 1994. "Rhetorically Covering Conflict: Gerald Graff As Curricular Rhetorician." In *Teaching the Conflicts: Gerald Graff, Curricular Reform, and the Culture War,* ed. William E. Cain. New York: Garland Publishing.

Malinowitz, Harriet. 1995. *Textual Orientations: Lesbian and Gay Students and the Making of Discourse Communities.* Portsmouth, N.H.: Boynton/Cook.

Martin, Biddy. 1988a. "Feminism, Criticism, and Foucault." In *Feminism and Foucault: Reflections on Resistance,* ed. Irene Diamond and Lee Quinby, 3–20. Boston: Northeastern University Press.

————. 1988b. "Lesbian Identity and Autobiographical Differences." *Life/Lines: Theorizing Women's Autobiography,* ed. Bella Brodski and Celeste Schenck, 77–103. Ithaca, N.Y.: Cornell University Press.

Matsuda, Mari. 1993. "Public Response to Racist Speech: Considering the Victim's Story." In *Words That Wound: Critical Race Theory, Assaultive Speech, and the First Amendment,* ed. Mari Matsuda, Charles Lawrence III, Richard Delgado, and Kimberle Williams Crenshaw, 17–52. Boulder, Colo.: Westview Press.

Matsuhashi, Ann, et al. 1989. "A Theoretical Framework for Studying Peer Tutoring as Response." In *Writing and Response: Theory, Practice, and Research,* ed. Chris M. Anson, 293–317. Carbondale, Ill.: National Council of Teachers of English.

Matthews, Nancy A. 1994. *Confronting Rape: The Feminist Anti-Rape Movement and the State.* New York: Routledge.

McCarthy, Cameron. 1994. "Multicultural Discourses and Curriculum Reform: A Critical Perspective." *Educational Theory* 44 (1): 81–98.

McClintock, Anne. 1995. *Imperial Leather: Race, Gender, and Sexuality in the Colonial Contest.* New York: Routledge.

McDowell, Deborah. 1995. "Transferences Black Feminist Discourse: The 'Practice' of Theory" In *Feminism Beside Itself,* ed. Diane Elam and Robyn Wiegman, 93–118. New York: Routledge.

McLaren, Peter. 1996. "La Lucha Continua: Freire, Boal, and the Challenge of History—To My Brothers and Sisters in Struggle." *Researcher* 11 (2): 5–10.

————. 1995. *Critical Pedagogy and Predatory Culture: Oppositional Politics in a Postmodern Era.* New York: Routledge.

————. 1994. "Multiculturalism and the Postmodern Critique: Toward a Pedagogy of Resistance and Transformation." In *Between Borders: Pedagogy and the Politics of Cultural Studies,* ed. Henry A. Giroux and Peter McLaren, 192–222. New York: Routledge.

————. 1991. "Schooling the Postmodern Body: Critical Pedagogy and the Politics of Enfleshment." In *Postmodernism, Feminism, and Cultural Politics,* ed. Henry A. Giroux, 144–73. Albany: State University of New York Press.

————, and Tomaz Tadeu da Silva. 1993. "Decentering Pedagogy: Critical Literacy, Resistance, and the Politics of Memory." In *Paulo Freire: A Critical Encounter,* ed. Peter McLaren and Peter Leonard, 47–89. London and New York: Routledge.

McLaughlin, Thomas. 1996. *Street Smarts and Critical Theory: Listening to the Vernacular.* Madison: University of Wisconsin Press.

McNay, Lois. 1992. *Foucault and Feminism: Power, Gender and the Self.* Boston: Northeastern University Press.

Merkin, Lewis, and Marilyn J. Smith. 1995. "A Community-Based Model Providing Services for Deaf and Deaf-Blind Victims of Sexual Assault and Domestic Violence." *Sexuality and Disability* 13 (2): 97–106.

Merrill, Marlene D. 1987. "Daughters of America Rejoice: The Oberlin Experiment." *Timeline* 4 (October–November): 12–21.

————. 1983a. "Radical Women and the Survival of Early Oberlin." *Oberlin Alumni Magazine* 79 (spring): 4–9.

————. 1983b. "Radical Women Helped to Save Early Oberlin." In *The Observer* 4 (March): 6, 4.

Miller, James. 1992. "Criticism As Activism." In *Fluid Exchanges: Artists and Critics in the AIDS Crisis,* ed. James Miller, 185–214. Toronto: University of Toronto Press.

Miller, Nancy K. 1991. *Getting Personal: Feminist Occasions and Other Autobiographical Acts.* New York: Routledge.

Miller, Richard E. 1996. "The Nervous System." *College English* 58 (3): 265–86.

————. 1994. "Fault Lines in the Contact Zone." *College English* 56 (4): 389–408.

Miller, Susan. 1991. *Textual Carnivals: The Politics of Composition.* Carbondale: Southern Illinois University Press.

Minghan, Ding. 1987. "Some Questions Concerning the Appraisal of the Boxer Movement." *Chinese Studies and History* 29 (3, 4): 24–41.

Minh-ha, Trinh T. 1993. "The Totalizing Quest of Meaning." In *Theorizing Documentary,* ed. Michael Renov, 90–107. New York: Routledge.

————. 1989. *Woman, Native, Other: Writing Postcoloniality and Feminism.* Bloomington: Indiana University Press.

Minnich, Elizabeth Kamarck. 1990. *Transforming Knowledge.* Philadelphia: Temple University Press.

Mitchell, Camille Hamlin. 1995. "Sexual Harassment of Undergraduate American Women: An Assessment of the Experience, Attitude, and Perception of Behaviors." Ph.D. diss. Cleveland State University.

Mohanty, Chandra Talpade. 1994. "On Race and Voice: Challenges for Liberal Education in the 1990s." *Cultural Critique* (winter): 179–208.

————. 1987. "Feminist Encounters Locating the Politics of Experience." *Copyright* 1: 30–44.

————, Ann Russo, and Lourdes Torres, eds. 1991. *Third World Women and the Politics of Feminism*. Bloomington: Indiana University Press.

Morrison, Margaret. 1997. "Celebrating Dis-eases of Women at Waytoofast." *Feminism and Composition: In Other Words,* eds. Susan Jarratt and Lynn Worsham, 206–14. New York: Modern Language Association.

Morrison, Toni. *Race-ing Justice, En-Gendering Power: Essays on Anita Hill, Clarence Thomas, and the Construction of Social Reality.* New York: Pantheon, 1992.

Mouffe, Chantal. 1992. "Feminism, Citizenship, and Radical Democratic Politics." In *Feminists Theorize the Political,* ed. Judith Butler and Joan W. Scott, 369–84. New York: Routledge.

Neel, Jasper. 1988. *Plato, Derrida, and Writing.* Carbondale: Southern Illinois University Press.

Newfield, Christopher and Avery F. Gordon. 1996. "Multiculturalism's Unfinished Business." In *Mapping Multiculturalism,* 76–115. Minneapolis: University of Minnesota Press.

Newton, Judith Lowder. 1994. *Starting Over: Feminism and the Politics of Cultural Critique.* Ann Arbor: University of Michigan Press.

Nichols, Bill. 1993. "Getting to Know You . . . Knowledge, Power, and the Body." In *Theorizing Documentary,* ed. Michael Renov, 174–92. New York: Routledge.

Norris, William P. 1992. "Liberal Attitudes and Homophobic Acts: The Paradoxes of Homosexual Experience in a Liberal Institution." In *Coming Out of the Classroom Closet: Gay and Lesbian Students, Teachers, and Curricula,* ed. Karen M. Harbeck, 81–120. New York: Harrington Park Press.

Nussbaum, Felicity. 1989. *The Autobiographical Subject: Gender and Ideology in Eighteenth-Century England.* Baltimore: Johns Hopkins University Press.

Oates, Joyce Carol. 1995. "Confronting Head On the Face of the Afflicted." *New York Times,* February 19, sec. 2: 1, 22.

Oberlin Shansi Memorial Association Newsletter. 1995. "The Boxer Uprising Symposium," page 1; "Class of '94 Plaque," page 2. No. 91, spring/summer.

Okely, Judith, and Helen Callaway, ed. 1992. *Anthropology and Autobiography.* New York: Routledge.

Perry, Ruth. 1992. "A Short History of the Term Politically Correct." In *Beyond PC: Toward a Politics of Understanding,* ed. Patricia Aufderheide, 71–79. Saint Paul, Minn.: Graywolf Press.

Phelan, Peggy. 1993. *Unmarked: The Politics of Performance.* New York: Routledge.

Plummer, Ken. 1995. *Telling Sexual Stories: Power, Change, and Social Worlds.* London and New York: Routledge.

Pratt, Mary Louise. 1992. *Imperial Eyes: Travel Writing and Transculturation.* London and New York: Routledge.

————. 1991. "Arts of the Contact Zone." *Profession* (91) 33–40.

Pratt, Minnie Bruce. 1984. "Identity: Skin Blood Heart." In *Yours in Struggle: Three Feminist Perspectives on Anti-Semitism and Racism.* Ithaca, N.Y.: Firebrand Books.

Probyn, Elspeth. 1993. *Sexing the Self: Gendered Positions in Cultural Studies.* New York: Routledge.

———. 1990. "Travels in the Postmodern: Making Sense of the Local." In *Feminism/Postmodernism,* ed. Linda Nicholson, 176–89. New York: Routledge.

Puar, Jasbir K. 1994. "Writing My Way 'Home': Traveling South Asian Bodies and Diasporic Journeys." *Socialist Review* 24(4): 75–108.

Rajchman, John, ed. 1995. *The Identity in Question.* New York: Routledge.

Ray, Ruth E. 1993. *The Practice of Theory: Teacher Research in Composition.* Urbana, Ill.: National Council of Teachers of English.

Rebolledo, Tey Diana. 1990. "The Politics of Poetics: Or What Am I, a Critic, Doing in this Text Anyway?" In *Making Face, Making Soul/Haciendo Caras: Creative and Critical Perspectives by Women of Color,* ed. Gloria Anzaldúa, 346–55. San Francisco: Aunt Lute Foundation Books.

Redick, Alison, and Sara Harris. 1991. "We're Gonna CRASH Your Policy." *Perspective* (October 3): 6–7.

Renov, Michael, ed. 1993. *Theorizing Documentary.* New York and London: Routledge.

Riccardi, Nicholas. 1993. "Student Faces Fire after Meeting." *The Oberlin Review* 122 (9) Friday, November 12: 1.

Rich, Adrienne. 1979. "When We Dead Awaken: Writing as Revision." In *On Lies, Secrets, and Silence,* 33–49. New York: Norton.

Ritchie, Joy S. 1990. "Confronting the Essential Problem: Reconnecting Feminist Theory and Pedagogy." *Journal of Advanced Composition* 10 (2): 249–73.

Roberts, General Henry M. 1951. *Roberts Rules of Order, Revised.* Chicago: Scott, Foresman and Co.

Roiphe, Katie. 1993. *The Morning After: Fear, Sex, and Feminism on Campus.* Boston: Little Brown and Co.

Roman, Leslie. 1997. "Denying (White) Racial Privilege: Redemption Discourses and the Uses of Fantasy." In *Off White: Readings on Race, Power, and Society,* 270–82. New York: Routledge.

———. 1993. "White Is a Color! White Defensiveness, Postmodernism, and Anti-Racist Pedagogy." In *Race Identity and Representation in Education,* ed. Cameron McCarthy and Warren Crichlow, 71–88. New York: Routledge.

Roof, Judith, and Robyn Wiegman, ed. 1995. *Who Can Speak? Authority and Critical Identity.* Urbana: University of Illinois Press.

Rose, Gillian. 1993. *Feminism and Geography.* Minneapolis: University of Minnesota Press.

Rose, Mike. 1989. *Lives on the Boundary.* New York: Free Press.

Rosen, Philip. 1993. "Document and Documentary: On the Persistence of Historical Concepts." In *Theorizing Documentary,* ed. Michael Renov, 58–89. New York: Routledge.

Ross, Andrew. 1992. "The Private Parts of Justice." *Race-ing Justice, En-gendering Power: Essays on Anita Hill, Clarence Thomas, and the Construction of Social Reality,* ed. Toni Morrison, 40–60. New York: Pantheon Books.

Royster, Jacqueline Jones. 1996. "When the First Voice You Hear Is Not Your Own." *CCC* 47. 1: 29–40.

Said, Edward W. 1995. "The Role of the Critical Intellectual." Lecture, May 10. Oberlin College, Oberlin, Ohio.

———. 1989. "Representing the Colonized: Anthropology's Interlocuters." *Critical Inquiry* 15 (winter): 205–25.

Salazar, Claudia. 1991. "A Third World Woman's Text: Between the Politics of Criticism and Cultural Politics." In *Women's Words: The Feminist Practice of Oral History*, ed. Sherna Berger Gluck and Daphne Patai, 93–106. New York: Routledge.

San Juan, E. Jr. 1991. "Multiculturalism vs. Hegemony: Ethnic Studies, Asian Americans, and U.S. Racial Politics." *Massachusetts Review* 32 (3): 467–78.

Scarry, Elaine. 1985. *The Body in Pain: The Making and Unmaking of the World*. New York: Oxford University Press.

Schleitwiler, Vincent. 1996. "Notes on Multiculturalism at Oberlin." *As I AM*, APA Conference issue (spring): 22–24.

Schilb, John. 1996. *Between the Lines: Relating Composition Theory and Literary Theory*. Portsmouth, N.H.: Boynton/Cook.

Schnell, Eileen E. 1997. "The Costs of Caring: 'Feminism' and Contingent Women Workers in Composition Studies." In *Feminism and Composition: In Other Words*, eds. Susan Jarratt and Lynn Worsham. New York: Modern Language Association.

Schutzman, Mady, ed. *Playing Boal: Theatre, Therapy, Activism*. By Jan Cohen-Cruz. New York: Routledge, 1993.

Scott, James J. 1990. *Domination and the Arts of Resistance*. New Haven, Conn.: Yale University Press.

Scott, Joan W. 1991. "The Evidence of Experience." *Critical Inquiry* 17 (summer): 773–97.

Selfe, Cynthia, and Richard J. Selfe, Jr. 1994. "The Politics of the Interface: Power and Its Exercise in Electronic Contact Zones." *CCC* 45 (4): 480–504.

Sekula, Allan. 1986. "The Body and the Archive." *October* 39: 3–64.

Severino, Carol, Juan Guerra, and Johnnella Butler, eds. 1997. *Writing in Multicultural Settings*. New York: Modern Language Association.

Shilling, Chris. 1993. *The Body and Social Theory*. London: Sage Publications.

Shirk, Margaret. 1993. "Eclecticism and Competing Logics in Composition." College, Composition, and Communication Conference. San Diego, Cal. April 1–3. Unpublished manuscript.

Shohat, Ella, and Robert Stam. 1996. "From the Imperial Family to the Transnational Imaginary: Media Spectatorship in the Age of Globalization." In *Global/Local: Cultural Production and the Transnational Imaginary*, ed. Rob Wilson and Wimal Dissanayake, 145–70. Durham, N.C.: Duke University Press.

Shor, Ira. 1993. "Education Is Politics: Paulo Freire's Critical Pedagogy." In *Paulo Freire: A Critical Encounter*, ed. Peter McLaren and Peter Leonard, 25–35. London and New York: Routledge.

Silverman, Kaja. 1988. *The Acoustic Mirror: The Female Voice in Psychoanalysis and Cinema.* Bloomington: Indiana University Press.

Simon, Roger. 1996. "Memories of 'That Which Has Never Been My Fault or Deed': Heteropathic Recollection and Transtemporal Aesthetics." Modern Language Association Conference. Unpublished paper.

Slater, Don. 1995. "Domestic Photography and Digital Culture." *The Photographic Image in Digital Culture,* ed. Martin Lister, 129–46. New York and London: Routledge.

Smart, Carol. 1989. *Feminism and the Power of Law.* London: Routledge.

Smith, Barbara. 1990. "Racism and Women's Studies." In *Making Face, Making Soul/ Haciendo Caras: Creative and Critical Perspectives by Women of Color,* ed. Gloria Anzaldúa, 25–28. San Francisco: Aunt Lute Foundation Books.

Smith, Sidonie. 1993. *Subjectivity, Identity, and the Body: Women's Autobiographical Practices in the Twentieth Century.* Bloomington: Indiana University Press.

———. 1987. *A Poetics of Women's Autobiography: Marginality and the Fictions of Self-Representation.* Bloomington: Indiana University Press.

———, and Julia Watson, ed. 1992. *De/Colonizing the Subject: The Politics of Gender in Women's Autobiography.* Minneapolis: University of Minnesota Press.

Smitherman, Geneva. 1977. *Talkin and Testifyin: The Language of Black America.* Boston: Houghton Mifflin.

Smolla, Rodney A. 1992. *Free Speech in an Open Society.* New York: Random House.

Sobsey, Dick, and Tanis Doe. 1991. "Patterns of Sexual Abuse and Assault." *Sexuality and Disability* 9 (3): 243–59.

Soliday, Mary. 1994. "Translating Self and Difference Through Literacy Narratives." *College English* 56 (5): 511–25.

Solomon, Barbara Miller. 1985. *In the Company of Educated Women.* New Haven, Conn.: Yale University Press.

Sommer, Doris. 1988. "Not Just a Personal Story: Women's *Testimonios* and the Plural Self." *Life/Lines: Theorizing Women's Autobiography,* 107–30. Ithaca, N.Y. and London: Cornell University Press.

Sommers, Nancy. 1993. "I Stand Here Writing." *College English* 55 (4): 420–28.

———. 1992. "Between the Drafts." *College Composition and Communication* 43 (1): 23–31.

Spain, Daphne. 1992. *Gendered Spaces.* Chapel Hill: University of North Carolina Press.

Spellmeyer, Kurt. 1989. "A Common Ground: The Essay in the Academy." *College English* 51 (3): 262–76.

Spence, Jo. 1995. *Cultural Sniping: The Art of Transgression.* London and New York: Routledge.

———, and Patricia Holland. 1991. *Family Snaps: The Meaning of Domestic Photography.* London: Virago Press.

Spivak, Gayatri. 1990. *The Post-Colonial Critic,* ed. Sarah Harasym. New York: Routledge.

———, and Ellen Rooney. 1989. "In a Word. Interview." *Differences* 1 (2): 124–56.

Spurr, David. 1993. *The Rhetoric of Empire: Colonial Discourse in Journalism, Travel*

*Writing, and Imperial Administration.* Durham, N.C. and London: Duke University Press.

Stanley, Liz. 1992. *The auto/biographical I: The Theory and Practice of Feminist Auto/Biography.* Manchester, N.Y.: Manchester University Press.

Stansell, Christine. 1992. "White Feminists and Black Realities: The Politics of Authenticity." In *Race-ing Justice, En-gendering Power: Essays on Anita Hill, Clarence Thomas, and the Construction of Social Reality,* ed. Toni Morrison, 251–68. New York: Pantheon Books.

Stanton, Domna C., ed. 1987. *The Female Autograph.* Chicago: University of Chicago Press.

————1986. "Difference on Trial: A Critique of the Maternal Metaphor in Cixous, Irigaray, and Kristeva." In *The Poetics of Gender,* ed. Nancy K. Miller, 157–82. New York: Columbia University Press.

Stepan, Nancy Leys, and Sander Gilman. 1993. "Appropriating the Idioms of Science: The Rejection of Scientific Racism." In *The 'Racial' Economy of Science: Toward a Democratic Future,* ed. Sandra Harding, 170–200. Bloomington: Indiana University Press.

Stevens, Patricia E., and Joanne M. Hall. 1990. "Abusive Health Care Interactions Experienced by Lesbians: A Case of Institutional Violence in the Treatment of Women." *Response* 13 (3): 23–27.

Stockton, Kathryn Bond. 1992. "Bodies and God: Poststructuralist Feminists Return to the Fold of Spiritual Materialism." *Boundary 2,* special issue on feminism and post-modernism, ed. Margaret Ferguson and Jennifer Wicke, 19 (2): 113–49.

Stone, Albert. 1991. "Modern American Autobiography: Texts and Transactions." In *American Autobiography: Retrospect and Prospect,* ed. Paul John Eakin, 95–122. Madison: University of Wisconsin Press.

Stranger, Carol. 1987. "The Sexual Politics of the One-to-One Tutorial Approach and Collaborative Learning." In *Teaching Writing: Pedagogy, Gender, and Equity,* ed. Cynthia L. Caywood and Gillian Overing, 31–44. Albany: State University of New York.

Sturgis, Alice. 1953. *Learning Parliamentary Procedure.* New York: McGraw-Hill.

Tagg, John. 1988. *The Burden of Representation.* Amherst: University of Massachusetts Press.

Tal, Kali. 1996. *Worlds of Hurt: Reading the Literatures of Trauma.* New York: Cambridge.

Taylor, Bryan, and Charles Conrad. 1992. "Narratives of Sexual Harassment: Organizational Dimensions." *Journal of Applied Communication Research* 20 (4): 401–18.

Tedesco, Janis. 1991. "Women's Ways of Knowing/Women's Ways of Composing." *Rhetoric Review* 9 (2): 245–56.

Thomas, Kendall. 1992. "Strange Fruit." In *Race-ing Justice, En-gendering Power: Essays on Anita Hill, Clarence Thomas, and the Construction of Social Reality,* ed. Toni Morrison, 364–89. New York: Pantheon Books.

Thomas, Nicholas. 1994. *Colonialism's Culture: Anthropology, Travel, and Government.* Princeton, N.J.: Princeton University Press.

Thompson, Ann, and Helen Wilcox, eds. 1989. *Teaching Women: Feminism and English Studies.* Manchester and New York: Manchester University Press.

Thompson, Becky W. 1996. *Names We Call Home: Autobiography on Racial Identity.* New York: Routledge.

Thompson, Becky W., and Sangeeta Tyagi, eds. 1993. *Beyond a Dream Deferred: Multicultural Education and the Politics of Excellence.* Minneapolis: University of Minnesota Press.

Tokarczyk, Michelle M., and Elizabeth A. Fay. 1993. *Working-Class Women in the Academy: Laborers in the Knowledge Factory.* Amherst: University of Massachusetts Press.

Tompkins, Jane. 1987. "Me and My Shadow." *New Literary History.* 19 (1). 197–200.

Torres, Lourdes. 1991. "The Construction of the Self in U.S. Latina Autobiographies." In *Third World Women and the Politics of Feminism,* ed. Chandra Talpade Mohanty, Ann Russo, and Lourdes Torres, 271–87. Bloomington: Indiana University Press.

Truth, Sojourner. 1990. "Ain't I a Woman." In *Issues in Feminism: An Introduction to Women's Studies,* ed. Sheila Ruth, 463–64. Boston: Houghton Mifflin.

Tryzelaar, Anneke. 1993a. "New Sexual Offense Proposal to Be Presented." *The Oberlin Review* 121 (21) (April 9): 1, 7.

———. 1993b. "Sexual Offense Issues Consume Campus." *The Oberlin Review* 121 (27) (May 28): 11.

Tryzelaar, Anneke, John Kearney, and David Schneider. 1993. "Students Storm Cox, Protesting Racism." *The Oberlin Review* 122 (9) (November 12): 7, 10.

Twentieth-Century Fox Film Corporation. 1991. *Sleeping with the Enemy,* dir. Joseph Rubin. Beverly Hills, Cal.: Fox Video.

U.S. Commission on Civil Rights. 1990. *Bigotry and Violence on American College Campuses.* Washington, D.C.: U.S. Government Printing Office.

Van Slyck, Phillis. 1997. "Repositioning Ourselves in the Contact Zone." *College English* 59: 149–70.

Villanueva, Victor Jr. 1993. *Bootstraps: From an American Academic of Color.* Urbana, Ill.: National Council of Teachers of English.

Volishinov, V.N. 1986. *Marxism and the Philosophy of Language,* trans. Ladislav Matejka and I. R. Titunik. Cambridge, Mass.: Harvard University Press.

Wallace, Michelle. 1990. "Variations on Negation and the Heresy of Black Feminist Creativity." In *Reading Black, Reading Feminist: A Critical Anthology,* ed. Henry Louis Gates Jr., 52–67. New York: Meridian Book.

Warner, Michael. 1992. "The Mass Public and the Mass Subject." In *Habermas and the Public Sphere,* ed. Craig Calhoun, 377–401. Cambridge, Mass.: MIT Press.

Waterman, Caroline K., Lori J. Dawson, and Michael J. Bologna. 1989. "Sexual Coercion in Gay Male and Lesbian Relationships: Predictors and Implications for Support Services." *The Journal of Sex Research* 26 (1): 118–24.

Weiler, Kathleen. 1988. *Women Teaching for Change: Gender, Class, and Power.* South Hadley, Mass.: Bergin and Garvey.

Wellman, David. 1996. "Red and Black in White America: Discovering Cross-Border Identities and Other Subversive Activities." In *Names We Call Home: Autobiography on Racial Identity,* ed. Becky W. Thompson and Sangeeta Tyagi, 29–42. New York: Routledge.

West, Cornel. 1995. "A Matter of Life and Death." In *The Identity in Question,* ed. John Rajchman, 15–32. New York: Routledge.

Wiegman, Robyn. 1995. *American Anatomies: Theorizing Race and Gender.* Durham, N.C.: Duke University Press.

Williams, Patricia J. 1991. *The Alchemy of Race and Rights.* Cambridge, Mass.: Harvard University Press.

Wicke, Jennifer. 1992. "Postmodern Identities and the Politics of the (Legal) Subject." *Boundary 2,* special issue on feminism and postmodernism, ed. Margaret Ferguson and Jennifer Wicke, 19 (2): 10–33.

Worsham, Lynn. 1997. "After Words: A Choice of Words Remains." In *Feminism and Composition: In Other Words,* eds. Susan Jarratt and Lynn Worsham, 329–56. New York: Modern Language Association.

———. 1991. "Writing against Writing: The Predicament of Ecriture Feminine in Composition Studies." In *Contending with Words: Composition and Rhetoric in a Postmodern Age,* ed. Patricia Harkin and John Schilb, 82–104. New York: Modern Language Association.

Worth, Fabienne. 1993. "Postmodern Pedagogy in the Multicultural Classroom: For Inappropriate Teachers and Imperfect Spectators." *Cultural Critique* 25: 5–32.

Wriggins. Jennifer. 1983. "Rape, Racism, and the Law." *Harvard Women's Law Journal* 6 (1): 103–41.

Wyatt, Gail Elizabeth. 1992. "The Sociocultural Context of African American and White American Women's Rape." *Journal of Social Issues* 48 (1): 77–91.

Young, James Edward. 1993. *The Texture of Memory: Holocaust Memorials and Meaning.* New Haven, Conn.: Yale University Press.

———. 1988. *Writing and Rewriting the Holocaust: Narrative and the Consequences of Interpretation.* Bloomington: Indiana University Press.

Zandy, Janet, ed. 1995. *Liberating Memory: Our Work and Our Working-Class Consciousness.* New Brunswick, N.J.: Rutgers University Press.

# INDEX

academic literacy, 8, 15
academy: as postcolonial site, 31
Ackelsberg, Martha A., xxxviii
activism: identity narratives, 75; and pedagogy, 89; as public art, 119–38; student, 71–89; teachable moments, 73, 75, 86–93
affirmative action policies, xxiv, xxvi
agency: xxxv, 138, 151–52, 153; and camera's gaze, 119–22; and critical witnessing, 138–41; and deconstruction, 26; dialogic nature of, 121, 124–30; and discourse, 60, 62, 65, 70, 129; and hate speech codes, 86; and the male gaze, 46–48; materialist feminist view of, 46–48, 74–75; and memory, 133; personal vs. political, 169n6; and postmodernism, xxxvii, 146; relational nature of, xxix, xxx, xxxvi, xxxvii
Aguirre, A., Jr., 162n8
"Ain't I a Woman?" (Truth), 65
Alarcón, Norma, xxiv, 70, 148, 153, 165n1

Alcoff, Linda, 125, 132, 133, 137
Althusser, Louis, xxxv
Altman, Meryl, 53
Anzaldúa, Gloria, 49, 50, 148, 160n5, 168n7; *Borderlands/La Frontera: The New Mestiza,* 48
Aronowitz, Stanley, 35
Ashley, Kathleen, 162n6
assimilationist pluralism, xxvi
Auslander, Philip, 152
authenticity: links to oppositional politics, 142–50
autobiographical acts: definition of, xiv, xxiii
autobiographical manifestos, 48; Combahee River Collective, 166n7
autobiographical scripts, xxi; and consensual relations, 97–103; institutionally driven, 143
autobiography: and authenticity, 17–20, 25–26, 72, 111; and capitalist ideology, 12; and commemorative practice, 71–93; contrary uses of, 95–118; and

197

WENDY S. HESFORD is assistant professor of English at Indiana University, Bloomington.

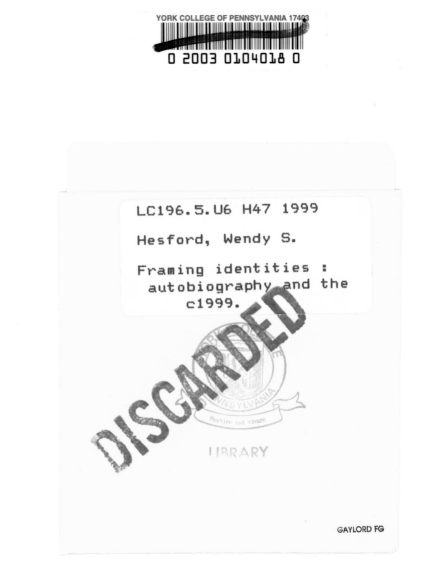